No One's Easy Daughter

Advance Support for *No One's Easy Daughter*

No One's Easy Daughter raises the voices of individuals striving to live an authentic religious life. Listen to their voices—those who stayed and those who chose another path. Notice, too, the voices become a collective as they merge into a communal life. These pages are filled with joy, sadness, fear, concerns for the world and an abundant love for Life/God. Enjoy the insights of these contemporary women religious!

Louise Akers, SC, D.Min., former Board member of Mary's Pence

Like guests at Judy Chicago's Dinner Party, these women bear witness to seismic shifts in the church and in society as their personal stories weave through each time period. By including those who left the order and those who stayed, we get a rich tapestry of experience and observation. I noticed particular voices, loved the texture in each section, and felt especially grateful for the conscious wisdom emerging in their later years.

Marjory Zoet Bankson, author of *Creative Aging*

No One's Easy Daughter is a treasure trove, with each story a precious gem. I've read them slowly, taking in the richness of each one, peeking behind the veil, as it were, and glimpsing the faces of these strong, beautiful women.

Their stories are told in simple, straightforward and unflinchingly honest ways that make them more powerful than many of the numerous mystical and theological tracts I've read over the years. They convey a fire within the writers' hearts that is tangible and, for me, sacramental in the way they enrich, inspire and communicate the presence of the divine in our lives.

There's passion for civil rights, assertion of women's freedom, rebellion against narrow ideas, openness and courage to change, moments of mystical experience, doubt, discovery, reconciliation, death of a spouse, a Nun celebrating mass in hurricane-devastated Honduras, and much, much more. All seem to have been enriched by the convent experience, whether good or bad, whether they remained Nuns or not. A strong sense of sisterhood among the Class of '57 pervades this book and strings the stories together.

As a man and a person who never had the convent experience, I deeply identify with the experience and journey of the women in this book. There is such great depth, wisdom and creativity in these pages. I recommend that they be read slowly, more than once, and used as sources of reflection.

Fred Brancato, PhD, author of
Ancient Wisdom and the Measure of Our Days:
The Spiritual Dimensions of Retirement, Aging and Loss

This candid, heartwarming book of valiant women engaging religious life on the threshold of Vatican II is well worth reading. In this compilation of stories and poems, thirty-some women recount their struggles, hopes and dreams as they entered the convent before the second Vatican Council and found themselves in the midst of tumultuous change. As young sisters, they realized the cost of personal growth sacrificed for the ideals of conformity and obedience. Each author eventually had to face the challenges of Vatican II and through their lives we see how God works in mysterious ways. Ultimately we see that the right road to God is the road of freedom in love.

Ilia Delio, OSF, author of *The Unbearable Wholeness of Being:*
God, Evolution and the Power of Love

I hold in my hands a valuable gift to the field of humanistic gerontology, revealing what it means to grow into our elderhood with purpose and spiritual reflection, while leaving a rich legacy for future generations to discover. It offers a stunning chorus of women's voices singing from the depths of their spirits, hearts, and memories, across 60 years of richly lived experience.

This compelling and beautifully crafted collective narrative weaves together soul-filled and deeply spiritual narratives of these "daughters" who were bravely in the front lines of some of the most important social, political, and spiritual movements of the past 60 years. I wrapped myself in the moving stories as the writers transitioned from youth, into midlife, and then elderhood—through alienation to grace.

The world needs this book now more than ever as humanity becomes increasingly polarized. These women embody what it means to question, search, serve, and act—on behalf of their deep beliefs for a better future.

Dr. Lyndall Hare, gerontologist, author of *In the Belly of the Beast:*
South African Women's Lives of Activism, Exile and Aging

Growing up in a Southern Baptist family, my knowledge of Catholicism and of Nuns came only through movies and by way of stories told by some of my friends who describe themselves as "Recovering Catholics." Reading *No One's Easy Daughter* was like looking into a mirror and seeing the face of each of the women, one by one, contributing to this marvelous and intriguing book. Reading their reflections, weaving in and through their eyes, I was able to perceive the vastness of their souls. What made them join the convent and stay or leave as they did captivated me. The fact that these women met in the 1950s and have continued to share their spiritual development and hunger for the great meaning and mysteries of life with one another gives this book a true profundity.

Their wide range of beliefs and experiences are the delicacies that create the compact whole. Through my own life's stages to the present, I have peeked into the depths of my inner self in a much different, although similar, way with these School Sisters of St. Francis in Milwaukee. This book has given me a deeper understanding of the humanness and archetype of Sisters and the reasons they accept their calling.

It seems as though the women's movement has its own chapter through the School Sisters of St. Francis's evolutionary and transformative consciousness. I want to meet all of these moxy women authors and personally thank them for this gift of expression.

Jean Harper, President and CEO,
Moxy Women.com and Women Taking Care of Business, Inc.

This stellar endeavor is a beautiful way of showing that everybody has a story to tell. The gripping stories of these 39 women harvest a collective wisdom and fashion a container for the Divine capable of firing our own hearts with new hope. In having the courage to tell their stories, the Convent Reception Class of 1957, in many ways, is telling our story even though the circumstances may be vastly different. What a legacy gift for whatever path others may be traveling.

Fr. Guerric Heckel, ocso, Trappist,
Founder and Director of
The Mepkin Abbey Institute of Contemplative Eldering

We've heard of "The Flying Nun," "The Singing Nun," and other public images of nuns. What we haven't heard are the genuine voices of women whose lives have been shaped by their monastic vocation. This book is a unique contribution to that unsuspected history, composed by Nuns and former Nuns who enable their voices at last to be heard.

Harry R. Moody, PhD., Retired Vice President, AARP, author of
The Five Stages of the Soul:
Charting the Spiritual Passages That Shape Our Lives

It is one thing to believe in a God who promises to turn our "wailing into dancing" (Psalm 30:11). It is quite another to know such a God, our Sister Sophia, "at the cellular level." These stories rise from circles of intimate knowing and welcome the reader exuberantly, with fierce hopefulness, into the dance.

Dr. Christopher Pramuk, author of
Hope Sings, So Beautiful: Graced Encounters Across the Color Line
and of *At Play in Creation: Merton's Awakening to the Feminine Divine*

A very worthy and unique contribution to spiritual memoirs. This is the kind of book that changes attitudes, changes perspectives, and changes lives—in good new directions! Read and be both challenged and inspired.

Fr. Richard Rohr, O.F.M., Center for Action and Contemplation,
author of *Falling Upward: A Spirituality for the Two Halves of Life*

An inspiring document that follows, for six decades, the lives of women, all of whom began adult life as religious sisters in the same congregation. Their collective story unfolds through many revolutionary changes in the church. This expertly interwoven narrative shows how these women—those who remained and those who left religious life—through searching, struggling and healing continued their commitment to spiritual growth and making their unique contributions to "renewing the face of the Earth."

Dr. Louis M. Savary and Dr. Patricia H. Berne, authors of
You Are God's Gift to the World and of *Why Did God Make Me?*

No One's Easy Daughter explores the common human question of how to live fully in the messiness of the world while opening to the deep spiritual love that gives our struggles meaning. As a Sufi, I know the importance of love. Reading this book is like sitting down for a cup of tea with a grandmother. It offers something rarely found in a book—wisdom.

Dr. Rebecca Schwartz, ND, LAc

This book carries the reader into a world normally cloistered from view, poignantly revealing it in a series of unforgettable vignettes. The true gift of the book, though, lies elsewhere. As it documents the personal struggles of commitment, doubt, revelation, hardship and love faced by these women, it opens the reader's heart to the mysterious journey we each undertake in our attempts to come to terms with our humanity in this world. As such, the book not only illuminates—it inspires.

Philip Shepherd, author of
New Self, New World: Recovering our Senses in the 21st Century

No One's Easy Daughter

Our Journeys of Transformation

EDITORS

MARY H. BER

MARY SUE KOEPPEL

MARY COLGAN McNAMARA

ROSE ANN TRZIL, OSF

IMAGO PRESS

TUCSON ARIZONA

Published in the United States of America by:

Imago Press
3710 East Edison
Tucson AZ 85716

Cover Art © Jane Ray (illustration from *Classic Fairy Tales* retold by Berlie Doherty, illustrated by Jane Ray, published by Walker Books)
www.janeray.com

Interior graphite drawings © Pat Baron Monigold
www.patmonigold.com

Cover Design and Book Design by Leila Joiner

ISBN 978-0-9981791-2-4

Library of Congress Control Number: 2017938087

Printed in the United States of America on Acid-Free Paper

All proceeds from the sale of this book will be donated to the School Sisters of St. Francis.

I want to know God
as the bird knows God,
lifting its wings;

as the cherry blossom rests
in perfect trust
on stem and air.

∼

fog
makes visible
the Breath

I am Your fog.

CONTENTS

FOREWORD

We experienced in Judy Chicago's iconic art exhibit *The Dinner Party*[1] the power of a group of women acting collectively to create one work of art. *No One's Easy Daughter*, written by a group of present and former School Sisters of St. Francis, is another powerful experience of a collective work.

Here the memories and reflections are gathered, one small piece after another, to create a colorful mosaic. The impact of the mosaic is the reliving of the inner story of the transformation of religious life for women living that life during the second half of the twentieth century to the present.

The mosaic is a triptych. The first panel carries memories of the time of entry and formation, an immersion into a different culture. What arises is a heavy feeling of tradition, conformity, fear, and at the same time, the deepening of spiritual awareness, the impact of powerful role models, and the fashioning of lifetime friendships.

The second panel follows the Second Vatican Council in the 1960s. Here the mosaic explodes with color. Piece after piece reflects a new culture arising: individual and group creativity, involvement in social protests and issues, freedom in personal and group lifestyles, opening to various approaches in spirituality and the re-thinking of a life commitment.

The colors of the third panel, now the reflections of educated women in their seventies and eighties, are deep and strong. These are quality reflections on the richness of a meaningful life, on the strength of long friendships, on the wisdom that can arise from challenges and suffering, on the peace of the approach to dying.

The facts of history have a soul. Whether you participated in or observed the facts of these years, in this mosaic you experience the evolution of the soul.

Francis Rothluebber,
President of the School Sisters of St. Francis 1966-1976,
Co-founder of Spirit Mountain Retreat Center
and of New Momentum for Human Unity

---

[1] *The Dinner Party* by feminist artist Judy Chicago is an installation artwork that celebrates women important to history. Thirty-nine of these mythical and historical women are represented by elaborate place settings arranged along a triangular table with another 999 women's names inscribed in gold scripts on white floor tiles. Chicago, who began the project alone, gradually guided scores of other collaborators to complete the piece that, after touring in 6 countries on 3 continents, now resides in the Elizabeth A. Sackler Center for Feminist Art at the Brooklyn Museum. Serendipitously, this book has 39 contributors and stands on an unseen floor of millions more sisters in spirit—those living, dead and still to come.

INTRODUCTION

We writers met as girls in a Convent Motherhouse between 1954 and 1956. In the summer of 1957, we became Nuns, Novices in the Order of the School Sisters of St. Francis in Milwaukee, Wisconsin.

Throughout history, Nuns seem to have been objects of fascination—secluded, mysterious, apart. We now invite you into that life and our stories, our journeys of transformation.

In telling our stories, we have come to realize that we are telling a much larger story, one in which you may be an intimate part. If you are near us in age, a story you are possibly already living. If you are younger, especially much younger, one waiting for you to carry forward into the future.

What is that story? The unfolding and blossoming of the Wise Woman Archetype. She who balances spiritual energies beyond gender and age, beyond religions and cultures. She who embraces and includes.

To the degree that you yearn for a world of meaning, justice and compassion, this book is your story as well as ours. In your hands may it be as if one or more of us writers sat down for coffee or tea at your table. What inner joys and struggles, early dreams and hopes, experience of injustice and global inequities do all of us share? How, for example, do we view God and the meaning of prayer? Or relate to our own aging and death and what may—or may not—await us beyond death?

Rather than a series of individual narratives, our story has become a collection of memories and reflections on the various themes of the human task of fashioning meaning within daily life. Narrative chapters link with lyrical chapters as we women share Glimpses of the Sacred.

As young women, we offer the Early Glimpses experienced in our fledgling understandings. These glimpses grow much more profound in our Later Life Glimpses of the Sacred. In the middle years, we write of searching for peace, of finding gentle strength, deep comfort, and wholeness. Here are love poems to the universe. Dreams and visions. Meditations.

The voices of classmates who have remained Sisters interweave with the voices of those who left—a polyphonic group memoir of our life journeys as women and spiritual seekers now in our 70s and 80s. We editors took as our primary task the collection, organization and arrangement of pieces within the whole, leaving each woman's individual voice true to her personal writing and/or speaking style. The intermingling of these stories, the poetry, the glimpses, the transformational undertones, all give *No Ones's Easy Daughter* a totally unique voice within the substantial body of literature about Convent life.

Those voices reflect a wide range of beliefs and experiences, all respected, all part of the whole, all metaphorical approximations of what lies ultimately beyond words and certainties. Collectively, they represent every person's inner journey.

We grew up in a much simpler-seeming world than the one in which we are now growing old. Choices and distinctions appeared clear-cut, at least until the cultural, political and religious upheaval of the 1960s. Suddenly the path ahead didn't seem as streamlined or easy.

Our book's title, *No One's Easy Daughter*, came out of that tumultuous reality and this poem by one of us:

MYSELF, COMPARING RELIGIONS

I would have been an easy worshipper of the sun.
One day's shining would have done or undone
the night names of god: the totem turtle
and the silver sway of axe or arrow,
golden calves and the myrtle
memories of head and marrow.

I would have been an easy atheist
upon beholding what the world missed
of mercy and of miracle. I sat
upon the Inca's eagle, land-locked flat
just centuries from blood's dying flight.
I was born the years that Dachau drank—
Third Reich's rite—
our hopes of heaven from an armored tank.

Yet today, hung between sun and slaughter,
I can be no one's easy daughter.

In Jane Ray's powerful cover image, we immediately felt the long history of rich symbolism involving women, water and wells. Nor could we miss its resonance within our own long life journeys. We are women rooted in the earth who continue to embrace the spiraling depth of the well and its invitation to paradox, cosmic consciousness and ultimately transformative wisdom.

The importance of *No One's Easy Daughter* will lie in whatever power it has to invite readers like yourself to consider the stages and wanderings of your own life journey. Like our lives, the book has three major sections— Early Life, Mid Life and Later Life. Within the sections, each of the 330+ pieces stands on its own and can be read as a short reflection or meditation.

We envision your hearing with an occasional shock of recognition— whether of pain or delight or both—echoes of your own inmost voice. The book will most certainly come full circle if you are inspired to reflect on, even to write and share your own transformational moments and memories.

So evolutionary energy on our beloved planet increases.

Mary H. Ber
Mary Sue Koeppel
Mary Colgan McNamara
Rose Ann Trzil, OSF

Prayer of Dedication to the Mothers

Mother Alexia, Mother Alfons, Sister Clara, we call on you. Come, each of you, to us in our endeavors. We are hungry for your words, your love, your sense of what is right for us.

We long to know the truth of you, of one another, of our universe. We pray— dream your dreams within us to wake us. Give vision to our eyes in dark of night.

Let the dreams of our hearts come alive and the heart of our dreams be true, bearing light from your ancestral fire.

With gratitude,
The Daughters of Your Lineage

PART I

EARLY LIFE

CHAPTER 1

WHY WE CAME

THE CANDY STORE WINDOW

"That's the one I want. Please, Mommy." I shout above the roar of the overhead Atlantic Ave El.

My nose is pressed against the cool glass of a Brooklyn candy store window on a stifling July afternoon. It is my sixth birthday and my mother has given me the choice of any gift in the store.

Just beyond the glass is an array of colorful dolls, clad in ruffled costumes. The one I point to is tucked between the wooden-shoed Dutch girl and the red-haired Irish Colleen. Its somber black dress and veil are sharp contrasts to the riot of colors that surround it.

A few minutes later I leave the store, clutching the Nun doll in my hand. Smiling to myself, I whisper, "This is what I will be when I grow up!"

YOU DON'T KNOW WHAT YOU ARE TALKING ABOUT

Once upon a time at a big family gathering, my grandmother asked me the age-old question, "What do you want to be when you grow up?" My four-year-old response was swift. "I want to be a Nun." And her response was just as swift. "You don't know what you are talking about!"

That is my earliest memory of my faith journey. But I never wavered from that decision. My incredibly happy childhood was colored with memories of the Nuns in the Sister's house, as we called their little home. I loved everything about the five Nuns at our parish. I watched and imitated everything they did—the way they held their rosaries, the way they folded their hands, the way they taught their classes.

And I loved everything about church, too. Rogation days, Forty Hours devotions, Stations of the Cross during Lent, Mass on Sundays and every school day morning were never a chore. I loved being around church. Deep in my young heart was a hunger for God.

When my two older Sisters entered St. Joseph Convent Motherhouse in Milwaukee, my desire to do the same became a passion. I read and reread their letters home. I looked at postcards and other pictures of their Convent and longed for the day when I would be there, too.

My desire to be a Nun wavered a bit in seventh and eighth grades. I had discovered boys—one in particular, who let me know there was more to life than a Convent. I thought a lot those two years about the possibility of just staying home and going to our public high school and being an ordinary person. But deep down I felt I was encountering a temptation that I needed to overcome. So, at the tender age of thirteen, going on fourteen, it was finally my time to enter St. Joseph Convent.

I Did Not Want a Life Like That

I had wanted to be a Nun for as far as I can remember—long before I started school. At the time I did not realize why I wanted to become a Sister. In retrospect I understand exactly why I made that choice when I was a mere baby. My parents did not have a happy marriage, so I knew I did not want a life like that. When I went to church or saw the Nuns who taught my older brothers and sisters, I observed how happy and seemingly carefree they were.

Besides, they would definitely save their souls—they would go to heaven. Of course, I wanted to be a Sister.

Ought To

"I have long curls now, because I'm going to be a Nun. Nuns cut off all their hair," I, a six-year-old, explained to my eight-year-old cousin sitting under the pine trees separating my home from the priest's rectory.

How did I know? What made me choose to become a Nun?

Perhaps it was my living next door to the Church complex: Priest's House, Catholic Church, Sisters' Convent, Catholic Grade School, the well-kept Cemetery behind the school. No mystery there.

Perhaps it was my godfather, a priest. As a child, I adored him.

Perhaps it was the cemetery I could see from my upstairs bedroom windows, a cemetery we played in as grade school kids. We sang the *Dies Irae, Dies Illa* during every funeral mass, even in summer. Life ended, I learned early.

Perhaps it was the Nuns—quiet, lovely, intelligent, friends to my mother who welcomed women with educations in a town where almost only she and the Nuns had studied beyond high school.

Perhaps it was knowing the only way out of our small town was through education and service. I always wanted to be a teacher. Nuns were teachers. I would be one.

But mostly, it was a choice for *ought to*, not *want to*, a life of the surest path to goodness, to holiness, to God.

I Joined for Sisterhood

Everyone in our new neighborhood at the edge of town knew it—this was the long-awaited week the Sisters would arrive. When I started out that sunny early August morning pushing my sister in her stroller, little did I realize how profoundly that walk would fashion my life.

Halfway around the block, they appeared—five vibrant young women, the youngest not much older than twice my nine years, each carrying a thick prayer book. All exuded excitement because while praying the Office in the local cemetery—no Church or Convent yet existed, only a school—they had watched snakes hatching beside a tombstone.

That was it for me. I was born, so it seems, wanting to be a Nun. Now I knew I wanted to be one of these Nuns and welcome snake-gazing into the bargain. I'll never know how my sister survived the rest of her flight home. Heart pounding, destiny calling, I careened to our back door, panting to my bewildered mother: "I've seen them! I've seen the Sisters."

Years later I discovered that others had entered the Convent for reasons related to God, some more specifically to Jesus, to winning heaven for choosing the harder path, to academic advancement, to family pressure, poverty or dysfunction, to general indecision about what to do next in life.

I joined for Sisterhood.

I PLAYED THE TEACHER, THE NUN, THE PRIEST

As long as I can remember, I wanted to be a teacher, and the only teachers I knew were Nuns. When we played, I was the teacher, the Nun. Sometimes I'd even dress up as a Nun. Well, sometimes I was the priest.

Once I started fifth grade, I got to stay after school to help the Nuns. And I came early to help. Anything they wanted done, I did—wash windows, put up bulletin boards, correct papers. I just liked being around the Nuns.

The School Sisters of St. Francis were friendly, happy—it was their spirit I really liked. I was going to be a School Sister of St. Francis.

WITH JOY AND SPIRIT

The tall, thin, stern woman stood behind her desk on a podium at the front of our third grade classroom, "How many girls have all ten of their conduct slips?"

Conduct slips… I was quite certain I had all of mine. I ducked down to reach my cigar/pencil box. There they were at the bottom of the box, all ten of them. I raised my hand.

Sister came down the aisle towards me and took the slips. After counting them she scowled and asked, "Are there any other girls who still have ten conduct slips?" She was clearly unhappy, but she finally turned toward me and said, "You will crown the Blessed Mother."

It was May 1st, the third and last time during the year that she spoke to me. I really don't think she knew my name.

Summer came and the release from school was welcome relief. A new subdivision was growing, complete with a new Catholic Parish, in what had been a cornfield just east of our home. That fall the new parish school opened.

My mother took me to register; we went into the fourth grade classroom. The Sister at the small desk reached out her hand to me, looked into my eyes, and with a friendly smile welcomed me. I was nearly speechless, but I couldn't help responding to her welcome. The room was small and bright, with pictures and a colorful quote on the front bulletin board. *What a difference,* I thought. *Maybe school will be fun this year!*

School was fun for the next five years. I found my new teachers to be inspiring, kind, and happy women. These Sisters talked with us, shared with us, encouraged us, and laughed with us. They treated each other with respect, and they opened to us a new way of accepting and respecting others.

During those five years I read all the books in the small school library and was allowed to read some books from the adult section. I was attracted to books about saints and religious who served the needy. I too wanted to serve God's people with the joy and spirit of my teachers. I wanted to become a School Sister of St. Francis.

NO CHICAGO-STYLE WEDDING

What started as a naïve infatuation with the lives of Sisters, their seeming other-worldliness and their mysterious ways of being, morphed into a sense of calling for my own life. My parents were devastated as I decided to answer this call and enter the community of the School Sisters of St. Francis. I was their only daughter, and dreams of a future Chicago-style wedding were dashed. No white dress and veil, bridesmaids and groomsmen. Just a Convent white veil ceremony shared by many others.

TO GET OUT OF THE HOUSE AND GO TO HIGH SCHOOL

"Why did I choose to become a Nun?" I don't remember ever having been asked.

Mine was not a spiritual journey. I went to the Convent because it was expected. My older sister was there and she was causing no one problems. I did hesitate at one point: *Who would stand up for my little brother if I left?* Well, at the point of that decision, my younger sister, who was pretty, more lovable, and still in grade school, showed to my thirteen-year-old satisfaction that she could.

So my aunt, who had prepared at least three of her daughters for the Convent, was allowed to collect the things I would need to have when I left home. I got new shoes! Also a brand new steamer trunk, now treasured by my daughter.

That summer I ran the hills and climbed the trees and enjoyed the back forty as much as I could—in preparation for letting go of my farm-life freedom.

The day we drove to the Convent in Milwaukee, we sang over and over, "Give me land, lots of land and the starry skies above. Don't fence me in." So somewhere inside I was making a choice to go to the Convent. But it was really the only way I could see to get out of the house and go to high school.

ABSENCE AND STARVATION

From early childhood, long before any new age-y stuff became popular, I had a strong, largely unconscious sense that several women murdered as witches had asked to coalesce their unlived energies into my current life. Even though I could never have expressed it in words as a girl, that inchoate sense of the unfinished lives of these murdered women played a huge role in my burning desire to join a Sisterhood of some kind, to find a place and way to reclaim lost female lives. That urgency drives me to this day and takes many forms.

Much later I would read Phyllis Chesler's painful truth about female children being starved for strong role models providing "…a legacy of power and humanity from adults of their own sex." My heightened sense of that absence and starvation is evidenced in one of my earliest, most persistent memories, the longing for an older sister. It was precisely that legacy of power and humanity for which I longed. Now I see it—the devaluing of the feminine in all its forms (the lives of women, animals, the environment, indigenous and developing cultures, etc.)—as one of the throbbing wounds of the planet we share.

INFLUENCE OF HOLLYWOOD

My grade school experiences always revolved around Nuns. I can't remember a time when I didn't want to be one of them. My parents were very active in the church and we spent a lot of time doing parish things. I stayed after school a lot to help my teachers with small jobs and enjoyed being with these Nuns. I had the School Sisters of St. Francis in first grade before we moved to another school run by other Franciscan Nuns.

Another influence during that time was, dare I say, Hollywood. A few years ago I watched *The Bells of St. Mary's* with Ingrid Bergman. I'm sure I saw this or a similar movie as a kid and was probably mesmerized by the floating vision of the Catholic religious. I'd like to say I entered with some lofty aspiration, but at fourteen years old I had not left childhood that far behind.

I Wanted to be a Missionary

I started thinking about religious life when I was in the fifth grade. I loved the Sisters I had in school and got to know them outside of the classroom because my dad would frequently take them to town for shopping or doctors' appointments. I usually got to go along. They were very friendly and very appreciative of the service rendered.

Reading books about missionaries also piqued my interest in religious life and I decided I was going to be a missionary. These plans got put on hold when I was in the eighth grade because my mother was very ill towards the end of that year. I decided that I would wait to enter religious life until after high school because I thought that I could only go to the Convent after eighth grade or after high school.

These plans changed again after I talked with a high school teacher I really liked. When the principal got hold of the story, she said that I could go even after ninth grade. It didn't take very long. In September of the year that I was to enter tenth grade, I found myself on the way to St. Joseph Convent in Milwaukee. I had some mixed emotions about going because my mother still was not very well, but she wasn't going to hold me back from my desire. I also think it was hard for my dad to see me leave home, but he never said anything to that effect.

To Find God

I had completed one year of high school and, after much pleading on my part, my parents had agreed to allow me to go nearly a thousand miles away to enter the School Sisters of St. Francis (SSSF) Community in Milwaukee, Wisconsin. I entered the Aspirancy program as a sophomore in the Convent high school.

I made the journey filled with the great desire to find God and give myself entirely to Him. I wanted to embrace the joy I had witnessed in the daily lives of the Sisters who had been my teachers for most of my grade school years.

I WAS FIRMLY DISCOURAGED

When I was growing up, the highest honor or gift to a family and a sure sign of God's blessings on a family was to have a son become a priest. The second best honor was to have a daughter become a religious Sister. As I grew up, I saw cousins become priests or Sisters and knew the high regard for them. While in seventh and eighth grade, I considered joining the Sisters. Because I was usually in trouble in school, I was firmly discouraged from taking my thoughts any further.

Our new high school was fortunate and very blessed because the best of the best in the SSSF Community were assigned to be our teachers since both the Community and the parish wanted this school to succeed. I saw and felt what being a Sister could mean in my life during the first two years of high school. So I talked with my favorite teacher. I couldn't believe that I would be accepted but I was. I entered after my sophomore year in high school.

IN A CONTEMPLATIVE PRESENCE

I chose Milwaukee and the School Sisters of St. Francis from an inner impulse. When I was thirteen, my mother took me to Milwaukee to see my two aunts who were School Sisters. I remember how I felt. The building was big and on a main thoroughfare. It had a black iron fence around it. The outside steps were wide and high. This did not look like any Convent I had seen in pictures.

My mother rang the doorbell. The portress opened the door. We entered the front door, walked up the steps and into the entryway. The portress asked my mother and me to wait in the art parlor. It was all so big with high ceilings, so quiet and full. I was in awe. I now know the feeling as one of being in a contemplative presence.

My child's heart and the romantic contemplative within me felt at home. And, as I remember the next four years of struggle through high school and adolescence, I now know I was already on the circuitous route of finding myself—and hence, God.

When I was seventeen, I wrote to Mother Corona and said that I wanted to come to Milwaukee and be a Sister. On the application blank next to "Why?" I said, "I want to be united with God."

I came to Milwaukee on September 6, 1956, expecting to be united with God.

SHE WOULD MISS HER ...

As a young girl, I never, ever considered the idea of entering a Convent and becoming a Nun. Not at age fourteen for sure. There was never even remote consideration until our parish pastor talked to me about his three sisters being members of the School Sisters of St. Francis Community. Oh, dear! That provided food for thought, and with gentle but clear persuasion I accepted the idea of giving it a try.

Why wouldn't the young daughter of an Irish Catholic family, a farm girl with nine siblings, want to enter the Convent? (Number ten was born soon after I became a Novice.) Well, for many reasons, a decision so bold, so dramatic might be in question. Maybe this child would miss her parents, her siblings, her mother's home cooking—as in her fried potatoes, which were the best in all the world, of course. The Johnny cake, the roasters of sweet corn, the peanut butter cupcakes. She'd miss fun times with the family, like family night at the outdoor theater and the buckets of freshly popped corn dripping in butter. In short, she would miss everything in reference to her family and life on the farm.

In what seemed to be no time at all, I found myself at the doorstep of 1501 South Layton Boulevard. With the badge of courage, two feet together and a trunk by my side, I was ready for boot camp, so I thought.

WAIT UNTIL YOU'RE SIXTEEN

What was it about the Sisters that made me envy their life so? Their kindness? The obvious care they had for us children? The secrecy of life behind walls that was hypnotic to a young girl? In many ways, the journey to the Convent was inevitable.

After grade school graduation, I announced to my parents that I was going to the Convent. They were somewhat stunned as I had never spoken about this before and promptly told me that I couldn't go until I was at least sixteen.

My mom was a convert to Catholicism and found strength and solace in the Catholic Church even though she didn't take the rules too seriously. For instance, every Friday we had coleslaw made with a bacon dressing. Of course we pulled out the bacon pieces and threw them away, but I lived in terror of inadvertently swallowing a speck of meat, which probably caused some stifled laughs from the priest in the confessional. At any rate, my mom was more or less neutral to the whole idea of my entering the Convent. On the other hand, my dad, a Catholic lifer, was opposed to this nonsense. Didn't I want to get married and have children?

Two years of waiting seemed long to me, but I decided to take advantage of the things that wouldn't be allowed once I joined the School Sisters. So I did teenage things at full tilt and enjoyed it all. During that time, my friends and I became part of the Young Christian Students, a social action group for teenagers that was similar to the Christian Family Movement founded by parents of a very good friend of mine. I spent hours each week at their home, which was always teeming with people—foster children, adopted children, foreign students, displaced persons, neighbors and us. In retrospect, being responsible for your world became part of my values and still influences my thinking.

I turned sixteen in April but waited until July to tell my parents that it was time for me to be going to the Convent. They honored their word, though reluctantly. The fourth of September was entrance day and one of the happiest days of my life.

PRE-FEMINISM CHOICES

I am seventeen years old. In January of my senior year, I am beginning to think about Life After High School. I know I'd like to become a writer, so I send for information from Marquette University's journalism program.

When I come home from school one afternoon, my mother walks out of the kitchen to meet me with an envelope from Marquette in her hand. "Honey, we can't afford this," she says.

Suddenly a number of things become clear. My mother's voice is calm, sure; that's because she's envisioning my taking a path exactly like hers. I've been in training: two years of shorthand and typing, one year of sewing. I'll work as a secretary for a brief time before getting married, settling down in the neighborhood, sending my kids to the parish school. In the Old Building (in contrast to the New Building, with its nice plastic desks and big windows) are some desks with the same wooden, varnished seats that have embraced both my mother's bottom and mine. Those seats are waiting for the bottoms of my kids.

Bab's Department Store, Kroger's Groceries, and Mr. Pomerantz the Tailor are also open for my patronage. The Altar and Rosary Society has dust rags waiting for me to use weekly—especially during the annual Holy Week Spring Cleaning binge.

All this despite the fact that I have not excelled in my secretarial studies, have not dated much during high school, and am clearly more interested in books than boys.

Books. College! How am I going to get to college? While I have excellent grades in English, I am not the all-around academic star that my friend is. She's won a scholarship to the only Catholic college within public transportation of my home. And, of course, I have to attend a Catholic college. Any other kind is a danger to my salvation—especially the University of Chicago, which is pink with Communism. Besides, the Nuns at our high school have said they will send our transcripts only to Catholic colleges.

I never thought of attending a community college, as my male cousins did several years later. One worked as a longshoreman and, after obtaining an Associate's Degree at a Junior College, went on to earn a law degree. The other became a CPA on the G.I. Bill after serving in Vietnam. These were choices that never entered my head during pre-Feminism days.

Society in the 1950s gave girls few options: we were expected to become stay-at-home mothers, raising children and caring for husband and house. Good Catholic Girls were also told about the possibility of being Nuns or of leading a Life of Single Blessedness. (I didn't think I wanted to know what that last was. I always thought of my sour-faced aunt, who worked as a secretary for a boss she worshiped. Single she was. But Blessed?) The Single Blesseds were expected to serve others in a career of Secretary, Teacher, or Nurse.

Feminism, which arrived during the social revolution of the late 1960s and early 1970s, had not yet told young women: "You can have any career you want. You are entitled to the same pay as a man if you have the same job. You are as capable, as articulate and efficient as men. Throughout the past centuries you have been oppressed by patriarchy in the workplace, in schools, in the Church. You can write as well as men—though you have not been published as often."

Some of us had felt the faint stirrings of the spirit of feminism by 1955, however. Why else would I have decided to become a journalist? Why else would one of my best friends, who predictably wound up in nursing school, yearn to become a doctor?

Why else was I determined to get to college, to escape my mother's life, which I saw as small and stifling? Her weekly laundering in a dark, cold basement. The hours of ironing that always followed a day later. Weekly trips to the grocery store and to the currency exchange where utility bills could be paid. The daily cooking of meals and the telephone calls to her best friend, my godmother, to exchange gossip and complaints about neighbors I never noticed.

I didn't realize until twenty-five years later that my desire for college was a subconscious reason for joining the Convent. It was certainly as strong as my very real desire to serve God as well as I could and to make the very best use of my life.

I'd been told that a religious vocation was a calling, that I'd feel it, and that its surety would sustain me throughout my vowed life. I spoke to one of my high school teachers about the fact that I didn't really feel a calling, but I knew I needed to make a decision about the rest of my life soon. (That's how it was in those days; life seemed so stable that one thought it was not only possible to make a permanent life choice, but imperative to do so only once— at age eighteen or very soon thereafter.) Sister said the Jesuits recommended folding a piece of paper down the middle whenever an important decision was required. List the pros on one side and the cons on the other.

OK! The pros had it. I was going to become a Nun.

But which order? Not the Nuns that taught me in either grade school or high school. They belonged to the neighborhood that was smothering me.

But the Nuns who taught at Alvernia High School—they seemed a different breed. Whenever I made the trip north for some meeting, I saw them smiling in the corridors, making ice cream cones in the cafeteria, chattering easily with the girls they taught. And those girls did all kinds of things that the ones in my high school did not. When we went to the same all-city Catholic functions, they seemed much more accomplished. They won more awards at speech contests and got more bills passed at mock sessions of Congress.

I wished Alvernia were not an hour and a half away by bus, so that I could attend school there. I wanted to stand among the girls in that plaid-skirted chorus who sang, "Most High, Omnipotent, Good Lord . . . ./Be praised . . .for Sister Moon and the Stars./ In the heavens you have made them/ Clear and precious and beautiful."

It would be some years before Feminism pointed at the skill, independence and efficiency of the Nuns who created and then ran the schools and hospitals that served American children and American sick people, particularly those in immigrant populations. But I instinctively decided to join the most efficient, friendly, and creative community I had ever met.

They were Franciscan, and that was a big plus because I was already a member of the Third Order of St. Francis; in fact, I was Prefect of our high school youth group. I already loved St. Francis, a brother poet. I couldn't hope that the poetry I was writing would ever equal the gorgeous glory of his, but I felt close to him in the spirit of word-making for God. I had my own leather-bound copy of *The Words of St. Francis*, knew his life, had given a speech about it at a Franciscan Youth Convention.

Having grown up surrounded by Chicago cement, I longed for Francis's feeling of closeness to nature. Probably I also subconsciously identified with his youthful rebellion against parents and society. In any case, I was glad that the community of my choice was Franciscan. I looked forward to deepening my insight into Franciscanism.

FROM A WPA PROJECT

My spiritual journey must have begun when I was born, the first baby born at home in the WPA (Roosevelt's Works Projects Administration) community. It made me a liberal and a nature-loving tree hugger—I must have been a budding Franciscan.

How could I not be attracted to the joy and love emanating from the SSSFs who came from Alverno and the Motherhouse to teach us Sunday school because we had no church or school at our parish until I was in seventh grade? They prepared us for first communion.

Eventually we did get a school; our principal and teacher became my sponsor when, after high school, I decided to follow my role models and enter St. Joseph Convent.

SEEKING MOTHERS AND DIRECTION

Looking back from a fifty-year perspective, I went to the Convent seeking mothers and direction. Since I lost my mother at four years of age, I did not have that directing, hovering presence and I became used to making my own decisions, directing my own life, and being responsible for myself very early.

When I reached sophomore year in college, I hadn't a clue about choosing a major. The guidance department testing showed that I could be an engineer, architect, or dentist. I remember the counselor, a woman, suggesting to me that, being a girl, I probably would rather be a teacher or journalist, which was second place in the testing. I had no idea how to pursue any of these careers nor any real desire to make a decision about them.

I felt at a dead end. I had transferred from my freshman year as an art major at a state university and come to a Catholic university seeking more insight into philosophy and religion. Those classes (along with the teachers and other students, most of them young men) left me uninterested and unfulfilled.

So I guess I said to myself, "I'll join the Convent." And somewhere in the depths of my being was also the idea that after the one decision I made, every other decision would be made by someone else. It was almost a feeling of relief. However, back then, had anyone asked, I would have said, "I am answering the Call. God has given me a Vocation!"

In Navy Blue Suit and Red Pumps

Life and Death have been closely connected for me most of my life. My rural childhood placed me in an environment rich in experiences of new life from the birthing of animals to the growing of much of the produce we ourselves consumed. The awesomeness of creation implanted in my soul a deep longing for silence, for contemplating God's magnificence in everyday reality as I lived it.

The seed had been planted in my soul early on. I was attracted to the spiritual dimensions of life and living, of loving and giving and doing for others by the inspiration of my parents and grandparents and other family members. I wanted to share my gifts with others without the responsibilities of family life.

My initial response to a call to join religious life was sparked by the joy and fullness of life reflected in the lives of some of my religious professors at Alverno College.

Because I entered the Convent after college, my entrance to formation and religious life was quite disappointing. I came dressed in a navy blue suit and red pumps. When I came out to meet my parents in my Postulant garb, my dad cried. I had never seen him cry except at the death of his parents, so I knew that this decision was going to be a challenge for both my parents and myself.

Chapter 2

Aspirancy

How Did It Begin?

The afternoon I, a freshman in high school, barely a teenager, arrived at St. Joseph Convent, a little Nun took me to a room full of dresses of all sizes and picked out one measured and made for me.

"Go behind that screen and change," she said. "You'll look better when you have these clothes on."

I doubted that would be true as I slid into the black dress, black cotton stockings and black shoes. When I came out from behind the screen, she pinned my long hair into a bun and hid it under a black, floppy veil.

I was relieved to hide my young womanhood and ready to sink into the experience of finding God. I felt excited, waiting like a *tabula rasa* ready to be written on by the spiritual life of the Convent. These next years would be the most challenging and stimulating years of my life.

The first two of those years my classmates and I were known as Aspirants, ones aspiring to a possible future as Nuns. During our first year of Aspirancy, we lived in the large Motherhouse while Marian Hall, a new home specifically for Aspirants, was being built across the street.

The glorious summer between those first two years we spent on the Convent farm, living in a huge, rambling farmhouse with deep and long porches. Some of us slept in the healthy fresh air of semi-enclosed, screened-in porches. Here we could listen to night birds and the sounds of wind and rain, sounds some of us missed in the large Convent in Milwaukee.

The second year we moved into the newly built Marian Hall across the street and lived somewhat separated from the rest of the Sisters, Novices and the Postulants. That year we were joined by more girls who had completed their freshman or sophomore years at their home high schools before becoming Aspirants with us.

All year long, summers included, we attended St. Joseph High School, taught by Nuns I deeply respected.

I sank gratefully into the beautiful liturgical rituals and the daily life of the Convent Aspirancy. I found it both challenging and exhilarating. So much to learn. So much to experience.

Chilled for Life

The wonders of high school took over my new world, especially Latin, English, world history and algebra. The teachers—each one's voice still echoes viscerally and joyfully from that long-ago place.

Our diminutive English teacher standing at the blackboard reciting Adelaide Crapsey's cinquain "The Warning" to us early in our ninth grade year. I still hold its haunting five lines by heart, feeling more deeply each passing year that "strange, still dusk" out of which death's fluttering messenger, the white moth, flew. I still hear the poet's final question as I heard it that day: "Why am I grown/ So cold?", leaving me chilled for life by both poetry and that white moth.

At Home

I immediately felt that the Convent was home. The first night, lying in my bed in St. Agatha dorm, I heard some stifled sobs and sniffling around me. I was sad that not everyone seemed as elated as I was, and instinctively knew I would never be homesick.

My God, at that time, was a personal God. I was engaged, as it were, to his son, Jesus. If I followed the rules and did my best, I would be rewarded forever in heaven. Earthly doubts and trials would give me an opportunity to prove my love for God.

Spunk

A relentless and powerful cloud of homesickness clobbered me on all sides. Culture shock did me no favors, either. An apparent lack of self-confidence presented me with feelings of frustration, loneliness, and a splotch of hostility. Thus, a heavy heart lined the halls with a bit of trouble for me beginning on day three of boot camp.

The Superiors called it rebellion and defiance. My Webster defined it as spunk—an honest response to rigid rules, far too much prayer time, just too much of everything except, of course, having some fun once in a while.

Eventually the homesickness faded. Institutional life slowly reached a comfort level. My lack of confidence, however, lingered; it wormed its way in and through most everything, especially my academic performance.

HOMESICK AT THE INHALING MONSTER

In our small town and even smaller parish, the lives of the Sisters intertwined so actively and constantly with those of my family that I didn't experience a terrible emotional rift when I joined the Community. The Sisters were already extended family to me. Best of all, now I had hundreds of older sisters.

Several classmates, however, had other reactions. I remember one girl in particular. It fell to all of us at regular intervals before breakfast to take the oily floor cloths we used under our mops to the dusting machine in the dark Motherhouse basement. That inhaling monster was a large, boxlike contraption much like an inverted vacuum cleaner. If we were exceptionally unlucky, we stood in a long line for our turn, thus losing precious moments needed to complete our daily work chores to the satisfaction of our superiors.

Somehow during those early four to six weeks while her homesickness lasted, this girl and I stood there together often, the whole line of us still within the Great Silence—she sobbing loudly over the breathy gulps of the machine and I desperate to comfort her without knowing how.

THOSE ELEPHANT EARS

No one warned me about the homesickness that would greet me every day, all day, at every meal (especially at every meal). The homesickness was like a coat that grew longer and longer as time went on. I missed my parents, my siblings, the farm—not the odors when the wind blew the wrong way, of course, but the fun we had there.

I missed Mom's cooking and her baking. She could cook anything and bake anything to perfection. As a matter of fact, she could have been awarded the blue ribbon at the Wisconsin State Fair many times over. Her peanut cupcakes were my favorite.

These square-shaped cupcakes were vanilla, with extra creamy frosting heaped with chopped salted peanuts. The thicker the frosting, the higher the peanuts. The head cook in the Convent never made peanut cupcakes.

She did gift us, however, with an amazing treat we called elephant ears. They were, without doubt, a runner-up to the cupcakes. The ears were huge, perhaps four inches in diameter, deep fried, topped with awesome frosting that had been drizzled on while they were still a tad warm. They were yummy and I always wanted more. One apiece. That was it!

COMFORTABLE

I remember being awed by the physical size of the Motherhouse and chapel. Outside of the Museum of Science and Industry, I had never been in such a large place. To this day I am very comfortable in large, older buildings with long corridor vistas, high ceilings and architectural detail.

STRANGELY LOVING WIND

Our lives were punctuated by prayer. The waking bell pierced our groggy worlds as an older Aspirant called out: "Jesus lives!" At that early hour and at that early age, how could we possibly have understood the challenge of our response—"Eternal love"? As we shuffled through predawn washing and dressing rituals, prayer continued. "As now I vest my body with my religious garb…"

Each room we entered carried not a number, but a name. A saint's name, most of them male.

No action or time period began without the reflection: "Place yourselves in the presence of God." We were reminded before algebra and world history, before lunch, before choir practice. Many times admittedly my mind had already leapt ahead to equations or wall maps, to food, to the Latin phrasings of Gregorian Chant.

One day, however, I was standing in the refectory with all the raw literalness of a fifteen-year-old and suddenly that phrase just stopped me still: *Place myself in the presence of God? How is it possible to be anywhere else? Wouldn't it be better to intone: Brace yourself in the presence of God? Be prepared. Brace yourself to embrace the unexpected, the unsought, even the unwanted.*

For the first time God swept through my life like an all-pervasive yet strangely loving wind. I could feel that presence pressing itself into my unknown future.

TEASING THE CITY GIRLS

The summer I remember most is the one we spent at the Convent Farm. I loved that summer. We teased the city girls by introducing them to cows and chickens. Besides taking sewing classes and botany, we weeded the garden, picked vegetables for meals, and I got to help catch chickens when they were needed for dinner.

I also remember thinking it was very funny when a cow grabbed the veil off the head of one of the Aspirants as we walked around the pasture saying our rosary together.

We slept in very crowded rooms but had a lot of fun waking up with rooster alarms and spending part of our day in the wonderful outdoors.

AT HOME ON THE CONVENT FARM

Being a farm girl, I felt totally at home on the Convent farm immediately. During our morning prayer, we could hear men's footsteps and their voices in the kitchen as they brought in the milk buckets from the barn. It made me homesick a bit, but I didn't care; it was comfortable and familiar.

I loved studying botany on the huge wrap-around porch. Science was never my strong suit, but searching for and then studying leaves on a farm porch was more like fun than work.

On Sundays for Mass we walked to different churches in the area where our Nuns taught and were then able to visit them in their Convents after Mass. I loved it! It made me long for the time when I, too, would be on mission. The Nuns seemed to have so much freedom compared to our very structured lives in formation.

I missed the second year Aspirants, who were spending their summer at St. Joseph Convent. But they did get to visit us on one occasion, and it was like a summer holiday! I remember playing ball in a huge field and wishing they didn't have to go back.

TABLE READER RENDEZVOUS

As a chubby, round-faced child, I did not have much self-confidence; however, I was very good at reading aloud. Because of my ability to inject interest and proper phrasing into my delivery, I was chosen as a regular table reader. I always looked over the material that I would be reading to give myself an idea of content and make sure there were no words I didn't know how to pronounce.

During one of my presentations the word *rendezvous* appeared. Undaunted, I simply pronounced it the way it looked: ren dez vus (short e's, the z sound of the second syllable, and short u and s sound of the third syllable). I had no idea it was a French word.

I kept reading—oblivious to the near-choking of the Aspirant Mistress. After the meal she diplomatically pulled me aside and advised me of the proper pronunciation of *rendezvous* and the importance of looking up unfamiliar words. To this day I can't see or hear that word without recalling this incident that took place so long ago.

SLEEPING, SEWING, MILKING, PICKING HEAVEN

I have fabulous, funny memories of our summer on the farm. There wasn't enough room for sleeping so two of us were put in a closet. The two cots could barely fit end to end so we had to crawl over each other's beds in order to get to them! We would laugh constantly as we maneuvered our way in and out of our beds. Oh, and was it hot in that closet. Hell warmed over.

One of the Sisters taught us sewing. I thought I would never forget how to do a flat-felled seam, but I have. Years later that Sister lived with us. Poor thing—I never learned to sew, to her utter dismay! I gladly ripped, washed, and ironed the habit pieces of others while they did my sewing. I still cannot sew.

The farm Sisters asked if anyone knew how to milk cows. Since my sister and I had grown up milking, to my delight we were allowed, when needed, to help with milking duty. I also remember a lot of apple picking, picking vegetables from the garden, and a lot of peeling and cleaning of fruit and vegetables.

The Motherhouse Chaplain came out to the farm for confessions. That could have been skipped in my opinion, but such was life in 1955.

Being a farm girl through and through certainly influenced my memories of the farm. I thought I was in heaven. I would have been glad to stay there forever!

HEIST OF CUPCAKES AND KOLACHES

During the early years of training especially, Visiting Sunday could never come fast enough or last long enough. Those of us with parents close enough for travel were the lucky ones. As you might imagine, our parents and siblings were just as excited about the visits. They would arrive with hugs aplenty, as well as packages of surprises. Some brought flowers, books, salve for acne, but mostly they brought our favorite bakery.

Those packages meant the world to me. Mom brought her famous peanut cupcakes. My friend's mother brought kolaches, the best in the world. I knew hers would take the prize even over those at the Czech bakery in Chicago on Cermac Street.

Oh, but no one ever told us that the wonderful packages given to us by our parents would not stay in our hands, on our laps or on our little shelves in the work area. Instead, the gifts were surrendered to respective superiors seconds after our visitors left. For later distribution.

No, no. This little detail was never mentioned in our handbook of rules/ regulations. The shock and disappointment were more than my heart (or stomach) could handle.

Others shared my sentiment. My dear friend was in disbelief. Before I continue with my story, I am compelled to tell you about her. Imagine the quiet in the Convent. Silence and quiet permeated the halls, dining rooms, dormitory areas, everywhere in the house. Not when she was around. She could speak without moving her lips. Her eyes did the talking, danced with laughter. The earth shook when she laughed out loud. At times, her laughter signaled a tad of mischief about to happen.

One fine day, it did happen! Both of us decided that the bakery our mothers gifted us with might stay in the superior's cupboards on the top shelf long enough to reach the stale stage. That just couldn't happen. Not to peanut cupcakes and the world's best kolaches.

The daring theft would take place during our first study time the day after visiting day. When all through the house the hallway floors would squeak in the silence, I would inconspicuously journey from the study hall to the area where the goodies were stored. After all, the frosting could melt on the cupcakes if we were to leave the box in the closet longer than a day.

Meanwhile my friend would cover for me while I made the journey to the closet, in hopes that no superior would notice the empty chair at my desk. My walk down the hall to the storage closet seemed more than just a block. Try a mile or two! My heart was pounding so hard I thought it would leap from my chest.

Once I entered the work area where the closet was, I prayed that the cupboard door would not be locked and ruin our whole plan. God was listening! The door was not locked, so I proceeded to maneuver the stack of packages to find our bakery. It took some skill to put all the packages back without leaving any empty spaces.

After a brief struggle to find both boxes, I gave a huge sigh of relief and proceeded with the goodies back to the silent study hall. I exchanged glances with my friend, a twinkle in her eye. Easy for her. I was the one who would be in trouble if caught.

I was caught. Didn't take a second. Before I even had a chance to open the boxes to share the goodies, a superior stood in the doorway. She was silent as she reached for the boxes. I was silent as I took a quick look at my friend. She did not have laughter in her eyes this time!

In one fateful moment, my ambitious intention changed to wanting the floor to open up and swallow both me and the bakery. I don't remember the consequence of my failed mission. I do remember I always wondered what happened to the cupcakes and kolaches.

THE WARNINGS

Almost from day one, the warnings began: "Avoid Particular Friendship." In equal parts serious and naïve, I struggled to understand. What was a particular friendship? How could a generic friendship even be possible?

Years later, when I realized the term referred to lesbian relationships, I wondered why our superiors had not been more specific. Sexually illiterate like many of my classmates, I still would not have understood what was meant, but at least a dictionary or encyclopedia, even in those pre-Wikipedia days, might have come to my rescue.

Another new lesson: "During recreation, don't spend all your time with the popular girls. Seek out those who might be struggling or feeling alone." Eager to become a good Sister, I did.

The result: Before our first month of Aspirant life was over, I was called into the Mistress's Office and accused, albeit kindly enough, of a particular friendship with a girl I didn't even like.

Second result: Never again in the Aspirancy did I seek out a waif or a stray!

IN THE WRONG RACKET?

It is a warm sunny day in early June. I am home for a three-week vacation from my first year in the Convent. I am sitting at the kitchen table with my dad. He is holding a beige-colored piece of paper in his large, calloused hand.

I'd entered the Aspirancy as a sophomore in the Convent high school. I had made the journey filled with the great desire to find God and give myself entirely to Him. I wanted to embrace the joy I had witnessed in the daily lives of the Sisters that had been my teachers for most of my grade school years.

The first days of the Convent were a shock to me. I knew that it was going to be strict and I had read about the rules and regulations that were going to seem strange to a teenager in the 1950s. I was ready for the 5 a.m. wake up call and all the prayers, but I couldn't find much of the joy. My greatest source of joy, fun and acceptance came from the other young girls who were my classmates. Most were from the Midwest and their simplicity and openness were delightful. Many are still among my dearest friends.

The best part of my day was the time spent in school under the spell of enthusiastic and caring teachers. I plunged into my studies with an energy I never knew I possessed. The one exception was our religion class, taught by an elderly priest, who just read from the book. We were expected to memorize material to be tested on. Even at that early age, I rebelled; I was looking for so much more.

My dad, a self-educated dock worker, is looking over the contents of the beige envelope—my report card. "Hmm, A's in history, English, math, and art, but a C- in religion! Did you ever think you might be in the wrong racket?"

A Bride of Christ

I had grown up in the 50s in a fairly typical Catholic family. We were obedient, how things looked was important and I was always nice to everyone. The town as well as my family had a strong German heritage so, at sixteen, I slipped easily into the School Sisters of St. Francis—a religious order with German roots. I loved the Sisters and I loved being a Sister.

In those days, I believed in a personal God who would watch over me and I believed that I was to become a bride of Christ—a lovely, comforting thought, except, of course, he was definitely the strong, silent type.

A Dozen Long-Stemmed Roses

During Advent and the forty days of Lent we received no letters or communications from our families. But for my birthday during Advent, my mother, who sometimes broke rules, sent me a dozen red, long-stemmed roses with the note: "Every girl ought to get a dozen long-stemmed roses once in her life." I remember being pleased and embarrassed as I opened the box and smelled the beautiful roses; then they disappeared, perhaps to the infirmary or to the chapel.

We kept no gifts, no matter who sent them.

Without a Mother

I had never been a really social person. So it amazes me now that I was always in the Penance Line for talking. I never learned how to keep the rule of silence. When someone needed something, I would always respond. Kitchen Duty, as penance, was an almost daily occurrence. In fact, I recall one occasion when I was not in the kitchen during recreation and I was not sure what to do.

Sleeping in a dorm didn't faze me. I'd never had my own room. But being a person who needs less sleep than most, I struggled. I had swollen glands forever, it seemed, and the infirmarian would make me a chamomile hot drink to take at bedtime. When I still couldn't sleep, I would crawl out the dormer window, sit on the roof and look at the stars while listening to the traffic on Layton Boulevard. No one ever told on me, and I certainly wasn't going to share that little bit of freedom with anyone else.

Somehow in those high school years I really developed only two friendships, still current today. One was with a gal who had the same back problem as I did. We were together as the rest did gym class. She was so smart (she liked math and science), but she treated me as a friend. The other came from a large family as poor as mine, maybe.

During sophomore year I realized what it meant to be without a mother. I was attracted to one of the House Sisters. She looked somewhat like the only picture I remembered of my own mother. I still have the book of poems I wrote about her. Sister did not allow me to attach to her. It hurt just a bit, but I was not surprised. I had never been close to a woman.

OUT OF MY ELEMENT

I had never been out of Chicago, so moving to the Motherhouse in Milwaukee to become an Aspirant as a high school junior was an amazing adventure and worry for me. I really didn't think I would miss the family I grew up in, but I did. Most of all, I missed my grammar school and high school friends who had accepted me as I was. They basically came from the same kind of home in which I grew up, so understanding was a given, without a lot of explanation. I was now with girls from many different backgrounds and I felt very isolated, overwhelmed and definitely out of my element.

I found our two superiors to be cold and demanding. I can look back and say that they were doing their jobs, but the hurt and confusion still live in me.

The Nuns who were our high school teachers helped me to cope with these challenges. Just like the teachers at my parish high school, they were the best of the best as far as I was concerned. They had high expectations for us. I found myself finally responding and trying to be a good student.

DARK NIGHT OF THE SOUL

To my dismay, soon after I arrived at the Convent at the tender age of thirteen, I started questioning my faith. I was not willing to just accept certain things and go on from there. I needed to go deeper. No assuming there is a God who always was and always will be. That was too easy.

I tried to talk to some classmates about my doubts, but no one was willing to go where I was. They always seemed to have the assurance that there is a God. I suffered from extreme guilt about my questioning. Most of the time, I tried not to think about my mental dilemma. This night of the soul that I experienced lasted throughout the Aspirancy, Postulancy, and on into the Novitiate.

Beginning of Contemplation

I can trace an almost direct line of grace from a book given to me as spiritual reading during the Advent season of my ninth grade Aspirant year to the books and realities that have most called my inner name for the rest of my life. That first book, Caryll Houselander's *The Reed of God*, already ten years old and well worn when it was placed in my hands, I opened. There glowed her first words:

> "That virginal quality which, for want of a better word,
> I call emptiness is the beginning of this contemplation."

With one sentence, the childishly romantic *Bells of St. Mary's* faded forever. I had entered a world of new music and silence, of both together in ceaseless paradox, of relentless openness to ongoing emanations that might choose to come my way from the heart of the universe.

In that prewinter dusk at age fourteen, wordlessly, I yearned to carry always what Houselander calls "a related heart connected to abiding beauty and indestructible light and life." I trusted that these years of formation—their struggles and small victories, their inevitable teenage angst and simple elations—would help set my heart on such a path.

My trust was not betrayed.

CHAPTER 3

POSTULANCY

LIFE AS A POSTULANT

After two years of Aspirancy, I became a Postulant, literally one requesting admission to religious life. Ninety-four young women aged sixteen to thirty became Postulants with me. That number dwindled to eighty-two before we entered the Novitiate.

Our Convent was a large, five-story building, several blocks long. It looked like an old college or huge hospital with lovely dormers and scrolling. Surrounding the building and its gardens was a tall wrought-iron fence that, we were taught, was not to keep us in but to keep the world out. More than four hundred women—professed Sisters, Novices and Postulants—prayed, worked, and slept in that building.

At one end stood a magnificent chapel patterned on the cathedrals of Europe, with high stained glass windows, mighty ceilings, a thundering organ, a faraway choir loft, marble terrazzo floors and white marble altars whose gold inlay sparkled in candle or sunlight. All day and all night, twenty-four hours a day, three hundred sixty-five days of the year, pairs of Nuns took turns praying for the world before the altar of our adjoining Adoration Chapel. We lived in personal poverty but surrounded by such magnificent music and art.

During my Postulancy, I completed my high school curriculum. I loved going to classes year round, which made it possible to graduate from high school in three years. Our teachers, among the best in a community of teachers, gave us an excellent background to support our future degrees.

Those who had already graduated from high school before entering the Postulancy attended Alverno, the women's college owned, administered and staffed by our Sisters.

One of our great joys as Postulants was learning to chant the eight official, beautiful prayers of psalms and lessons the Novices and Professed Sisters sang daily—Matins and Lauds in the morning; Prime, Terce, Sext, None throughout the day; Vespers and Compline late in the day. Prayer bound our days together.

We Postulants studied the Rules of the Community and prepared for the full life of the Nun.

MESHING AS A GROUP

I can still feel the welcome weight of our longer, heavier Postulant veil as compared with the wispy Aspirant one on the day we moved from Marian Hall back to the Motherhouse as Postulants, now only a scant ten months from becoming Novices—something we had been preparing for since we first set foot on Convent soil. How proud I was to place my hand just so to hold the new cape of our Postulant uniform together over my heart.

Over the next few weeks we new Postulants were joined by more than forty older, more experienced girls, some high school and college graduates, some with experience in the work world. To our sheltered eyes—veritable sophisticates. Together we were in large part farm and small town Midwestern girls with a sprinkling of city girls from Chicago and New York and four women from Central America, many of us the first women in our families who would receive a college education.

Because we former Aspirants knew the Convent ropes, we were excited and proud to be assigned as guardian angels to these newcomers. We had little appreciation of how it must have felt to them to be shepherded around by girls who likely reminded them of pesky little sisters left behind at home, particularly because between many of us there was an age gap of only two years.

It didn't help our meshing as a group that Sister Viola, the Postulant Mistress, seemed more comfortable with the former Aspirants, likely because she understood our self-contained, familiar Aspirancy world. So long removed from it, how could she possibly have understood the new world of independence, opportunity and leadership from which the older girls came? Even though we former Aspirants were ourselves only two years at most removed from that world, we too felt at times intimidated, at times intrigued by the wider worlds of these older sisters.

It would not be until the Novitiate that those distinctions began to dissolve at least somewhat and meld us truly into what we remain today, the Reception Class of 57.

FEROCITY OF THE INNER EXPERIENCE

In those early Motherhouse years, I passed the way a black person at that time might have been spoken of, most often pejoratively, as passing in white society. Looking back at that young girl, I know myself as the quintessential goody-goody, smiling and nodding.

No one could have known the expanse of what was going on inside me. I hardly knew myself. Since serious inner doubts about some aspects of religious teachings began for me by the age of four or so, belief has never been as important to me as inner experience. That experience, almost without realizing it, I pursued (and was pursued by) relentlessly.

The surface stumbling blocks of the institutional Convent superstructure I was able to ignore almost completely because of the ferocity of the interior experience offered by the prolonged periods of silence. My whole being thrilled with the almost undistracted devotion to study and reading, the art and sculpture we encountered in each corridor, the music I still hear in my heart's ear.

IT'S CONFUSING

My parents left several hours ago; they're back in Chicago now. So is my bedroom with its deep-sashed, filmy curtains and the closet where my pink prom dress and high-heeled sandals rest abandoned.

All my friends are back in Chicago too. And my beloved high school where I was editor of the yearbook and prefect of the Third Order of St. Francis.

Tonight I'm in this huge, vaulted chapel. It's dark outside now and dark inside too. Deep brown wooden benches filled with black-robed women. I'm kneeling in the front row, staring at my arm with its layers of black sleeve and cape. *Good Lord, I've made a horrible mistake.*

Afterward Postulants who have been Aspirants for one or two years, our guardian angels, take us to our sleeping quarters. Mine must be at least sixteen, but she has ten-year-old eyes. "We put shower slippers on our feet when we shower," she whispers primly.

"Well, I wash my feet in the shower." I don't even look at her as I speak. Are all the former Aspirants as blank-faced?

I steer clear of as many of them as possible. Thank heaven we College Postulants are bussed every weekday to a place where we can function as mature eighteen-year-olds. Sit me down in front of a book of literature, and I know who I am!

But it's confusing. I've never had so many rules to live by—some of them so minute. Be on time everywhere, especially chapel in the morning. Every Saturday afternoon, show the Mistress of Postulants two pairs of clean underwear and two pairs of clean stockings without holes. My stockings get holes very quickly, but I refuse to spend all Saturday afternoon mending them when I could otherwise be studying. I learn to show two mended pairs of stockings every week and to wear the ones with holes.

I try to obey the rules. I really do. Every morning I make a fresh resolution to do so, but at night, when I pull out my little particular examen book—alas, there are many infractions: I fell asleep during meditation again. Sister found dust in the corridor I clean daily. I laughed aloud in the dormitory just a few minutes ago when another Postulant got tangled in the curtains between our beds and stubbed her toe. I'll never make it to Nunhood.

And our Mistress of Postulants seems to have it in for me. She says I have spiritual pride and that I shouldn't be hanging around all the time with one other Postulant, that we should love everyone equally. What does that mean?

Has she ever been young? Has she ever been out of this huge Convent? Is she what I'm supposed to turn out like? I don't want to!

I'm not the only one confused. One day as we're riding to college, a twenty-two-year-old Postulant sits next to me on the bus. She's been part of the work force for four years. She looks at me grimly. "Every week the whole company payroll went through my hands, and now I can't fold rags correctly."

I commiserate. But, by this point, the bus has pulled up to the college. I grip my briefcase lovingly. It's Thursday, which means we don't have to go back to the Motherhouse for lunch. We eat with the college faculty and are supposed to use the afternoon for any necessary research. I don't have a paper pending, but my literature teacher said we're not going to study T. S. Eliot's "Four Quartets" because it's a difficult work, and we don't have time. Well, I found a commentary last Thursday on the reference shelf, and I'll have all afternoon to enjoy myself. Up in the library stacks where nobody has to know where I am and what I'm doing.

FROM MIND TO HEART

When I graduate from high school, my class rank is 14 out of 178. I am really smart. My understanding goes deep, and my memory is second to none. It's a good thing I'm smart because, heaven knows, I'm not beautiful—and a girl needs something to base her life on.

I'm entering a Convent where nobody knows me, but it won't take long before they recognize how smart I am and appreciate my contributions.

Only that's not what happens. My Mistress of Postulants seems to value other things more than intelligence—things like making a bed with military precision and getting to the chapel on time. Though I really try, I am not good at either. And then there is the really shocking accusation: she tells me I have intellectual pride. Sometimes it seems like a good mind is the only thing of myself I have to hold on to....

Recently, when I became a Sufi, I realized how right my Postulant Mistress was about intellectual pride, especially the amount of it that she saw in me. Like Buddhists, Sufis teach that the mind is usually a tyrant, a Master of Illusion and Deception. Sufis go to God through the heart; this seems to me a much deeper, more balanced, mystical process, rooted in love. I am learning how to make this shift.

I thank all my spiritual teachers—starting with my Mistress of Postulants, whose first lesson I wasn't ready to hear at the time.

A Relationship to All Life

As new Postulants, we were being taught the decorum of religious life. Don't bang doors, don't clang your silverware against the dishes, hand the serving bowl carefully and diligently to the Postulant next to you. Examples were many.

One day our Postulant Mistress said by way of encouragement, "You can tell a saint by the way he (I'm sure that would have been the pronoun of the day) holds things, picks them up and puts them down and hands them to others." The next day I, and probably many others, were 'wannabe' saints. The refectory and hallways were a bit quieter, I'm sure.

Today when I'm watering my garden, removing a dead leaf or flower, or when I am putting my dishes in the cupboard, arranging a table setting or changing the bedding, I often remember this teaching. The difference—I'm sure I don't qualify as a saint and it is not my wannabe.

What is present is a relationship to life—plants, dishes, bedding, the beautiful sickle moon or the purple finch nesting in my begonia plant. It matters not. The reverence within all life, including my own, is today's love creation.

Sister Viola, Mistress of Postulants

On a September day now misted to memory, we stood together as Postulants to begin life together as the Reception Class of 1957. There, too, stood the diminutive woman charged with our care.

What none of us knew, would never even have thought to ask, is when had this little Nun—to us elderly at sixty-four—with her slightly crooked walk and nervous hand gestures come to this Motherhouse building and Convent life. She was born in a century our eyes had never seen, in the final month of 1892. She became Sister Viola almost half a year before her sixteenth birthday and Mistress of Postulants before she turned 21. Her very first Postulant classes would, like herself, have been born toward the end of the nineteenth century.

We, on the other hand, her forty-third class of Postulants and ninety-some in number, were born in a century she had barely experienced except through the filter of life in a Convent. Her desire must have been to form us to fit the mold of that early community, the one she knew best, certainly the one she revered. Unbeknownst to us, possibly also even to her, we were to be her last Postulants. A transition class. End of the old. Beginning of the new.

Some, such as myself who entered as Aspirants immediately after grade school, knew her almost as an old maid aunt, peripheral, someone not to be taken too seriously. We still had, after all, our significantly younger and greatly respected high school teachers as guides and models.

On the other hand, those who entered after high school or college, older and more worldly-wise, met her as a first superior. For them she was the very face of life in the Convent, one with significant authority to shape and decide our futures and hopefully wisdom and experience to match. With the arrival of these Postulants who would spend their days at Alverno College away from the Convent enclosure, the clash of cultures—emphasis on rules, order and cleanliness vs. love for education, art, music and beauty—became more personally and painfully felt.

The buildings themselves, both beautiful in their own ways, epitomized the difference. The Motherhouse was massive, dark and old; Alverno College bright, airy and new. Life in the Motherhouse placed great value on simplicity, humility, punctuality, self-denial and blind obedience to God's will as manifested in the will of the Superior. Life at Alverno College invited intellectual curiosity and informed awareness of wider political, sociological, psychological and even theological worlds.

To a simple woman like Sister Viola, how could these older Postulants not have seemed exotic foreigners whose pride and independence stood in dire need of curbing? Within that creative tension, our own version of the medieval town and gown experience, our daily routines began—finishing high school, starting college or advanced studies. Accomplishing the many tasks large and small involved in institutional life.

Like my maternal grandfather, Sister Viola had a basketful of quixotic, mixed language words and sayings— "religious decorum, culture of the heart, *macht schnell,* alacrity, *dummkopf,* put on a happy face…."

When I asked classmates for their memories of some of these words, one sent this recollection: "'Go to chapel and pray!' One of us would barely get back from chapel and she'd say, 'Go to chapel and pray!'"

Another notes: "Somewhere in my cranial cavity the word (spelled phonetically) *Ouskilousken* harks back to the Convent, a description of our minds going off in a million directions or frenzied teenagers not having grasped the fine points of decorum."

As I sounded out the spelling of my friend's phonetics, I also could hear Viola saying that word. I emailed its phonetic spelling to my sister-in-law from Germany. She called back to say that the word must have been *ausgelassen*, whose meanings include high-spirited, skittish, rackety, boisterous, frolicsome, wild, kittenish, coltish, giddy. Such we certainly must have been—and Viola beside herself with concern that she would never be able to rein us in!

For me, no quote of hers was as trademark as "Two prisoners looked out from behind the bars./ One saw mud and the other stars." Lost on my naïveté was the analogy with incarceration. However, I didn't miss the implied approval of those who in dire circumstances could bring themselves to see stars and the suspected lack or character flaw in anyone who dared to catch even a glimpse of the mud.

As a group we lived on that slippery continuum from mud to stars. I was one who by disposition consistently saw stars. Now, with such strong tacit encouragement, that natural tendency became firm resolve. At the time I had no awareness of its downside—how such a view could blind me to the suffering of others and how it could proceed from a place of unacknowledged fear and distance me from my own pain as well. Others, good friends, lived mired in the mud. Struggling and suffering. And silent.

Memory inhabits much the same continuum. As we moved on beyond the Postulancy, life continued, as all life does, to offer both mud and stars. We continued to learn both coping skills and transformative spiritual and life-integration practices.

Some fifty years later when we started work on this book, our early silence was broken as seldom before. We began to admit to ourselves and to each other that both the mud and the stars, taken separately, were limiting and ultimately harmful perspectives even though remnants of those early patterns remained. Some who saw stars then—about life in general, about Convent life or Sister Viola—continued to see mostly stars. Some who saw mud continued to see mostly mud. Yet we are coming to see how these Postulancy memories fit into the integral fabric of the mud and stars of our whole lives.

Somehow, through all life's mud and stars, that early spark of *ausgelassen* still flames. It, too, has transformed and deepened into a mature and vibrant inner courage, allowing us to continue challenging our cherished assumptions and self-identifications and risking glimpses of still deeper vision. It encourages our movement from polarizing either/or positions to a more realistic and expanded view—the both/and of any healthy human life.

So, Sister Viola, hats (and veils) off to *ausgelassen*! Thank you for the stars you longed for us to see even when we couldn't and for the mud you wished to spare us even though you couldn't.

"Keep Me, O Lord, As the Apple of Thine Eye"

I remember once when I was having a bad day, Sister Viola told me to say, "Keep me, O Lord, as the apple of thine eye; protect me under the shadow of thy wings." I said it over and over, and it got me through the day. Over the many years, I have repeated that prayer when in need. That prayer has helped me.

More than the Curriculum

Our teachers, like the women who had taught me in grade school, conveyed more than the curriculum requirements for our high school and college education. They shared their faith and opened our minds far beyond our immediate surroundings and lifestyle.

However, I often wondered about the minutiae of instructions and corrections that seemed to be the focus of the weekly conferences from our Mistresses. I kept hoping to learn more about prayer, the interior life, and relationship with God.

5:30 a.m. Meditation

I remember vividly trying many mornings during 5:30 meditation to get into a smelly fishing boat with the grimy disciples and never quite managing to do so. The method itself (Ignatian) may have suited men but didn't seem at the time the most inviting to teenage girls.

How our superiors must have struggled to teach it to us! Very likely their souls longed for more, even as ours did.

PART OF SOMETHING LARGER

Despite the regimentation and the barebones lifestyle—how we dressed, worked, ate, slept, prayed, sang, recreated—I felt happy to be part of such a large group where I always found someone to talk to and work with. There was a certain comfort for me in the order and predictability of each hour of each day.

I felt our class bonded because of common feelings, values, joy, suffering, inconvenience, and at times, insanity. It became evident that each classmate possessed her own unique talents, all of us complementing each other in some way. I felt that I was part of something larger than family or neighborhood or school.

Though I could not have verbalized it then, I felt the definite contrast between all the ideas and life of St. Francis that we studied and the reality of being in an essentially German-influenced community: authority, discipline, order, hierarchy, sameness, judgment, conviction, punishment, fear, etc.

This culture was the direct opposite of the one I had come from in my family, which had influences of farmers, artists, and union workers. Not much religion and a rather loose day-by-day operation for all, but an appreciation for and knowledge of the natural world.

The Postulant Mistress in desperation one day accosted me and said, "I know what's wrong with you. You went to public high school and you were raised by a Protestant grandmother." Of course, she was right. I had gone to public high school and did not have the experience of many other Postulants who had gone to Catholic girls' schools where they got to know the Nuns.

Attending Alverno College provided that experience for me. It opened my eyes to many different challenges and insights and for the first time I felt I was really learning. In my classes at Alverno, I experienced strong, smart, highly educated and successful women who not only challenged us, but also supported our talents and directed our efforts in each class. These women, at that time almost all Sisters, were great mentors and I cherish their example to this day.

One day at Alverno I was with another Postulant who said, "Let's go see Sister Augustine (Alverno's president at that time) and tell her what a great job she's doing." So we went to her office, knocked on the door and were admitted. My friend said, "We just wanted to tell you that we think you are doing a wonderful job here at Alverno." And then we told her how much we liked being there and what a great place it was. I don't remember her reply, only that she smiled and was kind to us and chuckled a bit.

ISIS OF THE BLUE NILE

On important days like the feast of St. Francis, patron of the Community, and Christmas, Easter, and other special holidays like the Fourth of July and Mardi Gras, we might be treated to a full-length feature film. We saw these movies with several hundred Postulants and Nuns sitting on hard wooden chairs in St. Joseph Hall. A movie projection 'booth' showed 16mm films with pauses as the film reels were changed.

If a movie were about to show a man and woman kissing or getting intimate in any way, the Sister projectionist would slide her black scapular in front of the light to block out the scene. You can imagine how our imaginations worked overtime developing that scene.

Most of the movies were the Legion of Decency's rating: safe for children. That meant we saw movies about dogs. Too many dog movies.

Finally, one feast day the buzz was, "Tonight's movie is *Isis of the Blue Nile!* That can't be a dog movie!" Well, imagine the sighs when onto the screen leaped Isis of the Blue Nile—a four legged, sophisticated golden retriever. There were no scenes to block out.

GOD MUST WANT ME

There was a mantra, I don't recall whose, "If you continue to do that, we will send you home." I believed it. So when it came time to receive the veil as a Novice, and they hadn't sent me home, I figured God must want me to be a Nun. I surely was not holy enough. And I could not meditate, so I was sure that I wasn't good enough. But no one else seemed to be either.

They never did send me home—even with chronic illnesses that the doctor said would go away if I went home. I guess they knew what home was like for me, or maybe they guessed. I don't recall feeling sorry for myself.

FEAR AND ITS CONSEQUENCES

My initial impressions of the Convent pretty much met my expectations. I was prepared for a disciplined life: the rules of silence, custody of the eyes, retreat days, daily work, Saturday's chores and mending, early rising—all of these were expected and accepted joyfully. Not all was positive though. People are flawed—and I found that this included the superiors whose responsibility it was to guide us. Naively I expected them to be perfect, to be loving.

Having grown up in a spontaneous and happy environment, I was not prepared for the experience of fear that entered my life—fear of my superiors, fear of the Mother General, fear of all authority figures. I don't know where this fear came from; I'd never known fear in my family or school life before. My parents were strict, but lovingly strict, and *lovingly* is the key word here, I think.

During our formation years in the Convent, I never felt our corrections, our penances, many of our instructions were given out of love or out of interest in us personally, but to preserve order and to be sure we did not upset the perfection of the rules we were meant to follow. I remember vividly the nervous anxiety I would feel every time I had to report back to a superior after fulfilling a task or to apologize for something I had done wrong. On many occasions I felt close to tears and had to muster all my courage even to approach the superior.

I mention this because I believe this overarching fear did two things to me. First, it affected my relationship with God. God could only love me if I were perfect and, at that time in my young life, perfection meant doing all the externals exactly. I did not know the meaning of grace until a few years ago. Secondly, it closed something inside of me—the willingness to dare, the spontaneity and creativity that I remember in myself as a child.

LA GENTE VALIENTE QUE SE TRASLADA A OTRO PAÍS (THOSE VALIANT ONES WHO UPROOT THEMSELVES TO ANOTHER COUNTRY)

Repare usted la gente valiente que se traslada a otro país a seminarios o a conventos. Lleva su valija, pero deja su convivencia social, se desviste de todo. Ya trasladada a veces te quedan algunos segundos para respirar, si es que respiras y dices: "No te abrís mas, recuerda lo que decía tu abuela, tu papa, tu mama… "hay que saber afrontar la vida".

Y afortunadamente te encuentras con buenos maestros que te adoctrinan: "Human Rights," "In god we trust," "to be or not to be," "'Honest' Pretension" y caminando las grandes distancias dentro de los edificios, le das vueltas y revueltas, en la cabeza, a esos credos—y mucha otra gente se ve seria y pensativa, quizá por lo mismo. Tienes que estar pendiente porque repetidas veces, te vuelves a perder, a perder entre tanta gente, donde comes, donde duermes, donde estudias y mucho mas donde rezas. Muchísima gente—y tu sola.

Sin embargo a pesar de todo, se crece. Eso si.

THOSE VALIANT ONES WHO UPROOT THEMSELVES TO ANOTHER COUNTRY
(LA GENTE VALIENTE QUE SE TRASLADA A OTRO PAÍS)

Consider for a moment those valiant ones who uproot themselves to another country to seminaries or convents. Such a one carries her suitcase but leaves behind her social support system and way of life; she divests herself of everything. Now transplanted, she may breathe in rare seconds, if she breathes at all, and say: "Don't open yourself any further. Remember the words of your grandmother, your papa, your mama… 'You have to know how to face life.'"

Fortunately you find yourself among good teachers who instill within you: "Human Rights," "In God we trust," "To be or not to be," "'Honest' Pretension." And walking the great distances within the buildings, you turn these beliefs over and over in your head. Others view you as serious and thoughtful, perhaps for that very reason. You need to be vigilant because time and again you get lost, lost among so many people, where you eat, where you sleep, where you study and many more wheres. So many people—and you alone.

Nevertheless, despite everything, you grow. That for sure.

EASY AND DIFFICULT

Some of the aspects of my new way of life were very easy for me and some were very difficult. Getting up at 5 a.m. was not a big deal for me because I had been doing that at home. It was easy also to follow most of the rules we had, but some of them did not make sense to me. I had had more responsibility and opportunity for making decisions at home than I felt I was being given in the Convent. Because I was very shy, I did not speak up for fear of being sent home.

I spent one year as an Aspirant and one year as a Postulant before entering the Novitiate. Those years had their ups and downs. Many times I wished I could share with someone what was really going on inside me. When I did try, it seemed as though it was always in the wrong place at the wrong time. Ultimately, I decided that things had to get better as time went on.

I did not form any close friendships because, by the time one began to develop, other Sisters felt that I was smothering the person, or the Sister herself had chosen another path.

SAN SERVING WITH GRACE, CARE AND KINDNESS

One of our tasks as Postulants, and later as second year Novices, was to wait tables at the Sacred Heart Sanitarium for people undergoing treatment. ('San serving' we called it.) I don't remember whether it was for all three meals, but I do remember serving beautifully cut grapefruit, among other fruits, for breakfast and setting lovely tables for evening dinners.

There were two dining areas, one dark room with white tablecloths with expensive china and beautiful rugs for wealthy patients and the other casual for patients who seemed more like ordinary people. We Postulants began as servers in the casual area and later were moved to the dining room where patients dressed for dinner (women in long gowns, sometimes with much jewelry, and men in suits, sometimes tuxedos). At tables that seated six or so, we served each guest individually from platters and dishes as we moved from one guest to another like servants in 20s and 30s movies. Someone said later that these old, frail men and women included movie stars. I do not know if that was true because these guests never spoke to us young Nuns, and the Sisters in charge of the dining rooms and kitchens maintained privacy.

We were to serve everyone the same—with grace, care, and kindness. And we were grateful for the patients at our Community's Sacred Heart Sanitarium. Its international reputation brought patients from many countries and helped support our educations as well as the numerous works of our Nuns for the poor and downtrodden.

SMALL PRICE TO PAY

Those formation years provided rigorous academic and crowd control disciplines. After all, we lived in a home of hundreds of women. We were responsible not only for our own Convent food, laundry, cleaning and maintenance, but also for helping with the laundry and food service of our community-owned mental hospital and our world-famous sanitarium.

Many the trips we took through dark, damp underground tunnels, veils flying, pushing straw-smelling carts of dirty sheets and bed clothing! Looking back, I consider that physical labor a small price to have paid for the excellent education we received. To this day, many young people have to take on similar jobs with little hope of ever receiving the quality education we did.

We had, after all, entered a burgeoning religious order that faced the unexpected need to place more emphasis on order than on religion or any kind of spiritual formation. Our religious instructions focused often on how the rule would keep us if we but kept it. Such axioms hardly nourished the idealistic dreams many of us had before we entered.

What We Lived On

My most treasured childhood Christmas gift ever came in my eighth grade year—a portable Olivetti typewriter. Televisions were just beginning to enter middle class households with computers as yet decades away. In our circumscribed 1950s world, most of us had very limited access to the outside world.

Within the Convent, even the limited outside worlds of our early lives shrank dramatically. We lived on the strength of each other, what Erving Goffman in his dense but brilliant book *Asylums* describes as the 'underlife' within total institutions, and of whatever inner worlds we, largely individually, were able to create and sustain. Even under the ever-watchful eye of superiors, the underlife we shared as late teens and twenty-somethings was vibrant and thrilling, exploits that continue to unite us in nostalgic laughter while creating much deeper bonds many, many years later.

Like Big Sisters

The graduation ceremony for us forty-some Postulants who finished high school that spring was a sad, solemn affair in St. Joseph Hall. By taking heavy course loads, even in the summers, we had worked hard to finish all our high school classes in three years.

Our families were not invited. I remember the Sister Principal on stage handing out diplomas; perhaps there were a few speeches and a song or two. Finally it was over and, as new high school graduates, we began excitedly talking and laughing.

Our Postulant Mistress swung her large rosary beads and stopped all talking. "Go to the chapel and say the Stations of the Cross," she commanded. So off we went to celebrate our graduation via the way of the crucified Jesus.

The college Postulants, like big Sisters, horrified that we graduates were given no time to savor our accomplishments, put together a celebration of skits and poems to acknowledge our big day. It was the first time I felt the older women really cared about us and understood the level of our young sacrifices. We were not just naïve little lambs.

THE TRANSFORMING LIGHT OF GOD

I was asked by Sister Viola to create the lyrics to our class song, words that musicians in our class would put to music. I was thrilled to be asked. Poetry was something I'd loved and written for as long as I could remember. Perhaps this wonderful task would lead me to feel more a part of St. Joseph Convent.

We had a class motto: *Nothing is impossible for those who will and those who love.* And we had a patron saint—chosen pretty much because our Mistress of Postulants had suggested him: Saint Ignatius of Laconi. Nobody had ever heard of him before that. I doubted that I could work the motto into a poem, but I'd have to mention our patron. In order to do my best, I went deep inside. This is what poured out:

> When the vines of the harvest are heavy with fruit
> And the sun rises purple and flame,
> Oh, the Master is anxious to gather the grapes.
> Come, Sisters, and work for His Name.
>
> Who will teach us to sing of a crucified King?
> Who will teach us to smile in the song?
> For we cannot tremble at His wounded touch,
> And we must not fear to love too much.
> His hope lies in the strong!

Oh, glorious Ignatius,
Wise with the wisdom of simple men!
Oh, glorious Ignatius,
Strong with the strength of Christ.
Teach us the wisdom of souls that give,
That we may die and God may live.
Show us the price of reaping souls
And the courage to pay the price.

Ignatius, Ignatius,
Glorious Ignatius,
Our radiant light.

I recall thinking, years later, that all my pain during the Postulancy had been sealed into those words. What a terrible picture of my future service of God! The last three lines had been added by someone else. The musicians? Our Mistress of Postulants? At the time I resented someone tacking all that light on to the darkness I'd written about.

Now I'm grateful. Because, whether we stayed or left, the Light of God continues to transform us. That's what this book is about.

WAITING AND WAITING

I decided to enter the Convent in November so I would be part of the Reception Class of 1957 because a good friend from my high school was already in that class. Entering the Convent was a rather scary step; I figured that having a friend already in place would make it seem less scary.

My first six months were uneventful. I made new friends, got used to new classes with new teachers, made some inroads into the spiritual life, although I never could figure out what I was supposed to be doing during meditation. I found my niche by keeping my head down and blending in.

And then my friend was sent home, a term meaning that somehow she had been found wanting. But now I had new friends, good friends, and I didn't even think of quitting. Graduation from high school was approaching at the end of May, then Reception retreat, then Reception into the Novitiate, June 13, the class of 1957.

The first bombshell to hit me was the principal informing me that in all probability I would not graduate with the others because I did not have enough credits. How could this be? If I had remained at my local high school, I would have had five or six credits beyond the requirements. Was not that school staffed by the same order of Nuns? I took the college prep track there. What did they mean: I didn't have enough credits?

I'm surprised I had the nerve to voice my concerns to this woman whom I barely knew. I guess I was no longer keeping my head down. Scenarios of being held back to graduate with the Aspirant class behind me were torture. In the end, after an agonizing week, I got the news that yes, indeed, I had enough credits to graduate. I don't know what kind of math was involved; I just know that someone went to bat for me and I am still grateful. I would have missed out on being part of a significant adventure with some of the people I still hold very dear.

Another bombshell awaited. Because of the size of our class, it was decided that it would be split into two sections, a June Reception and an August Reception. Those Postulants who entered before September 8 would be in the June Reception and those after would be received in August, essentially putting the high school Postulants in the early one and the college and post-college Postulants in the later one.

While the high school students had classes in the Motherhouse, the college Postulants were able to go to Alverno College, mingle with lay college students and be away from the watchful eyes of our Postulant Mistress for part of the day. She meant well, but she was elderly, possibly in pain from ailments of the elderly; her moods and behavior were erratic. It made for tension in the Postulancy, and the prospect of having to wait two months to move on to the Novitiate was a great disappointment.

Then we were physically split into two groups, even with the suggestion that we have no contact with the other group. I am not sure how it happened or who initiated the thought, but something wonderful began that summer. We refused to be separated spiritually and emotionally. We couldn't wait to come back together once more as a class in the Novitiate.

CLOSE FRIENDSHIPS

I was prepared for friendships, but not with the depth or height or breadth I experienced in the Convent. These friendships were not dependent on the clothes you wore, or the grades you got, or your good looks. These grew out of shared experiences, common goals and dreams, discussions of literature, and our deep longings to know the God we came to serve. Almost all of my closest friends are still those that began and were nurtured over fifty years ago in the Convent. "For My Friend" was written in those early years.

FOR MY FRIEND

You are always gift
when you come—
newly wrapped to
each moment.

Your greeting (remiss of
card and postage)
occasions out of
nowhere
a birth day and
I am a Yes older.

SILENCE, SOLITUDE

For me the call to religious life came before Postulancy. The Postulancy and Novitiate solidified my being. I could not have had a better experience. I was shocked later to find that not everyone loved the Postulancy and Novitiate. Silence, solitude, these were the epitome of religious life. For me Novitiate was the end, was everything I would have been happy to have my whole life.

CHAPTER 4

NOVITIATE

LIFE AS A NOVICE

After nine months as a Postulant, I delightedly became a Novice. On our Reception Day into the Order of the School Sisters of St. Francis, our Mother Superior handed me a new name on a three-by-five white card. That name was to hide my old identity from the world.

A Nun cut my hair to within an inch of my skull and shaved around my ears so none of my hair could escape from beneath the veil. She covered my head with a white cotton cowl. Over the cowl I wore a white veil that hung in folds almost to my thighs.

We Novices learned to sit up straight. Everyone could tell if a Novice had broken that rule because her veil would be creased by the pressure of such leaning. Good Novices went for two years without resting their backs.

Around my body hung layers of a black serge habit that reached about an inch from the floor. Black stockings and shoes completed the habit. Thus, except for face and hands, I was covered in yards of wool. Because Novices owned no coats, this wool was wonderful in the northern winters where temperatures often reached zero or below, but the same black habits became sticky problems in the hot summer. In one-hundred-degree heat, the smell of wet, sweaty serge in laundry rooms, kitchens, and gardens couldn't be erased by incense.

The rising bell clanged at 5 a.m. and we, in our dormitories of fifty or so white-curtained cells, responded. One of my little pleasures occurred each Sunday—we slept until 6 a.m. Our daily schedule was fine for the early riser, who I am not, and for someone who can function well on less than seven hours of sleep, which I cannot. I, who seldom can sleep before midnight, after hours of exhausted tossing, finally slept only to be awakened in the best hours of my sleep to begin the day all over again.

Once every two weeks we were awakened by twos between 1 a.m. and 4 a.m. to take our turns for an hour in the Adoration Chapel for special prayer watches. I loved these hours of special prayer in the middle of the night—but for years was perpetually exhausted.

Most mornings by 5:30 we had taken a sponge bath, dressed without mirrors, and walked the several blocks through the Convent halls to the chapel.

There we said traditional morning prayers in English, sang the beautiful hours of the Office in Gregorian Chant, meditated for half an hour, and attended a celebration of holy Mass. Each morning as I watched the hundreds of women move quietly to the front of the chapel to receive Communion, I felt deeply moved that they had invited a young girl like me to join them. These hours of the morning were the most profound hours of my day.

After Mass, we cleaned the Convent. My task usually involved scrubbing a large bathroom of six toilet stalls, four bathtub stalls, and four hand sinks. Sometimes a Nun came to check that we Novices were doing a good job. I knew her white glove usually fingered only the chrome around the faucets, so I kept it sparkling.

Every Saturday we pinned up our skirts and rolled up our sleeves to clean intensely, doing what other housekeepers might do once a year. Our Convent shone spotlessly. I have never experienced that intense cleanliness anywhere else, not even in a hospital. No home has ever smelled as aromatic as that mix of beeswax, polish, and incense.

While we cleaned, Nuns in the kitchen prepared our breakfast consisting of a piece of fruit, a bowl of hot oatmeal, a slice of bread, and a protein, usually a slice of cheese. We ate in large refectories where eight women sat at each table and shared food. It was assumed by the Novice Mistress that all food would be eaten because nourishment was necessary if the body were to accomplish the day's work and prayer.

Partial fasting was mandatory on some days, when less food was served, but we were still expected to finish all the sustenance at the table. Not for us the luxury of deciding when to fast or abstain. A distinct part of living in community was this acceptance of the decisions made by others. We acted without our own will, whether it was in the amount and kind of food we ate, the types of books we read, or the time we rose or went to bed. All of the minutes of the day were prescribed; choices were not given. But this was not all negative. Not having choices freed one, provided more time to concentrate on spiritual experiences, to meditate.

As a first year Novice, each morning and afternoon I helped wash the dirty laundry of hundreds of Nuns and several large hospitals operated by our Community. At first, I was in charge of great circular commercial-size machines that washed or dried sheets and towels, but after I caught my arm in one of the spinning cycles and almost twisted my elbow out of its socket, I was assigned to iron altar linens. During our manual labor in the laundry or kitchen, we prayed aloud together. At noon we ate our main meal and then attended chapel to chant the short Sext and None hours of the Office. Twice a day, after each main meal and prayers, we recreated for about a half hour.

Most of the time I lived awe-dazzled by the art, wide-eyed at the liturgical ceremonies, humbled by the hundreds of dedicated women who opened their home and way of life to me. Sister Archelaus, our Novice Mistress, moved among us as an inspiration and spiritual leader, teaching us, guiding us in the ways of the religious life we were to live.

At the noon and evening meals we were served generous portions of traditional European cuisine, the best of which I have tasted only in a few fine restaurants. The cooks, some from Europe, prepared balanced meals of fruits, vegetables, beef, pork, and poultry produced largely by the Nuns on our community farm.

Like many people in farming communities, we ate whatever was in season. When tomatoes were plentiful, for breakfast we Novices were served sliced ripe tomatoes instead of apples or citrus fruit; dinner included hot tomato soup, hot diced tomatoes as the day's vegetable, perhaps sliced tomatoes as salad, and tomato sauce on the meat. Supper again dished up sliced tomatoes or diced tomatoes. Coffee breaks doled out tomato juice. This red menu, with small variations, lasted for days.

Once, after days of eating tomatoes in every guise, we were served what looked like strawberry shortcake. We secretly breathed relief until we tasted it—tomato shortcake with pink tomato frosting.

Choir Novices finished the day's manual labor early and joined the choir Postulants for an hour of practice. Here I learned with surprise that I had a respectable contralto singing voice. In choir I was introduced to the magnificent melodies of the polyphonic composers and Gregorian and Liturgical hymns. Only the Vienna Boys' Choir, which I later heard in Vienna itself, can equal the clear, high voices of the Nuns' choir singing on Christmas Eve or at dawn on Easter morning when melodies soared and echoed from the cathedral ceilings.

After choir practice, we gathered in chapel to sing Vespers, pray the rosary, and read writings of the great thinkers of the Church.

At 6 p.m. we ate another balanced meal of a protein, salad, vegetable, starch, and dessert, then recreated for half an hour, perhaps walking in the garden (which I loved), playing cards (which I hated) or just talking to each other. We lived the Convent dictum: hands off, arm's length, and so for almost all those years I was in the Convent, I never touched anyone or even shook hands. This absence of touch was one of my most profound losses. By 7:30 p.m., we were again in silence, this time to study until 9 p.m. when we attended chapel again to say evening prayers and to chant Compline, the last soothing prayer of our Liturgical Day. Lights were out by 10.

Night, from Compline until after breakfast, was called the Great Silence, and no one talked except in dire emergencies. Night was to be the time of uninterrupted communing with God.

As second year Novices, in addition to our prayer and work in the Motherhouse, we attended Alverno College, the college created and staffed mostly by our Nuns. This second year I settled into a time of challenging study and deepening spirituality, learning new ideas and great literature, enjoying the deep richness of our college faculty, the art galleries, the library, the women students, the new theology, the music, and the drama, all in the security of the Novitiate life.

Part of the wonder of the Novitiate—learning about God, having no obstacles to prayer times, studying the vows, having freedom from worries about ordinary financial issues, all while nesting in a group of wonderfully educated women leaders. Women's liberation, as I read of it later, need only to look for inspiration to our Nuns as mentors.

The White-Veiled Innocent

The romantic aura that swirled around Convent life, both inside and outside the walls, found its vortex in the Novice—the initiate, the white-veiled, the innocent, the perpetual bride. In our ears rang words such as those of Gerard Manley Hopkins' "Heaven-Haven"—"And I have asked to be/ Where no storms come…"

Perhaps we believed these words. Undoubtedly we longed to believe them as we knelt breathlessly at the altar rail that summer morning of our Reception with our new name, as yet unknown to us, folded between our trembling fingers for the Bishop to read out to the world. "You have been known as Pat, Jeanne, Sandra… You will now be called Sister Mary…."

Decades later I read in Joan Ohanneson's *Scarlet Music* her prescient words about a young woman entering Hildegard of Bingen's Convent in the 1100s. The young woman curtsied to the Magistra, rose slowly and asked: "Am I truly entering the gates of Paradise, my lady?"

The Magistra assured her that much would depend on what she brought inside these gates and who she became when they closed behind her, adding "There will be many surprises."

In ten centuries, had much changed? We, too, knelt there, the youngest among us sixteen, the oldest thirty-one, our faces radiant, unafraid of surprises and awaiting some version of paradise. Forgotten or denied was the reality that the *tabula* wasn't *rasa*. We weren't blank slates. Neither were those charged with our care.

Charged principally with that care during our two Novitiate years stood the tall, elegant, silent, formidable figure of our Mistress, Sister Archelaus. Even as Aspirants and Postulants living in the same building with her for one to three years, few if any of us had ever heard her speak, still less experienced her trademark chuckle and quick handkerchief to the mouth to stifle outright laughter. No square of cloth, however, could cover the participatory twinkle in her vibrant eyes.

What, tucked deep within the designs of our souls, did we bring inside those Novitiate gates? Who would we become? And what would be the surprises?

A Day of Love and Promise

The memories I have of our Reception Day are beautiful—a day of love and promise that still remains today. I would not trade it nor change it in any way. How blessed we were and are because we responded to a call.

"Trouble Getting Your Duds On?"

I believe there is something human in every spiritual event and something spiritual in every human event. Thus, I share my experience of Reception Day.

In my eighteen-year-old self I suppose I embraced the right reasons for wanting to be a Franciscan Nun. I wanted to serve others in joy and simplicity as St. Francis did, to exult in the music, beauty and dance of creation, to become a selfless bride of Christ. Though my actions that day spoke these lofty ideals outwardly, my inner self was reacting to things much more mundane—the crude chopping off of my hair, the antiquated name that I thought I'd have to bear forever, and masking disappointment with a smile as I told my new religious name to my parents. Then there was the problem of all the new bindings around my face and forehead. I couldn't wait to take them off!

That same night I remember the stifled chuckles as we witnessed each other in the dormitory during the Great Silence. There was supposed to be no talking and the keeping of custody of the eyes during this time, but many expressions spoke volumes as we took in the various forms of crew cuts and chop jobs.

The next morning I was late for chapel so in all humility I did what was expected and knelt before our assistant Novice Mistress, acknowledging my transgression. Instead of a reprimand or doling out a penance she said, "What's the matter? Have trouble getting your duds on?" To this day, I'm grateful for her humor.

Rich, Dark Brown Hair

I do remember that I weighed close to 200 pounds on Reception Day, and my hair was the only part of my physiognomy in which I took pride. Having it cut felt like a real loss.

I remember that some of the girls had shoe boxes for their shorn locks, which they intended to give to their parents. I thought that a splendid idea, so I presented my shoe box to my astonished parents. When they clearly didn't know how to respond, I probably took the box back and changed the subject. I remember throwing the box into the incinerator.

My heart turns over with a pang even now at that memory. My hair was a rich, dark brown when I was eighteen. It was thick and long. Now it's thin and gray.

Intimacy with the Great Mystery

At the time Reception Day was a huge event for me. Novices seemed closer to God than anyone else on the planet, and I guess I believed that this same intimacy would occur automatically when the white veil was placed on my head. Strangely, all these years later, very few memories of that day surface.

I do remember the excitement of getting to curl my very long hair one last time. We were to walk down the aisle as brides of Christ. At one point in the ceremony, we left the chapel with a folded veil in our hands to be met by a professed Sister, who cut all those curls off and dressed us in our spotless white veils. I also remember kneeling at the altar railing to hear my new name from the Bishop. It was a shock! I had not asked for that name, and it might have been a little harder to accept if my dad hadn't liked it immediately. "I like it!" he said later in the garden. "The name has dignity." The rest of the day is a blur. There was a bit of trouble eating with all that tight new material around our faces and chins, but we got used to that soon enough!

And, as for Intimacy with the Great Mystery, the new white veil did not automatically produce it. There were new glimpses, and the journey has continued this past half century with moments of great clarity but more often, with the daily, hourly stretching of faith.

From That Moment

Our Reception Day is one not easily forgotten. The day outdid itself with more rain than had been seen in a very long time. The half of our Novitiate class that would be received later in the summer spent the day mopping up floodwaters in the Motherhouse basement music rooms.

Those of us being received didn't worry about the rain. We were excited about getting our habits, white veils, and new names.

I don't remember much about the ceremony, but at some part we left chapel and went to St. Joseph Hall where a professed Sister of our choosing was waiting to cut our hair and dress us in our new habit and crown of artificial white roses.

After we returned to chapel, we went up to the communion rail and were given a slip of paper with a new name. From that moment we were Sisters.

She Was a Saint

In the spring of 1957 I was seventeen years old. I had just graduated from St. Joseph Convent High School and now awaited Reception. I remember kneeling in the Mother General's office making my formal petition to enter the order and wondering what I would do if she said, "No." Becoming a Nun was all I had wanted since childhood.

I clearly recall walking down the terrazzo aisle of the Motherhouse chapel on Reception day. The ceremony was carefully choreographed with nothing left to chance after hours of practice. This was a monumental day in my young life, and it was the first in a series of events where my parents would be observers and not participants. Detachment from my family was well under way. This disconnect with family would last the rest of my life. It was a happy occasion, but the following day reality set in with a new superior in charge, a whole new litany of dos and don'ts in the Novitiate and the mandatory marine style short haircut.

I hated the name I was given. I met an older Nun one day shortly after Reception; she told me she knew the *real* Sister who had had that name, and she was a saint!

Is Your New Name Really—?

I had asked for a simple name—Sister Peter Marie. I really wanted that name, and it was hard to share the Novitiate with the young woman who received it a year later. Instead, I was to be called Sister Peter Nolasco, the five-syllabled name of a Nun who had just died.

My little Sister's eyes were like saucers when I met my family later: "Is your new name really Sister Peter-in-Alaska?"

Young Bride of Christ

Reception Day was everything a young Bride of Christ could hope for—my family somewhere in the full chapel, the splendor of the chapel itself, glorious music, a meaningful ceremony, the anticipation of receiving the habit and a new name and the real beginning of life as a Sister. I didn't give much thought to the mechanics of changing from the Postulant's uniform and special bridal veil to the Novice habit.

Needless to say, the donning of the habit was no small thing. Fortunately we had a senior Sister who helped us pull, tuck, pin and fold as necessary. But, before any of that, we had our hair cut. So, in a matter of minutes, in relative silence, forty or so young women (my friends!) sat and had their hair trimmed, cut, butchered, removed by forty or so other women, none of them trained as barbers.

When I looked up, the humor of the situation swept over me—we more or less looked like palm trees with tufts, twigs and branches of hair sticking out in all directions. My overwhelming thought was, "My God, does anyone else think we look like palm trees? Is this not hilarious? Can I laugh? No!" After we were properly garbed, the solemnity of the occasion returned, stifled my perverse humor and the day proceeded as expected.

My Mom's Name

My most memorable moment on Reception Day was receiving the name I asked for, my mom's name. She had died when I was thirteen months old. I remember asking my dad what he thought of my new name. His wordless response was spoken so deeply in tear-filled eyes. I'll never forget our glances meeting in profound communication.

Formal Entry

Reception Day—a day Postulants are conditioned to look forward to with joy and great anticipation. Mom and Dad took off work and my whole family came to Milwaukee from Illinois. I remember feeling awkward in the new habit, especially the veil.

During retreat I had written down three names, one of which I hoped would be my religious name, all the while knowing I could very well end up with a long forgotten saint's name from some middle European country. There were Sisters in the community already sporting some very interesting creations. When the Bishop took the little slip of paper from between my folded hands and read my new name, I could hardly believe my good fortune. Later, I learned the previous owner of that name had been a humble elderly Nun, a person much beloved by all.

Reception Day was formal entry into the community of strong, intelligent, spiritually rich women. The class of 57 was just starting to become the cohesive group of such strong, intelligent, spiritually rich women whom I have been so fortunate to know for more than fifty years.

WE DON'T DO THAT

A few weeks after our Reception, Sister Archelaus, our Novice Mistress, passed out mail already opened and read by her or the assistant Novice Mistress. Most envelopes held photos of family members posing with happy Novices in their new white veils crowned with flowers on Reception Day. I did not get a letter, but then Sister Archelaus called me to her desk and opened an envelope with pictures from my family. "Who is this?" she asked, pointing to a picture of me standing between my cute little brothers aged six and eight, smiling shyly in their new suits. I was bending down, affectionately holding an arm around the shoulders of each little guy.

"Those are my two little brothers," I explained proudly.

"We don't do that," Archelaus said.

I was astounded. We did not touch even our own little brothers? "No," Archelaus said. "We do not do that." That privation of touch stayed with me, governed my many years in the Convent.

SISTER ARCHELAUS ASKS HOW

Our Novitiate was a third floor, large, sunlit, double room with rounded tops on the tall windows. These lovely windows reaching almost to the ceiling could be opened or closed only with a twelve-foot, thin, round, wooden window pole. Radiators for winter heat stood near the windows.

Once a Novice opening a window dropped the long window pole down a radiator pipe hole. We split our sides with laughter at Chapter of Faults when the Novice confessed, "Sister, I lost the window pole."

I recall Sister Archelaus asked, "Sister, how did you manage that?" and swiftly covered her mouth with her large hanky. Archelaus could not keep a straight face!

In long rows, small individual desks, one for each Novice, faced the front where our two Novice Mistresses had larger desks facing the Novices. Sister Archelaus sat on a large platform with a book rack on her desk. For some reason I was fascinated with that book rack. I guess I was intrigued with what those books were all about.

Because my Nun's name began alphabetically with a "T", I sat in one of the last rows of the second room. I was always pretty distant from Sister Archelaus as she gave instructions, so it was quite easy for me to hide, as I often did.

It Was Safe, Nourishing, Good and Very Pleasing

I remember the hours during the day as being very regular. When the bell rang for a meal, everyone simply stopped what she was doing and went to eat a nourishing meal. When the bell rang for prayer, everyone stopped what she was doing and went to pray and praise God.

I remember Reception Day—wearing a white veil with a ring of flowers around our heads. It was very good.

I remember sitting in the visitor's room waiting to lock up for the night with another Novice. When it was time to lock up, I remember walking down the halls making sure that this door was locked and that window shut on my route. It was a small responsibility, but I felt I was doing my part to see that all was well for the night.

The Perpetual Adoration Chapel also comes to mind. When it was my turn to pray at night, I remember a Sister coming to tap me on the shoulder to get up in the middle of the night to take my hour in the chapel. It was an hour to pray and reflect. It was such a good practice.

These are just some memories that come to mind. It was safe, it was nourishing both physically and spiritually. It was very good, and I think a time very pleasing to God the Father, Son, and Holy Spirit.

I Liked

What I really liked was working with two classmates who are still close friends, one in the bakery and the other in the refectory. I remember feeling so proud to wear the veil. I remember another classmate's laughter and happy heart that kept me sane.

HOPPING ON THE WAGON

As a first year Novice I was in charge of the cleaning materials. I cannot remember the name of the little room on the fourth floor where supplies were stored. When the Novices had a large-scale cleaning job, it was my responsibility to have all the materials at the job site. One of our classmates, whose warm smile I can still remember, operated the nearby elevator.

I used to take wagonloads of dirty rags to the laundry after big scrubbing jobs. (Even today I always have a cupboard of folded rags in my laundry room.) Sometimes I would use the steam tunnel to go to the laundry. There was quite an incline in the tunnel as you reached the Motherhouse elevator.

One day, when I was returning through the tunnel from the laundry with an empty wagon, I decided to hop on the wagon and coast to the elevator. I didn't realize how steep the incline was until it was too late and I was speeding toward the elevator. The wagon upset and I took a header down the concrete floor, of course sporting a white collar and white veil. The trick was to get up to the dorm and change dirty collar and veil without being discovered by the authorities.

WHAT WON OUR HEARTS

Alas, my early Convent years used to look very dark indeed: the vastness of the St. Joseph Convent complex—tunnels that ran for blocks from the basement all the way up to St. Mary's Hill, the mental hospital, and to the laundry, and to the Sacred Heart Sanitarium. The residue of German language and culture. What seemed to me—who had done very little manual labor up to then—a painful emphasis on scrubbing floors, scouring huge kettles, mangling sheets during ninety degree temperatures wearing face linens and skirts made of six and a half yards of English wool. All of this exacerbated by the fact that I couldn't manage to get to chapel on time and spent much of my Postulancy washing dishes during recreation and much of my Novitiate kneeling for breakfast.

I had a tough time especially during Postulancy: always late for morning prayers, constantly given penances for infractions I couldn't seem to help, slow and awkward at the hated manual labor, accused of particular friendships. I felt my superior had it in for me. I became very self-conscious, afraid I was constantly watched and evaluated.

Sure enough, I was almost sent home right before Reception. Sister Archelaus had to have known about that. But she never mentioned it, didn't seem to pay me any special disciplinary attention. Gratefully, I began to relax. I was so thankful to her; she just left me alone.

There were also lovely little Name Day gifts that now live between the pages of my beat-up Bible. There were college classes that gave me a professional foundation I still count on. I formed friendships I continue to cherish.

At St. Joseph Convent I did find the beauty I thirsted for. I found it in the statues of Sister Helena and the music of both Sister Cherubim and Sister Theophane. Oh, yes! I became part of a choir that sang, "Most High, Omnipotent, Good Lord...."

I now had some music to go with the words I loved during high school: "Be praised, my Lord for Sister Moon and the Stars..." and "The Lord bless you and keep you...." I had a drawing of St. Francis holding a bird in his hand, a Name Day gift during Novitiate, and a packet of note cards that illustrate some of Sister Helena's work.

What we most complained about was not the manual labor or the obedience but the absence of spirituality we had come seeking. Although we didn't find a spirituality we understood at the time, we did find art. Especially for those of us from middle class backgrounds, that was a great gift. Only a few of us had upper class backgrounds and had already been exposed to great art.

It was art rather than religion that won our hearts. It was what we created together as women that sings in us now.

I realize now that as a teenager I wasn't ready for the spirituality that I was longing for. That came many, many years later.

SHOCK

My greatest shock was to see the minutiae of supposedly necessary rules and regulations that governed our lives as new recruits. The letter of the law seemed more important than the spirit of the law. My heart moved from acceptance of this way of living to hoping for a different future—a way of living more in tune with the world from which I came and to which I intended to minister. That prayer was answered within ten years when John the XXIII called for a complete renewal in the Church with Vatican II.

POSITIVES AND NEGATIVES

Leaving home at fourteen created a disconnect with family and relatives. It also affected my memory of events from early years.

Not having been away from home that much, I wasn't always comfortable in big groups of people and at that time I was shy. I think during high school years most adolescent girls learn social coping skills—dealing with peer pressure, handling friendships that succeed or fail, learning self-defense. We never had that opportunity since we were so busy being Christ-like and not having Particular Friendships. I don't always deal well with other women. I am missing that cunning clique savvy you learn in your youth.

I did not experience much kindness at the hands of the superiors. In training we were stripped of our identity, deprived of human friendship, and subjected to public humiliation. I'm rather proud to have survived the dealings I had with them. I read this description of military life in Paul Fussell's *Wartime: Understanding Behavior in the Second World War*: "Generating maximum anxiety over matters of minimum significance." This sums up the gist of a lot of my life during that time.

However, I am grateful to the fellow Nuns who impacted my life in a positive way. I had the opportunity to live and work with some very talented women. I received an excellent education and acquired habits of self-discipline and structure that have been invaluable in my personal and business life.

My deepest gratitude of all goes to the Community's wonderful artists who believed in me and my future as an artist. These women taught me to build an interior catalog of images, seemingly inconsequential sightings— the way a shadow spreads itself at a certain time of the day, the magic of light entering the iris of the eye, the way a color changes as it rounds an object, the way a leaf curls into itself—observations that never cease to fuel a sense of wonder. To this day I can't understand why most people can't take joy in these simple things I treasure.

I remember one of those artists, Sister Helena, introducing me to that lovely saying, "If you have two loaves of bread, go, sell one, and buy hyacinths to feed your soul." What they taught me about seeing has provided hyacinths for the rest of my life.

CELLS, SHOWERS, DIRTY WASH, LIVER
DUMPLINGS, EFFICIENCY

It defies reality almost to comprehend how so many Nuns slept on the top floors of the Motherhouse where most of the dormitories were. Think about it. Probably four hundred or more Sisters, each in a cell with a bed and small stand made private by curtains that closed all around, the space probably not more than six by eight feet.

Then you have the 'daily shower'—the parade to the bathrooms to fill the wash basin, then dump it, then fill it again, all of us carrying a pan of water to our cells each night and washing ourselves and brushing our teeth, then lining up to dump the dirty water back in the common bathroom. Using baking soda for toothpaste and deodorant. And the same thing happened each morning.

Wasn't it our choir directress who said to all of us one time to please take care in cleaning our teeth and the rest of us? I think she was overwhelmed by one hundred smelly post-adolescents all breathing out at her.

I remember collecting all that terrible wash in the bathrooms and how we were assigned to certain bags. It amazes me to this day the efficiency of it all—everyone getting her own clean laundry back.

The dining experience was the utmost of efficiency. Sisters, Novices, Postulants and Aspirants all ate at the same time, in their different refectories, sat in assigned seats, kept custody of the eyes and silence while we passed the food to each other for three meals a day plus morning and afternoon snacks. All the food prepared, cooked, transported, cleaned up by the Sisters themselves, slave labor provided by those in training. For entertainment, one Sister sat on a raised platform and read inspiring works to us. I learned to eat food I had not tried before, some tasty, some not so good. But you had to eat what was on the table, and you were hungry, so it didn't matter.

I remember gagging on liver dumpling soup and hoping that I would get only one in my soup bowl, then having a classmate at the end of the table dishing out the soup and giving me three or four because I sat next to our Superior. That meant my bowl was the second one filled, while those at the end of the table got mostly juice and one dumpling.

I especially liked celebrating St. Nicholas Day, December 6. When we arrived in the refectory, at each of our places were an apple, an orange, and some holy cards. To this day, with my kids and grandkids, I do the same. It's a nice celebration before Christmas that they look forward to and enjoy. They get little presents.

THINGS I WANT TO FORGET

Cloth sanitary napkins
Parsnips
Darning on Saturday morning
Corn bread with syrup for dessert
Chapter of faults
Tomato shortcake (remember gleaning the tomato fields?)
Winter bloomers (and I don't mean flowers)

THINGS I DON'T WANT TO FORGET

Christmas Eve
Choir
The passion vine that bloomed near the back door of Alverno College
The mock orchestra in the Novitiate
Burying the 19-year-old Novice, Sister Rosarian

NOVICES PRACTICE POVERTY, OBEDIENCE, CHASTITY

Some Novices found preparing for the vows of poverty, chastity, and obedience difficult.

Some resented poverty because it meant doing manual labor. We Novices did peel hundreds of pounds of potatoes and wash bushels of fruits and vegetables. We helped in the Convent bakery and the print shop. Some of us were wait staff in the sanitarium dining rooms. Novices did the laundry—ran the huge washing machines and the heavy mangle for the hundreds of sheets and bedding (not just for the Nuns, but also for the nearby sanitarium and the mental hospital run by the Nuns). Some Novices wondered why they had to work like this during the week and then get down on hands and knees every Friday evening to scrub the Convent Chapel terrazzo floors.

But most of us knew that if we young, healthy Novices did not do the manual labor in the Motherhouse, who would? Surely the grumbling Novices did not expect outsiders to clean the Convent, prepare the food, do the laundry. Who would pay for that? We were poor. Yes, we were cheap labor, but it offered us our opportunity to support our communal life and pay for our fantastic educations.

Poverty to others was a problem because it meant having little privacy. Novices slept in large rooms, in individual cells, each consisting of a single cot, a chair, a wash stand with basin, a drawer, and box for clothing. Poverty meant having no control over the snorers, the sleep walkers, the insomniacs. Poverty meant having to stand in line for a toilet, a shower, water.

Poverty meant eating what was served, whether you liked it or not. Poverty meant never having money to leave the Convent grounds. Poverty meant not driving. Poverty meant wearing some pieces of clothing until they made good rags. Poverty meant using cloth instead of disposable sanitary pads. (We were ecologically advanced in our poverty; the laundry washed these cloths sparkling white and we used them again.)

We had no money in our pockets, but we shared a sturdy roof, good food, clean rooms. Because of our beautiful chapel and magnificent liturgy, the splendid art and music, and the mentoring of the fantastic women, our lives were richer, not poorer, than those of many others.

For some Novices, the vow of obedience became a roadblock. We had to learn to live in a group and do as the group was to do. We had to follow rules made for the good of the whole. For many, especially those from small families, and the free-spirited individualists, the loners, and the mavericks, this was difficult.

No facet of a Novice's life was her own to choose. Everyday decisions were made for the group—when to eat (three times a day when the bells rang), and where to eat (sitting in the refectory at assigned places), and what to eat, when to rise, and when to go to bed, what to wear, when to sing the liturgy, when to quietly meditate or study, when to talk, when to read, often what to read, when to work, where to work—these decisions were not our own.

Because these day-to-day choices were removed, we were to have more time to be with God. Some of us, unconcerned about minor daily choices, did find these experiences freeing. Others resented giving up their free will.

The most difficult issue of obedience probably would concern our work and our mission groups after Novitiate. Who we lived with (fifty Nuns of all ages or perhaps a tiny group of all older women), where we lived (inner city ghetto, or suburbs, or small farming community), and what our life's work would be (teaching elementary, or high school or college; nursing in a clinic or hospital; home making; managing schools or hospitals or the Motherhouse), were not usually our decisions to make. These decisions, made independently for young Nuns by superiors, sometimes took much prayer and soul searching to accept.

The vow of chastity, too, became a problem for some as they longed for children and family life. Some Novices found solace seeing themselves as young brides of Christ. Some of us, though, never really believed God was so substantially human.

As a young Nun, I had decided not to marry or have children and didn't think of chastity as a loss, but rather as a gift giving me time and energy to devote to others.

Perhaps not being in love in my late teens made my giving up sexual intimacy a simple decision, like giving up smoking or drinking. Besides, in the late 50s, the pill was not yet integrated into our culture, so recreational sex was avoided by nice girls; it was not really a choice we considered. And the vicarious experiences of many novels and great books of literature told me much about the human condition. I'll not soon forget my young fascination with the *Canterbury Tales*. For sensual imagery, there was the beautiful *Song of Solomon*. Think of all the pubic hair in John Updike's writings. Chastity for English majors was not as much a mystery as it was to some Nuns.

Giving up the chance to have children was another issue we had to face. Because I had younger brothers and sisters whose diapers I had often changed, whose feeding and crying I was often asked to attend to, and whose delightful little lives I had shared ever since I was old enough to remember, I knew something about a household with children. As an older teen, I didn't yet feel drawn to have babies of my own. I thought being a teacher, extra-curricular advisor/coach, and friend of hundreds of young, high school teens a year would amply satisfy my maternal instincts.

So the vows were not my problem. But who was God? My relationship to God? Ah, that problem would be mine for my life.

FEELING SPECIAL

During the Novitiate, I had two things that made me feel special. One was a real blessing. I got to help Sister Sacristan take care of the flowers and keep the beautiful marble altars clean.

The other was catching the sheets as they came off the mangle. If I had the right partner (and I don't remember who), we could catch and fold the sheets neatly without any piling up.

One thing that has been a lifelong comfort and sanity saver for me has been singing in the choir. That started in seventh grade. Then I think they tolerated me because they felt sorry for me. But I learned to sing alto with them. In the Convent choir, I was a second alto and returned many years later to be part of the choir for the Centennial Celebration of St. Joseph Chapel.

PEAS, PRINTING, PENANCE

Even though there were hard times throughout our formation years, I can truly say that I don't regret a bit of it. It is so amazing to me what details one remembers and what great things are forgotten! Peas on movie night, square dancing, kneeling on the floor in the refectory for penance. And did I ever have a whopper one month because I ran a dolly of one thousand Father Francis books into the newly installed door to the kitchen. A fellow Novice and I were in a hurry to get to religion class so as not to get in trouble.

I learned how to pack books for shipping during my time in the printing room. I loved working in the printing room and in the laundry. I used to have to put on a black veil when running those big washing machines.

CELEBRATING FEAST DAYS

What I really liked in the Novitiate was the way we celebrated feast days with a special Mass, special food, visiting with the professed Sisters, and a more relaxed schedule.

SEPARATION AND RESENTMENT

As first year Novices, we were separated from the rest of the community except for special occasions. We were not allowed to speak to anyone outside of the Novitiate without permission. My sister entered as an Aspirant the year I became a Novice. We would pass each other in the Motherhouse hallways and could not speak to each other. I resented this a great deal, especially when she went through some very serious physical problems, which eventually caused her to be sent home.

Family Visits

During formation, visits with family took place at the Motherhouse, usually in the garden, and they were scheduled very infrequently. I was, therefore, surprised when my Mistress of Novices told me one day that family members awaited me in the garden outside the kitchen.

I didn't stop to ponder this delightful news. I rushed outside to find my uncle, who had driven one hundred miles to bring me a package. My seven-year-old sister had come with him. She was sitting on a bench where the Sisters who worked in the kitchen used to rest sometimes after a day of feeding four hundred women three meals.

And she was eating one of Sister Almerida's huge apricot-filled cookies. She had no time to run and throw her arms around me—too busy licking the frosting. Sister Almerida herself, supervisor of the kitchen staff, sat beside her smiling, as if she had nothing else to do in the middle of the afternoon. "I catch them with my cookies," she said.

I was touched by the scene—so much like something that might have occurred in a neighbor's back yard at home. My experience of life in this great building was so organized that it often felt regimented. I thought, "This is how it must have been when the community was smaller."

I was right! A few years later, when I was part of a smaller mission in Chicago, my mother used to drive the twenty miles across the city to visit me on a Sunday afternoon. The first time she came, the Sister who cooked for us served her the same delicious Sunday dinner we'd been served. They talked for a little while afterward. When she learned that Mom's favorite dessert was blueberry pie, she had one waiting every time Mom came.

A Novice's Death

In the winter of 1958-59 the Asian flu raged through the Motherhouse sending most of the Novices, Postulants, Aspirants, and Professed Nuns to their beds. In the epidemic, one of the young Novices from the class behind our own died. On her deathbed, she was allowed to make her vows.

For some Novices, whose parents and grandparents still lived, her shocking death was their first experience with bereavement. I shall never forget the devastated faces of the young Novice's parents as they sat by her plain, open casket, in a classroom cleared out to serve as a makeshift wake room.

These shattered parents helped prepare me for my own family's response to my young brother's death just a few years later.

MYSTIC OF THE NOVITIATE

I loved her. I still love her. That is the truest and most honest thing I can say. Feared mightily by many. Majestic mystic. Sister Archelaus, the tall, elegant Mistress of Novices. She'd held that post since the year before I was born.

"The last laus [louse] in the house," as she occasionally referred to herself with that shamanic yet mischievous twinkle in her eye.

We had one of those mysterious energetic connections. I could feel emotions as they passed through her. I watched her come close to inner death herself as the young Novice Rosarian lay close to death and eventually died on February 27, 1959, during the Asian flu epidemic.

I myself fell seriously afoul of her only once in my two years as a Novice. The big talent show. Our group was going to be a sort of Barbershop Quartet and wanted a good name and outfit. We got clean, white rags from the scrub department and pinned them down the front of our long black scapulars. Voilà! The Skunk Hollow Sweethearts.

Well, lo and behold, the next day we learned, kneeling before her penitently, that we had "desecrated the holy habit." I don't remember what, if any, punishment we actually received. All I remember is that she could hardly keep from laughing. Nor—aghast as I was for having offended her—could I.

The night we entered our retreat for First Profession of Vows, she offered us chocolate candy from boxes she must have saved for that occasion, cajoling us with another of her memorable lines: "Take lots. Take two."

I remember sensing her grief as she moved among us with her candy. It was clear to my heart that she had grown to love us deeply. Years later I overheard my mother say to one of my aunts about my entering the Convent, "Just when she became old enough for me to really talk to, she left home." That night Archelaus seemed to mourn losing us just as we were growing mature enough to be companions to her mighty soul.

This woman, with all the ethereal, eternal echoes I sensed (and still sense) in her, anchored, epitomized, embodied my Novitiate. I can summon back the grace and stress, the pain, potential and power of those days by inviting her into my world now from beyond the grave. And now I can truly talk to her.

THE DYE HELD

We were Postulants only a short while when we heard the dictum: Never one, seldom two, always three or more. I didn't think much about it. Eventually I learned it was the PF scare—Particular Friendship that could easily morph into a lesbian relationship and violate a future Sister's vow of celibacy.

That has never been what a particular friend has meant to me. I've always had best friends, one to whom I could tell my life and she to me. My best friend from high school and those through other periods of my life are still my friends though many miles apart.

I know quickly who will be my best friend when I come to a new situation.

I came to St. Joseph Convent on September 6, 1956. Several other new Postulants came a few days later. We welcomed the new arrivals. I saw an attractive young woman come into the back entrance of the Convent with her family. I liked her and spoke to her immediately. I still remember that she was both attentive and genuine in the midst of the hellos and goodbyes in the crowd. In the Postulancy, because our last names were both toward the end of the alphabet, we were assigned seats next to one another. The 'dye' was cast—multi-colored, I would say.

Later when we were in the Novitiate, our names did not bring us together but the dye held—there was no fading. It is a very particular friendship with many stories.

One major story: We were first year Novices. I had received a call from my family telling me my brother had been paralyzed from the neck down. I wanted to talk with my friend. After lunch and before kitchen duty, I went to her music practice room in the lower level of the Convent. We talked as fast as we could. When I got to my duty in the kitchen I knew I was three to four minutes late.

Sister Almerida, the very kind and generous cook in charge of the kitchen, was not there. She had put a second year Novice in charge. Great Power. I, the first year Novice, was late and the Novice Mistress needed to know!

A day or two later my friend and I were called separately into Sister Archelaus's office. We both received a penance—a week of kitchen duty during recreation period. My friend the first week and I the second.

Many years later when Sister Archelaus, beloved to so many of us, was at Maria Linden retirement center in Rockford, I went to visit her. She could hardly speak due to a throat condition but her mind and presence were as strong as ever. As we reminisced, the incident of my friend, myself and the kitchen penance came into the conversation. Sister Archelaus smiled and said, "I was just a little concerned that you might be depending a bit too much on your friend. You needed to get stronger on your own." This wise woman knew me as she knew so many of us who passed through her care. When I think of her today and sense her presence, I feel the dignity and integrity that she still offers us.

My particular friend and I are still particular friends—no generality between us. Whoever knows us knows we are friends. We are both School Sisters in our seventh decade. It is now the twenty-first century and Convent times have changed. We and our brothers and sisters of the world know and continue to live within love for which the human heart is made.

SCRUBBING LESSON

On Friday evenings every inch of the Convent terrazzo corridor and chapel was scrubbed on hands and knees for the coming Sabbath. The scrub room Novice prepared pails, folded absorbent rags, a kneeling pad and scrub brush for each of us. We worked in pairs—a second year Novice with a first year Novice. With 150 Novices trained well in scrubbing and silence, it all happened quickly and efficiently in an hour or less.

One Saturday morning, Sister Archelaus called my partner and me to the corridor we had scrubbed the evening before. In her serious voice, "Sisters, look at this." Every two feet or so there was a gray streak with irregular edges about two inches wide. We had not overlapped our scrubbing.

That evening when the other Novices were headed to bed after night prayer, my partner and I went to our corridor with our buckets of water, rags and brushes. We put in our second night of scrubbing, this time with large overlapping suds and scrubs. When we finished, my Novice partner said Sister Archelaus had told her we should go back to the Novitiate. We went, not knowing what to expect.

There on the ledge as we came in the door were two candy bars. We felt again the human kindness of our stern, strong, and very human Novice Mistress.

The Woman We Admired

Sister Archelaus, one of the first great mentors of my life. On my first evening in the Novitiate, she invited me to help her collect some things from an adjacent room, all the while asking me about my family (supposedly a forbidden topic) and putting me totally at ease, not just for that night, but for my entire two years with her. She was tall, regal in her walk, and holy, almost other worldly. We did not need to discuss a deep spiritual life; we saw her living it, drawing us into that realm with her.

After a few months she asked me to take care of her personal items, and I'll never forget the time this busy woman (the one so intimidating to some Novices) asked me if I'd seen her clean wash that hadn't come back from the laundry. Of course I had not, but that was her way of sending me on a laundry search to handle something for which she had no time.

Molding 150 or so Novices each year into fine Nuns was no easy task, but she did it, gently and most effectively, with her example. What a lonely life she must have had, literally raising hundreds of women from teens to maturity, year after year, 24/7 with only a week long retreat once a year for respite. And she was teaching Bible history and taking advanced university courses. Later, any of us with a difficult teaching assignment needed only to remember her dedication and holiness.

The Hidden Wedding

Joan, one of my close high school friends, had been conflicted for a long time about whether to join the Poor Clares or to marry her boyfriend of two years. As she asked, I had been praying that she decide according to God's will.

During a family visit I learned that Joan had married that fall. "But, of course, you know," my mother said. "Joan sent you her wedding pictures." I wept inside. I could not let my mother know I'd never gotten the pictures.

"Why not!" I railed inside. "It wouldn't have hurt my vocation. Joan, beautiful Joan, my soul-Sister! A bride! But I can't see her."

FROM MORNING GARBAGE DETAIL TO EVENING COMPLINE

Another Novice and I had an unusual daily work assignment. We had to carry large, heavy galvanized steel garbage cans from the Novitiate building all the way to the large incinerator near the power house about half a block away. We then dragged them up a flight of steep stairs, pulled opened a heavy cover, lifted up the cans and dumped their contents into a blazing fire.

This was especially challenging in the winter. I spent many a frigid morning on my backside sliding on that Wisconsin ice. Because the two of us were not the most enthusiastic cleaners, we thought that this was the greatest job ever. We did it so well (probably because we were strong as bulls) we got to keep the job for most of the year.

Once when we were emptying the cans, my fountain pen slipped out of its holder and fell right into the furnace. My first thought was, "Sister Archelaus is going to kill me!" When I told her of my carelessness, she opened her desk drawer, pulled out a pen that was much better than the one I lost and simply said, "Don't let it happen again." When I asked her for a penance, she simply waved me out of her office. Now I realize that she understood what a physically demanding job we had.

We Novices were the first class to receive the new Divine Office books. We were trained to find our way through the labyrinth of hours and special feast days. I loved the liturgical journey. I still have my Breviary and often say morning prayer with it.

Likewise, I treasure the quiet moments when, at the end of our monthly meeting of the Women's Group at my Episcopal Church, this gentle group of women softly recites in unison the powerful prayer of Compline. We smile and say that we put the world to bed and pray it into a peaceful night's sleep. Funny how I have come full circle in prayer and community. I have found such wonderful love and acceptance from these women of strength and generosity.

EARLY THEATER

Without radio and TV in the Novitiate, we made our own entertainment. Some of us created silly or serious plays and skits for feast days. A few of us wrote poems that classmates performed in a kind of choral reading, almost like a Greek chorus. The skills I gained by writing pieces for an audience, hearing others deliver my words, and understanding how an audience reacted to them stayed with me. Later I used those experiences as I coached students to win forensics competitions.

NEWS?

For an entire year, we first year Novices had no access to radios, TVs, newspapers, or magazines and as a result knew very little of what was happening in the rest of the world.

So I vividly remember when the Motherhouse Chaplain, before his weekly lecture, called our Novice Mistress outside the Novitiate door. From my desk near the entry, I heard him ask her, "May I tell the Novices that the Russians have successfully launched Sputnik?" That's how we learned about the famous first satellite.

One evening Sister Archelaus announced that Fidel Castro had been elected President of Cuba. We were told that was good news, an answer to prayers, because he would rescue the country from tyranny.

When my beloved Milwaukee Braves won the 1957 World Series, I unearthed the news in an old newspaper lining a newly scrubbed terrazzo floor.

GREAT FULFILLMENT

The second year of Novitiate was a joy for me because I embraced Alverno College and my studies with gusto. I felt more confident and was more comfortable as a Sister. The year flew by and before I knew it I was professed and teaching in a large suburban school near Milwaukee. I found such great fulfillment as a teacher and have been blessed with the joy of touching the lives of so many students, young children, teenagers, and incarcerated adults. The seeds for this calling were sown those many years ago by that great and strong woman, Sister Archelaus, and our brilliant Sisters who taught us at Alverno College.

EXHAUSTED, ANGRY, ALWAYS STRUGGLING

As a second year Novice, I attended classes at Alverno College. I found this to be most difficult. We were expected to excel with grades as well as classroom participation. And yet, we were not given the time to study because we had chores and other religious training classes once we got back to the Motherhouse. After chores, training, prayers, meals, early bed and early rising, I found myself exhausted and angry and always struggling to keep up.

ASKING TO RECONSIDER A DECISION

My music tests, probably because I had taken piano lessons since first grade, turned out well, prompting the head of the Music Department to sign me up for a college major in music—with composition, organ, violin, voice, etc. I was horrified when I was given my college schedule. I knew my talents were not in music and, for the only time in my Convent life, I asked that a decision about me be reconsidered. A respected Nun, one of my college teachers, had said something I will never forget: "Life in the Convent is hard enough without spending your entire life doing what you do not like."

So I approached my Novice Mistress and asked her to end my music curriculum. "If not music," she asked, "what do you want to teach?" She listened and approved changing my college major from music to English literature. I was relieved and happy.

THE NOVICE WAS MISSING

The biggest shock for me was the day we were in line to ask to make first vows. The Novice who was to come after me was not there, and I couldn't understand why. It really shook me up because I was excited about taking the next step. Needless to say, that experience stayed with me for a long time.

FIRST PROFESSION CEREMONY

After two years as a Novice, we took for one year the temporary vows of poverty, chastity, and obedience in a beautiful ceremony called First Profession of Vows. During part of the ceremony, we lay face-down on the chapel floor while other Sisters covered us up with a huge, black cloth called a pall. Lying under the pall symbolized our death to the world.

In the ceremony, we received the black veil and a simple gold band for our ring finger. And we were crowned with thorns, not flowers as on our

Reception Day, symbols we wore all day, even as we visited with our families who had come to support us in the ceremony.

Because we had lived a life of poverty, chastity and obedience in the Novitiate, I did not find any difficult transitions into the vowed life. By then, the vows were part of my lifestyle.

Ought To What?

All through my years in the Convent, I chose *ought to*. Even under the black pall during my first vow ceremony, I wanted to jump up, throw off the pall, and say, "No, I won't." But *ought to* kept me face down on the cold terrazzo floor.

Ought to what? I thought God expected me to lead the best life I could, a life of self-denial, dedication, and service to The One Who Is. (Some people's problems with Father or Mother God never made sense to me because if God were God, God had to be beyond maleness/femaleness. Talking about such differences seemed a waste of energy.)

Praying to God was difficult. I yearned to learn how to meditate but never quite understood how to do it. What we were taught—picturing the events of the New Testament and reflecting—made little sense, although interesting sometimes to an active imagination. God had to be bigger than the person revered in the Gospels. But no one talked about that.

Celebration of Survival

To me, Profession Day was a celebration of survival. I had made it through all the calculated character building or destruction of the Novitiate, and now I would be sent on my first mission. I have a photograph that my father took of me on that day. It looks like a studio shot with soft lighting and a profile portrait pose. Maybe this picture shows what the day meant to my father. I look at it and wonder how I was ever at that place in my life.

I Had a Future

Profession Day. "Thank God I made it!" Thank God Novitiate is over. Now I set new goals and I really look to the future. Yes, I loved my ring, the black veil, and the solemnity of taking vows, but mostly, now I knew I had a future.

WITH NO DOUBTS

My father, who lived into his nineties, was quite a storyteller. We always encouraged him to talk about his past and enjoyed the colorful embellishments that changed from one telling to another.

One day, in the last year of his life, he said to me, "Do you know the hardest day of my life?" Of course, I was very curious to hear the answer from this man who had lived through two world wars, the depression, and the loss of many people near and dear to him. "Well," he said, "it was that day they put that black funeral cloth over you." I realized with horror that that was my Profession Day, one of the happiest days in my life.

My father continued, "I bet I never told you that before."

"No, you never did," I agreed. I somehow knew that what my dad had just shared was true, and that was one story that would never change.

For my part, I approached Profession Day with no doubts and felt deeply sorry for the few people in my class who, I suspected, were struggling with the magnitude of what they were about to do. I so wished that we could talk and I could share part of my certainty with them. The black funeral pall was indeed a meaningful symbol to me, and I fully embraced the concept of being dead to the world.

CHAPTER 5
EARLY LIFE GLIMPSES OF THE SACRED

WE CANTORS

We cantors stood upstairs at the choir railing in the chapel. The cathedral ceiling swooped and arched above us waiting to catch and swirl our chanting and hurl it to the heavens.

It was easy to be mesmerized by the sound and by the strange power of the moment. What if I read the wrong page? What if I started on the wrong note? What if I stumbled or mixed up the words?

Time to start. Softly sound the pitch pipe, set my mind, breathe in the air always scented slightly with incense and then spin out the beautiful words. Back and forth—the dance of a single voice alternating with the rise of many voices breathing together, praying together. What moved me most was the singleness of purpose. Here we were, four hundred women with one objective—praising God at this moment in time.

LET WHAT IS BE

I remember sitting in our Novitiate study hall one sun-filled fall afternoon. Totally unbidden, a prayer slipped into my awareness:

Let what is BE.

I felt an inner expanding of myself into the wholeness of that day, neither sublimation nor self-sacrificing surrender but rather a full and rounded, invigorating embrace of the IS-ness of each moment. Over the years that prayer has become the core of my existence.

THE GREAT WHITE SILENCE

Is there anything as lovely or as silent as Convent gardens under a foot of fresh snow? From the third floor Novitiate windows we looked down to the Convent gardens lying quietly after the blizzard. No wind. Nothing moved in the great, white silence. Trees from smallest twigs to large branches cuddled snow. Snow smoothed out gravel walks, winter flower beds and dried stalks. Bushes sat as igloos.

Then a cardinal flew from the trees, a tiny red dot against the white. Our Convent existed in the middle of an industrial city, so pure snow like that of my northern Wisconsin home was rare. But here it was. Silent, profound, reverent as our own Great Silence. What a wonderful gift for my first Christmas as a Nun.

THERE IS NO GOD

The introduction to Convent life was hard for me, not because we scrubbed floors and had to keep silent. Not because I was homesick, but because of what I heard being said about God. On a rainy, cold November afternoon, I sat in St. Joseph Hall with ninety-some other Postulants as our Mistress pointed to a yellowed cardboard flip chart. That triangle, we were told, represented the Trinity—God.

Something in me closed or, as I see it today, maybe opened, and I fell through into a "there is no God" space of fear, terror, and isolation. The romance, yearning, and child's surety of God was gone. This period lasted seven years.

I knew that leaving Milwaukee and returning to my family wouldn't make any difference. The no-God-space was in me; it would be in me wherever I would go. And it has been. But it has become less frequent and less intense. I know now that this space is invitation.

ONE GRAIN[1]

Here I lie
In the sand-strewn silence of the ocean floor
Where seaweed, tangled, lace-like, cloisters me,

[1]First printed in 1963 in *Vision* magazine of Alverno College

Gray shelled, from the coral-hued anemone.
My hope lies in one grain of sand,
At first unfelt
Yet the core of all my weaving,
The reason for my shell-life and my singing.
My hope lies in one grain of sand,
So placed
That when the doom of shattered-shell death
Breaks my citadel,
My margarita will rise full-formed
Above the sea swell.

NOURISHMENT NEEDED FOR OUR SOULS

ARCHITECTURE: We had the best teacher of all—lived ritual amidst exquisite music in a startlingly beautiful architectural and artistic space. All of this pulsing sound vibration came to us within a luminous architectural structure of white Carrara marble with stunning mosaics and stained glass images hovering over us. Most of the nourishment I needed for my soul came from this beautiful Liturgy that was an intimate part of our days. Our souls were honed in a way that no words could ever have accomplished for us at those young ages.

THE CHOIR: From the first moment I heard the Convent choir, I felt transported to another realm. This was true whether it was their delivery of great polyphonic music or simple Gregorian chant. Even our daily chanting of the breviary has instilled in me a profound love for the psalms.

GREGORIAN CHANT: The Choir loft was the best place in our Convent: four wooden tiers, one hundred fifty voices soaring over a "chapel" big enough and ornate enough to have passed as a cathedral.

Every morning the chants wandered reflectively over the Sisters below, giving them time to sink into various parts of the Mass: *Gloria*, Glory to God in the highest; *Credo*, This is what I believe; *Benedictus qui venit in nomine Domine*, Blessed is He Who comes in the name of the Lord.

Our singing of Gregorian Chant had no pauses. We were taught to breathe separately when necessary, then rejoin the group as the melody rose and fell, expanded and faded.

One morning, as I tried to take such a breath, it stopped halfway up my throat, halted by the grace of the choir directress's hands. For a moment I could see her fingers actually rounding the music that came from our voices, shaping it, into the sounds that rolled over the railings of the choir loft. That musical sculpting awed me into silence.

THEATER OR WHY I MISS THE MOTHERHOUSE AT CHRISTMAS: In the world, Christmas-related stuff floods the market often before Halloween stuff is off the shelves. The material aspect of the holiday leaves in its wake a calendar day devoid of spirit and meaning.

That's why I miss the Motherhouse on Christmas Eve. It was theater at its best, a night of wonderment. After all the silence and starkness of Advent, the sights and sounds in the chapel were magical. The beautiful Nativity scene and the music and choir pieces made the chapel so not of this earth.

THE ANNUNCIATION[2]

A breath
Shook the wheat shaft.
A grain drank in its strength,
Lost nothingness in falling,
And died.

NOVENA[3]

Descend,
Seven-star splendor
On this shadow-pained cenacle
This unshining, shattered upper room of me.
Fireflame now.
Kindle *caritas.*

---

[2]First printed in 1957 in *The Little Portion* magazine of St. Joseph Convent High School

[3]First printed in 1961 in *Vision* magazine of Alverno College

NO NEED TO LEAVE DIMINISHED

As a young Nun, I was fortunate to stay at Alverno College to finish my BA degree before being assigned to teach high school. Those two years changed my life. I remember that each morning the college priest/theologian, Raymond Parr, preached a short sermon. For months, I couldn't follow what he was saying, although the faculty who heard him, too, revered his words. Then one morning, I sat up. "Did he just say that?" I looked around to see if others were as spellbound as I.

I had just caught the wave-length of a theologian speaking insights that years later appeared in print written by world famous theologians. Here was the truth not hemmed in by simple catechism questions and answers. Here was my opening to de Chardin, Hans Kung, Schillebeekx, and Martin Marty, Harvy Cox, Paul Tillich, etc., theologians who have shaped my thinking.

And in literature classes I met T.S. Eliot, whose Buddhist-laden words in the "Four Quartets" and "Ash Wednesday" felt absolutely right, true. I began to relax into a deeper reality that held me quietly—without fear, anxiety, contrition, guilt, *ought to*. The richer, profound spirituality began to wipe away the fears, the silly mini-concerns of a semi-cloistered young woman. In the large scheme of the universe, I had been wasting energy and so began to move beyond the pettiness of religious decrees and doctrine.

While this inner self was learning a spiritual life, I was learning amazing things about art, music, literature. Before entering the Convent, (before television), I'd never been to an art gallery and now each meandering through one left me with an ache. All I can say is the art by the Nuns was so beautiful it stunned me, left its mark in my gut. In the Convent, I heard my first live concerto, first violin solos, timpani drums, four-tiered great pipe organ solos, music by Palestrina, a hundred-plus women's choir singing four-part harmonies *a cappella* in the magnificent basilica we called our chapel. The world famous women musicians/composers and artists of our community are gifts to the hundreds/thousands of women who lived with them and their art.

Rich was our life in art and music and literature. Women left the Convent for many reasons, but we did not need to leave diminished.

Where do these reflections lead? To my deep love and respect for the women with whom I shared my life in the Convent.

Prayer[4]

Lord,
Spring of the green,
Maker of the new pulse—
Up-
Bubble of water,
And of the wind with the young-love sigh,
Eternal Master of the quick-created moment:
Give me a spirit that floods like a stream in ice-break,
Round, pregnant thought plopped as perfect as rain
Over and down through the brown earth of me.
Give me April fingers, green like new tulip shoots,
And hair that rises to meet the wind,
And stout
Hard feet for splashing,
And the night rain through my veins,
Thoughts like young grass,
And the strength to run through
Them now as light and liquid as a child.

Awakening the Cellular Memory

As the memory of our religious instructions by the Convent Chaplain and the Mistress of Postulants came to mind, I attempted to write about them and about the group activities of square dancing and volleyball. When I re-read what I had written, I felt the words and energy so negative and bitter that I deleted them, knowing now that it is better not to send such negative energy into the universe.

As I reflected on what I wrote last evening, I wondered about the subtle but definite experience within me. It was not the words I wrote, but rather that those words opened a cellular memory unopened but active these past fifty-five years. Last evening's feeling was a viscerally remembered hatred and rage against what I perceived as the ignorance and superficiality of the spiritual teaching we were receiving.

---

[4]First printed in 1960 in *Vision* magazine of Alverno College

During the sport's activities, I felt chunky, clumsy and self-conscious. In my 18-year-old mind I blamed the teacher for these feelings. My rationalization: We were in the Convent to learn about God, not physical fitness.

I know now in my seventy-four-year-old consciousness that all of the energies that I carry are my responsibility. They are allowed both for transformation and for the deepened and expanded presence of healing in the universe.

Today I am filled with gratitude for this knowing. Rather than blaming other people or circumstances, I have learned to ask the question, "What is my part in this energetic exchange?" The answer always gives me a bit more of myself.

It is a gift that brings me peace. I feel it carrying the power to heal what, a mere fourteen hours ago, had still been an unidentified open wound from my younger days, a darkness. That darkness has come to light within me and for this I am grateful. In this moment, I have forgiven those who gave us the very best they knew and forgiven, as well, my own ignorance and my judgment against them.

MARANATHA: PRAYER FOR THE SECOND ADVENT[5]

Apoc. 22:20

Unless the grain of wheat, the in-sin-born,
In-sin-grown flesh-seed, falling, die, itself
Remains un-Hosted, and the wafer worn
Of sacrament becomes the shell and shelf.
Unless the chrysalis, the Christ-caught one,
Is silvered, silent, in the dark silk first,
Unknown will be the gift of Savior-sun,
Unfought the dark-won death of pupa-burst.

O Christ! the beast oppresses, the world-weight,
Tipping our fleshly scales against the law
Of mind and weighing will. The late,
The last Advent unkernel us and thaw.
Free us, weeviled in the cosmic cocoon.
Beat down the beast and come, Lord Jesus soon!

---

[5]First printed in 1961 in *Vision* magazine of Alverno College

DREAMS

One of my most important spiritual practices began during Novitiate: paying attention to my dreams. In that Novitiate dream *I am walking through a dense fog—white on all sides, above and below. As I plod along, I find myself chanting rhythmically:*

> *Am I Mary?*
> *Am I Sister Mary?*
> *Who am I?*
> *Am I Mary?*
> *Am I Sister Mary?*
> *Who am I?*

I awoke in the midst of the chanting and immediately felt intense relief. My problems at St. Joseph Convent were simply caused by an identity crisis; I was really OK otherwise. This experience taught me how dreams can explain situations in one's life. *The next significant dream occurred while I was teaching high school in Chicago. In this dream I am an eight-year-old boy in Indochina. Some of my friends and I are playing in the jungle when word comes that the Communists are almost upon our village. I am given the task of warning everyone so they can flee a massacre.*

Heart pounding, I speed off, running until I drop from exhaustion on some vegetation at the edge of the jungle. For one moment I look across the sand to the sea beyond and then bury my head in my folded arm. I am in despair of fulfilling my duty and terrified for my own life. When I hear footsteps approaching, I tremble. This is the end! But I am just too tired to move away from my own death.

However, when I timidly raise my eyes a few inches, I see the feet and robe of the wise old man of our village. "Oh," I cry out, "the Communists are coming! And I'm supposed to warn the village. And I tried. I really tried. But I'm so tired. I just can't run any more."

He nods gently. "Poor little one. Yes, you are so tired. That's because you spend all your energy shouting and flailing your arms around like the giant crab grass you are lying on." He points at the thick-jointed foliage beneath me. Then he gestures toward a little river flowing down to the sea. On the other side of the river some cattails stand in the shallows. "You should grow strong and silent like the river rushes. Poor little one. Yes…." Then he picks me up and carries me to safety while I look into his glowing face.

After that dream I really tried to be more self-contained, more of a listener, less into every activity swirling around me. I'd learned how dreams can contain real guidance.

Eschatology[6]

I have a tongue within the bones of me
Tense with a word I would be born to say—
One pregnant word that searches silently
The break between the spirit and the clay.
The bones have but one master. I am two,
And each of me cries with a different claim;
So when I charge the bones, they ask me who
Commands it, and I cannot give a name.
But there will come a wholeness from the fire
That fuses me, an essence from the glow.
The Potter's voice will thunder my desire.
I shall command the bones, and they shall know
I have been spoken; it is time to speak.
And from the flame of me that word shall streak.

[6]First printed in 1961 in *Vision* magazine of Alverno College

PART II

MID LIFE

CHAPTER 6

CRITICAL DECISIONS

FORCES OF CHANGE

Our formal formation years came to an end in the summer of 1959 with our first Profession of Vows. Despite the desire of the Vatican Congregation for Religious that Sisters continue in training until we earned our first degrees, the practical reality of classrooms without teachers spoke with the louder voice. A few of us moved to Alverno College to complete our undergraduate degrees. Enclosure ended for most of us, however, as with trunks packed we boarded cars, trains and buses to our first teaching, nursing and housekeeping assignments.

Forces of change had been stirring throughout the 50s. Even enclosure couldn't fully protect us from them. During that late summer exodus from the Motherhouse, we did not return to the world we left, to the country we left, nor to the Church as we knew it. That placid, certain and circumscribed existence of the 50s no longer existed.

Describing those drug-laced 60s into which we unknowingly headed, Paul Kantner, co-founder of the Jefferson Airplane, is credited with saying, "If you can remember anything about the 60s, you weren't really there." But for us, it was the mid-to-late 50s that we had missed, living as we did during Aspirancy, Postulancy and Novitiate in relative isolation from the outside world.

Neither we nor the world could have predicted the perfect storm of cultural, social, political and religious factors awaiting this next phase of our lives. Behind us lingered the ethereal echoes of Latin Gregorian Chant; ahead loomed a world of burgeoning protest songs.

We heard Bob Dylan's iconic *The Times, They Are A-Changin'*—for us they certainly were—and Joni Mitchell's *Both Sides Now*. We would be challenged to look at both sides, not only of life and love, but of almost every *given* in our lives. Civil rights struggles, with their Black Panthers and the Chicago Seven; the Vietnam War in which many of our students fought and some died; the Cuban Missile Crisis; the assassinations of JFK, MLK and RFK; the construction of the Berlin Wall, Communism in Russia and China, Mao's disastrous Cultural Revolution; the Space Race; the beginning of the Information Age; systems thinking and chaos theory; Vatican II, of course, and an influx of transformational theological thinking and books; the death of God movement. In Africa alone, thirty-two countries gained independence from their European rulers during that single decade.

How could such cultural and political upheaval not steer us toward more personal independence and inner freedom? John XXIII's stated intention to convene the Second Vatican Council in the early 60s and JFK's pledge to land a man on the moon by the end of that same decade book-ended the personal, community-wide and Church 'moon landings' we would soon experience.

That perfect storm would see some of us re-evaluate and reverse decisions we had made a decade earlier, bearing—in the language of that day—the stigma of a lost vocation. Others of us would deepen and broaden those same early decisions, receiving—again in the language of the day—the gift of perseverance. To the outside world those choices of leaving the Convent or staying looked miles apart. At the time they felt far apart to many of us as well.

Within each of us, though, those decisions seemed organic outgrowths of lives led with honest questioning and integrity and an expression of deep inner destiny. From that wider perspective, vocation is not something one starts and stops, loses or ever leaves behind. Rather, it is an intimate pebble dropped from the heart of Sacred Mystery into each personal pond, flowing out from there in concentric ripples across a lifetime.

COST OF THE DECISION

I was among the few selected to spend the next two years at Alverno College to finish our degrees. We moved to the college campus where only four, not sixty Nuns shared a dorm room. Luxury! Our study room was a renovated sun porch where papers on desks fluttered in winter drafts. One term I carried twenty-one semester hours, in addition to all our regular hours of prayer and community activities. I remember being so pressed for time, I studied for French vocabulary tests only while running down four flights of stairs on the way to class. Teachers at Alverno were so fine that in all my graduate and postgraduate courses, I met only one professor who held a candle to them. For me, these two college years, when our main goal was learning, were idyllic spiritually and intellectually.

With my degree earned *cum laude*, I was assigned to a high school to teach freshman English, speech and religion. Because the school was new, many of the fifty best of the Convent's 3,000 teaching Nuns had been assigned to the school to ensure its success. I, fresh from college, was unbelievably fortunate to begin teaching among them. In teams, we planned courses and made our daily lesson plans. I learned from masters and taught among them, the most creative women I have ever worked with. Amid their excellence, I was an ordinary, creative teacher. Ten years after I left the Convent and won the state Professor of the Year award for excellence in teaching, I could only wonder what awards would have been given to my Convent mentors.

Daily life as a teaching Nun of the 60s was much the same as when I was a Novice—rise at 5 a.m.; morning prayers, lauds, meditation, Mass until 6:30; teaching duties until 5 p.m.; prayer, Office, reading; dinner; evening recreation; study time; prayer; 10 p.m. retire. We spent weekends praying, preparing classes, and doing chores.

For years, I traveled almost every Saturday to chaperone and judge tournaments with the school's forensic and debate teams. I was advisor to the yearbook and newspaper staffs during the interesting days of underground newspapers. Summers I attended graduate school and earned my MA.

I appreciated my fellow Nuns. I will never again have the opportunity to live closely with hundreds of Mother Teresas. The women I lived with molded the souls of American farm, small town, and city kids. They helped ghetto kids read and write their way out of poverty.

Our Nuns taught self-sufficiency to the women of Appalachia. Nuns operated our women's college to accommodate women's needs by creating some of the first weekend college classes. These Nuns began, forty years ago, exemplary programs for the retired elderly in need of physical and mental stimulation. They were among the first Nuns on the civil rights picket lines. These were the women of prison ministry, the women of hospices. These were the women of underground Catholicism.

I was one of them.

And yet I left them. I left the Convent.

Why? I had entered the Convent as a young woman who accepted elements of medieval Catholicism. But even as a teenager I sometimes wondered if parts of the traditional teachings were too simple, too stringent, too unyielding to attribute to an almighty God.

These doubts magnified during my college theology courses. At first I sat in classes listening to what I thought were traditional explanations of religious teachings overlaid with some liberal theology. Gradually, though, I began to understand the far-reaching implications of what was being said. The theology I was hearing was gently calling into question my own beliefs.

One day the theologian talking about the trinity stated the reasons why there probably wasn't any trinity: God was beyond man's puny explanations of three persons in one God. I was shocked, but the idea made sense. I was going to have to change.

Day after day, in course after course, through college, through postgraduate courses, I listened, discussed and argued. I was doing what many young Nuns were doing. The Catholic Church opened up in the 1960s and 70s through the work of its Ecumenical Council, Vatican II, and embraced a Christianity that welcomed diversity, questions and profound studies of mysteries.

How could I teach in religion classes that there was just a single religion's answer when many religions pose the same questions about good and evil, about the beginnings and end of life, about a source of reality greater than the God explained by a Bible of the Judeo-Christian tradition? Other religions preach virgin births, messiahs, redemption through faith or good works or both, miracles, sin, salvation. Rituals and sacraments offered human beings a means of coping with the exigencies of human existence. But now I was asking: Were the rituals of one religion as powerful and symbolic as those of others? Certainly I could no longer teach a single, best road to salvation.

As a young girl, I had the threat of punishment and eternal damnation to keep me pure and good. Later I had my belief in the Church and the life of a Nun. Now, if I left the religious life, where would I find holiness? Wouldn't it be easier to forget the questions and just try to be a good Nun?

No.

I could no longer do what I did well—teach young adults in the Catholic school about the Catholic faith and shape the minds of the next generation— as a Nun.

I wanted to be holy, had chosen religious life as a special way to holiness. If I left the Convent and traditional Catholicism, would I find a spiritual life that was so essential to my own well-being? Plainly, I feared an empty life that rested without the spiritual underpinning of the Convent liturgy.

Even though my faith in a supreme being and the ultimate goodness of humanity was greater than ever, my Nun's habit and Nun's name contradicted what I believed. To be true to my convictions, I had to get a divorce from the Convent.

Leaving the community of those marvelous women was the hardest thing I have ever done. The women who shared my life in community, the teachers and nurses, the artists, writers, hospital administrators and college professors—these people could not easily be dismissed from my life. I had matured among these fantastically talented, brilliant women. They had mentored me—a young girl from a small town—into one who now understood the exigencies of feminism and racism, art and philosophy, commitment and modern despair, platonic and sexual love, myth and religious symbolism. With them I had escaped the narcissism of most teenagers and a dependency on males to make my life meaningful.

My life, my point of view, my trust in women would always be marked by their greatest gift to me—the security and independence of my own person. That security helped me change my life.

I anticipated the cost of my decision. I would lose my mentors and my friends. I would exchange a religious community of noble women who would always look after me, no matter what pain or trauma I might face as I grew older—cancer, stroke, Alzheimer's disease—for a life where I alone was responsible for myself. To leave the Convent would bring insecurity about my future, a sense of tension, and a loss of the peace about everyday living I had always experienced.

I wrote to the Pope, using the form letter, "Humbly prostrate at your feet, I ask to be absolved of my vows...." Sometime later I received his dispensation from my vows of poverty, chastity, and obedience.

At the Convent we had a little goodbye ceremony: I hugged my superiors, thanked them for their check of $300, and sobbed my way out the front door.

I felt like someone newly independent who immediately had to find a place to sleep, food, clothes, a haircut, and a paycheck to supply these daily needs. I spent most of the $300 on the deposit and rent for an apartment. It was lovely, had one bedroom and a privacy I'd never had. Only I had the key to the front door. My father loaned me money to see me through to my first paycheck. Friends lent me a bed and a dresser. My mother gave me kitchen items.

My new life could have been difficult, but I was lucky. I began teaching immediately in a new college, so my first paycheck came within weeks. With a used sewing machine, I created my own clothes, though I bought sweaters and suits at thrift stores. I searched the newspaper for estate sales because I decided that I might as well buy good used furniture as cheap new furniture. I learned to cane chairs, refinish wood pieces, sew window coverings. One of the men with whom I'd been teaching helped me buy my first car. I started to make new friends.

I saw a world with strange inventions and lifestyles in a drug culture I could not have imagined. When I could, I sat in the public library studying magazines and newspapers to find ads (what new things did people buy?) and photos (what did people wear and do?) and articles (what did people think and say?). I walked the malls to watch people and study how young women acted. In supermarkets I marveled at the new fast foods (waffles for toasters, microwavable popcorn, fat-free ice cream), the unexpected fruits and vegetables (kiwi, raspberries in January), computer scanning at checkout counters. I started to adjust.

Using my skills honed in the Convent, I became a leader, a catalyst at work. I started innovative programs. I served on state committees, was elected to a board of directors and a president to thousands in an important organization. I wrote government grants, published in professional and popular journals, was a department chair, consulted around the United States.

I saved and soon made a down payment on a lovely old brick duplex. I lived alone, found good people to rent the downstairs apartment to cover half the mortgage.

On weekends I sat in different churches to listen and watch. Then, through a friend, I found a church where almost every week the cleric dealt with questions very similar to the ones I had asked. He offered new insights to the spiritual life.

I settled. I found peace within myself. And still I longed for God.

DISCERNMENT AND THE NATURE OF VOCATION

In the bicycle-filled summer before we entered the Convent together, my friend and I made a girlhood promise. If either of us ever felt like leaving, she would say nothing to anyone for two weeks. If the decision to leave persisted after two weeks, she would tell the other. Neither of us ever left then; neither of us ever felt like leaving.

Yet today I am married, a mother, a grandmother. She is a School Sister of St. Francis. Our story takes some reflection about staying and leaving, about default and decision, about discernment and the nature of vocation itself.

I know Sisters who wonder occasionally if they stayed by default, just as I know married women who wonder if marriage has become a default choice for them. I know many women who left religious life and continue to carry their communities joyously into every aspect of their present lives and others who take pains to hide the fact that they ever darkened a Convent door.

Perhaps each of life's decisions—large or small—holds elements of both discernment and default. There are certainly mornings in every life when we get out of bed by default. The majority of days, however, we live by decision and ongoing discernment, the deepening knowledge that this is indeed the place of our destiny. As Hamlet knew: "There's a divinity that shapes our ends,/ Rough-hew them how we will."

JOLTING KNOWLEDGE

One of the hardest things during the four years I spent at the Motherhouse and also during the summers at Alverno was the jolting knowledge that some classmates were *disappearing*. One day they were next to you in chapel; the next day they were gone, never to be seen or heard from again.

The experience was disconcerting. Did they leave by their choice or were they sent home? Were they ill, did they have a nervous breakdown, did they do some unspeakable evil deed? Would this happen to me? Was I on the edge of disappearing? Not until years later did I hear some of the details.

I COULD NOT

When I was to be professed as a Nun and take vows, I realized that I could not go out and give children religious instruction that I was having difficulty accepting myself. So, at the very last minute in June 1959 after completing two years at Alverno College, I decided that I had to leave the Convent and the religious life that I thought would bring me happiness and be my salvation. My sister, a professed School Sister at the time, didn't even know I had left.

After those years in the Convent I spent about a year working on my father's potato farm. After the harvest season, I decided to drive to California with my brother who had just gotten out of the Marines. He wanted to return to California where he had been stationed and where our grandparents, several aunts and uncles, and sister lived. I decided to venture westward and join my sister who lived in South Gate, California at the time.

There I attended Sawyer Business School in Los Angeles where I learned the fundamentals of data processing and worked at the Western and Southern Insurance Company until they closed the Los Angeles branch office. My career in aerospace started when I was hired at North American Aviation in Downey, California to support the newly won Apollo contract.

"Why Are You Crying?"

During formation I thought I was on the straight path to sainthood and perfection. I loved all that the Convent and my classmates and mentors meant to my spiritual development.

What was that about pride preceding the fall? Not very well prepared to teach high school students, I struggled to keep up with them. I loved teaching but it was exhausting—physically, mentally and emotionally.

It didn't help that those were times of change within the church and society—ecumenism, civil rights, etc. Hypocrisy haunted me, and the mantra of "ours is not to question why; ours is but to do or die" did me in. I couldn't help but question and the answer for me was to embrace change and uncertainty.

So I left the Community in 1965 while my classmates were making their final vows. With tears streaming down my face, I was asked by our Mother Superior, "Why are you crying? Isn't this what you wanted?" She really didn't understand what a lot of us were going through at that time.

The First Protest Picketing by Nuns in the U.S.

I had no understanding of social justice work as I was growing up in a rural, Catholic, farming area. Because, in entering the Convent, I came into a traditional formation program, a sense of that kind of work did not develop there either.

My first assignment was teaching in a Chicago high school in the early 1960s. I'd never been in a big city before. What happened there opened boundaries for me and helped me to cross borders beyond my experience.

First of all, an older, more socially conscious Sister said my whole outlook was "very provincial." I had to look up the word "provincial." When I found out that it meant "narrow in outlook," that made me angry. I thought, "This is not going to be true."

The second event occurred when I was going to school for my Master's at DePaul University. Some of the other Sisters who taught at Alvernia with me were studying at Loyola University that summer. When the Sisters discovered that African-Americans attending Loyola could not use the swimming pool, five of us picketed in front of Loyola in full habit. This day was the first time in my sheltered life that I saw hate in people's eyes.

Our protest picketing hit the newspapers, evening TV news, international news. After this, more and more religious joined civil rights demonstrations, but we were the first religious in the U.S. to do so.

BANNER OF RIBBONS

My conversion to Unitarian Universalism occurred in the mid 60s—years before I even knew about the Unitarian Universalist church. Here's how it happened: I had been a Nun—a Sister, for about ten years. I had taken vows of poverty, chastity and obedience and was teaching music at a high school operated by the School Sisters of St. Francis. At that time the Catholic school system was in full swing and bursting at the seams with huge classes and overcrowded classrooms. The schools needed teachers so badly that we Sisters were often sent out to teach before we finished our college degrees. While this may have been a disadvantage for the students and a little nerve-wracking for us, nevertheless it meant that summers were always much anticipated and appreciated for we got to return to Alverno College in Milwaukee to finish off six to eight more college credits.

So summer meant a release from classroom teaching and a noisy, chatty, warm reunion with my friends from the Novitiate. I was stimulated by college classes in a nurturing environment. I loved it! Every Monday evening we trundled to the college auditorium to hear a lecture from the chaplain. I must admit that I often spent the time dozing or daydreaming.

However, one Monday evening a guest lecturer was introduced. He came on to the stage carrying a banner of ribbons. They were, he explained, symbols of the many gifts and talents each of us was given. He went on to clarify that each of us had a unique collection of ribbons—a personalized banner, so to speak, that represented our potential as an individual human being. "Sin," he said, "was the failure to reach this potential."

Well, I became fully awake; lights went on, cannons exploded, my mind raced through all kinds of possibilities. *If sin was the failure to reach my potential, what about eating meat on Friday? What about missing Mass on a holy day of obligation? Were they sins or not? What did my banner look like? Was I using my gifts? Was I reaching my potential? What were my gifts anyway? What were the expectations I should be living up to? And how was I going to figure this all out?*

I remember going for a long walk and pondering these many questions—questions I continue to live with.

Our day-to-day lives as Nuns were totally focused on teaching—we even had Sisters who would cook for us so we would be free to pray and prepare for our classes. My day began with meditation and prayer, followed by playing the organ for at least one Mass, a quick breakfast (usually in silence), a full day of teaching both private lessons and classes, a short gathering to chant the afternoon prayers of the Divine Office, then more music lessons, a supper followed by rehearsals for a variety show, or school musical or some other ensemble group. It was a busy and focused life not unlike many lives today. I liked the efficiency of it all and appreciated the times of silence. The friends I have from my Convent days are still friends, not because we shared so many feelings (who had the time?) but because we shared the common and unique experience of religious life.

The changes that were taking place in the church and in society at large during the 1960s emphasized a more personal, responsible approach to spirituality and to life as a whole—at least to me—so when I heard the banner lecture, everything began to fall into place. Jesus evolved from spiritual spouse to admirable historical figure. The vow of obedience was not as important as a personal quest for truth and meaning. The vow of poverty still made sense, and even though most people hadn't made that vow, they too seemed to struggle with keeping things simple and responsibly managing stuff in their lives. The vow of chastity was… well, what was that all about?

After a lot of thought, I decided that my life would be more purposeful and I could better reach my potential outside the order. So I left the School Sisters and moved to Milwaukee to teach and finish my Master's at the University of Wisconsin-Milwaukee.

Then a few years later I married and we discovered the Unitarian Universalist Church. That church has not only given me a community of companions and fellow travelers; it has also inspired me to continue the journey, the quest, the discovery.

An early belief of mine transferred seamlessly into Unitarian Universalism. The Catholic Church had taught the doctrine of the Mystical Body of Christ: we as individual members of the church were part of Christ. I interpreted this to mean that everyone was more or less sacred and deserving of respect at the very least. Imagine my delight when I read the UU principles, especially the "inherent worth and dignity of every person" and "the interdependent web… of which we are a part."

The idea of the Mystical Body of Christ hit me full force during my first year of teaching. The ramification of this belief was that absolutely everything was divine. A popular book at that time was *The Divine Milieu* by Teilhard de Chardin, and reading it drove home the sacredness of the world.

I clearly remember how I felt when I went into the Convent—I was absolutely sure that being a Sister was the right thing, the only right thing for me to do. Now, decades later, I am not sure about a lot of things but confident that as long as there is a community of Unitarian Universalists, I will be both challenged and supported to create a banner that will make the world a more wholesome, strong and beautiful place.

THINKING OFTEN OF MY AGE AND MY ABILITY TO HAVE CHILDREN

After leaving the Motherhouse to go on mission, I remember thinking often of my age and my ability to still have children. As the time drew closer to final vows, I found myself struggling with the idea of promising to spend the rest of my life as a religious. Eventually in that final year, I knew that I could not walk up to the altar and promise that. As I struggled with the decision of staying or leaving, I was fortunate to have Father Parr, Alverno's chaplain, as an important source of support during this time of uncertainty.

Shortly after vow preparation day, I wrote to my provincial superior asking for another year of temporary vows because I felt that I could not make final vows just then. Sometime later I received a letter that said that I did not receive the vote to make final vows nor to renew temporary vows and that I should see Mother soon to make arrangements to leave. This was in June.

So I had to leave. I remember being called to Mother's office just before I left. Mother, her assistant, and some others were there. Mother said, "Remember—you have the vow of chastity until August." Her assistant said, "We're going to miss you around here."

I suppose the moment was similar for all who left in those days. I changed clothes in a closet. My superior on mission was there to help. (They had bought me an outfit and my dad had brought some things, including a pair of my cousin's shoes that didn't quite fit.) I walked out the front door, into the car and was on my way home. I remember that I had grown my hair out somewhat, but the temples had been shaved so the hair wouldn't show under the veil. Later when I went to the beauty parlor to get my hair cut properly, the beautician asked about why I had those large shaved areas on the sides of my head. I told her I had a rash and that was the only way it could be cured.

Of course, leaving was the right thing for me. I had grown intolerant of the demands and limitations of religious life. But it was traumatic for me to be forced out alone, apart from all those I knew and had bonded with. The intellectual and religious perspectives acquired at Alverno made it difficult for me to return to the Catholic parishes as a layperson. So I didn't.

My family was happy that I had returned. Luckily my grandmother lived to see all of my children. She and the rest of my family were a great support for me as I made the transition to a new life.

I NEVER LEFT

I had to leave the Convent to be true to myself, to my lifelong need for silence. When I left the Convent, I was told by a friend, "Your home is your cloister." I love silence. My home is silence, solitude. For me these are the epitome of religious life.

I left because I had to. But I never left. I still feel like a Nun.

I WAS HAPPY

I don't think I made a decision about staying or leaving. I was happy doing what I was doing. There were always people around to support me. People who challenged me and helped me grow. I've always appreciated those people.

When we changed back to our given baptismal/legal names, I told my fifth and sixth grade students that I was going to leave them, and they would have a new teacher the next day. I told them good-bye and that I had enjoyed teaching them very much. "Your new teacher is Sister Julene. Please be good to her."

The next day I came back to the classroom and announced, "Hi, I'm Sister Julene."

When we could take off the habit, I asked my high school students if I should keep the habit or get rid of it. They said, "Get rid of it. Then we won't be afraid to talk to you." So I went and bought a blue/grey short skirt and a white blouse and wore them the next day to class.

BECAUSE I WANTED TO BE AN ARTIST

I left the order because I wanted to be an artist.

I had been assigned grade school teaching positions for the six years I was in vows. I was supposed to be teaching high school art but there was a short supply of elementary teachers in the order. I enjoyed teaching but I knew I did not want to do it for years.

I chose to leave when it was time to make final vows. I was ushered in the back door of the Rockford Provincial house and put in one of the parlors with a hide-a-bed. There was an appearance before the council and a document to be signed promising not to seek recompense for services rendered. I was taken to the train station very early in the morning and sent on my way to Chicago. It all felt like what today is called a covert operation. Nevertheless, I was on my way back into a world I had left at the age of fourteen.

I would like to include, at this point, some thoughts from *The Spiral Staircase* by Karen Armstrong, who speaks of the religious life in those days as "a conditioning," so much so that leaving was not like a simple change of job or house. During our years of formation we were isolated both from the outside world and from the rest of the community. For that reason, "the whims and moods" of those in authority "acquired monumental importance." Punishments felt like cosmic events. In loneliness and misery, there seemed no possibility of comfort. Young as so many of us were, we had scant outside experience to draw upon. We had been segregated, deprived of normal affection and faced situations designed to test our mettle so that we might become totally self-reliant and no longer need "human love or approval."

A scant three years later, I was married; my son was born in 1968 and my daughter in 1971. For years I had nightmares about going back to the Convent with family in tow. I would tell the Nuns emphatically that I was just coming back to volunteer my time.

I'm not sure I was an ideal candidate for motherhood. I was not as warm and human as I should have been. I was still in the mindset of Convent discipline and fault-finding. Not exactly the attitude for creating a loving, nurturing atmosphere for children.

The Foundation

At the end of the Novitiate, we made our first profession of vows and could be assigned to missions in whatever field we were being educated and trained. However, some would be chosen to remain at Alverno College and finish their education. At one point during summer classes, names would be announced over the public address system. I kept asking God to let me stay at Alverno.

After the last name was called—and it wasn't mine—I was still sure that I would be staying in college. Nothing had been said officially but I felt God had heard me. Three days later, I found out I would be going out on mission to teach second grade. I had about twenty-four college credits to my name.

Because I knew nothing about teaching or classroom management, I was trained by an experienced teacher on a daily basis. She was strict and very capable so I learned quickly. I found religious life to be difficult and sought refuge in lesson plans and doing artwork for our community celebrations. I had never considered myself artistic in any way, but those projects kept me going. The superior we had was the youngest in the community and she was bound and determined to assert herself as the superior. At the end of that year, I was fortunate to be transferred to another mission.

During the following five years that I remained in the community, I struggled with depression and ulcers. I knew that I was not fitting in as I was expected to, but I stayed. I was blessed with a superior who nurtured and nourished me with her strong sense of community, observance and obedience to the Rule, respect, responsibility, creativity and human compassion.

Changes were coming to the religious life as I envisioned it when I joined the community. I knew that community living would be radically changed. Because I was not even able to live religious life as it was, the idea of radical change was too much. I left the community. I left people whom I loved and who loved me and set out on the rest of my journey.

That journey has been amazing. I know that my ten years in the community have been the foundation of all that I have experienced since I left.

COMMITTED

In the1960s, scripture and theology courses as well as new ways of looking at community and religious life began to answer many questions in my soul. I started to feel free and at the same time more committed to living as a religious woman.

That commitment never changed.

"YOU DON'T KNOW ANYTHING"

My leaving had two parts. Both were salted with tears.

First, I met with the Mother Provincial from Chicago. She was kindness itself, gently suggesting that I keep my profession ring and wishing me well. A few years later, when I met her at a gathering and thanked her for that kindness, she turned joyfully to her companion, another Community administrator, and exclaimed, "See! I always said we should be understanding!"

My second leave-taking was scheduled at the Chicago Chancery Office, where I had to sign my severance documents. At first I was confused: where was the kindly older priest who'd helped me with an issue in the past? Now the papers were presented to me by a fresh-faced young man who looked no older than the seniors from the final high school class I'd taught as a Nun.

My hand shook as I signed the papers. There was no going back at this point. My vows broken. And all the beloved Sister-friends I was leaving; their hurt faces sifted through my mind. Along with the dear fifth graders who had formed my first class. Patrick, whom I had to remind to wash his face when he went to serve a funeral Mass. Roger, who accompanied our Christmas carols with his drum. And whole families of kids I'd taught. Their class plays and the literary magazine we'd produced together. The roses that one class brought me at graduation. What now? Could anything ever be this good again?

The young priest cleared his throat and started advising me, "As you begin your new life...."

I stared at him through tears that were hot and bitter. "Little boy," I thought, "you don't know anything."

A BETTER FIT

I finally realized that the vows of poverty, chastity and obedience might fit better on someone else.

I DID NOT CRINGE

"Your Mother mourned for you every day of the last ten years," accused my Uncle, the Priest, shaking his finger at me during his eulogy for my Mother. Her casket lay ten feet from me. Hundreds of women and men in the church listened to him blame me for making a decision that brought my Mother such sadness.

But his words did not make me cringe.

I knew the truth of my Mother's reaction in ways he did not. When I told my mother I was thinking of leaving the Convent, she said, "Oh." Then she looked out the window and changed the subject: "Isn't that a beautiful sunset?"

My Mother did not talk about my choice. She didn't understand enough not to be sad, but she was sad with an intuitive understanding that gave me total permission to do what I did. I think she was a little worried by my decision because she was an extremely intelligent woman; she knew that, if she understood why I left the Convent, she would have to question her own beliefs. So she chose not to confront the issues.

To me, however, she was neither resentful nor unloving. A very feminist woman herself in everything but the Church, in a way she was proud of my independence.

Yes, I had left a lifestyle she and my Father had honored. Once I had brought them a faint bit of glory when I took the black and white habit and the vows that made me a Nun.

For sixteen years I had lived a life of poverty, chastity and obedience. For sixteen years I had tried to work out my destiny with Jesus Christ. It was a long sixteen years during which I gradually came to an existential decision that I had to live a life truer to my beliefs. I no longer believed fundamentalist doctrines of the Church like the improbable Assumption of Mary into heaven, the infallibility of the Pope, eternal punishment, and original sin. I could no longer be a Nun expected to represent these ideas.

Such doctrines were the beliefs of my Uncle, the Priest. My faith was deeper than those dogmas. So when he accused me of making my Mother continually mourn, I could ignore his criticism. He didn't understand my Mother. She understood me.

POROUS BONES

i.

Taking Vows

Under the black pall,
my tight face nudged
white terrazzo floor.

They said, "She dies."

They rolled back the pall.

They said, "She rises,
enters a new life."

But under the pall
I pondered: Do I dare
hurl back
the black sheet
stand up

flail the silence
shout, "No. No."

ii.
How the Decision Came

Not out of the blue,
not from on high.

I took off my veil,
wrapped it
in a brown paper bag,

the gold band
still warm from my finger
slid into the bag

which crackled a dying organ chord
as I punched the air out
and walked with it
to the Motherhouse.

I'd written the Pope
"Humbly at your feet. . .
a lost vocation."

"I dispense you from your vows."

Those cold stone floors
couldn't make me holy.

Convents birthed saints
or miscarried dry wombs.
And I couldn't see myself a saint.

iii
Burning

How then did that life pump into my bones,
burn my flesh,

whisper to me
in the quiet of nights
and the quiet of days,

twist my arms out of their sockets?
How did it spade my soul?

BEING A WOMAN

Perhaps the historical purpose of wearing a habit was to adopt the dress code of the common working person, but my twentieth-century understanding concluded that we wore the habit to hide individuality. We were draped in black and white so that only our faces and hands were visible. At best we were gentle, caring, neutered blobs without too much personality and certainly without sexuality. At the time I didn't think about the habit as a negative thing. It made life very simple; I never had to think twice about what to wear in the morning!

During the mid-60s as we began to follow the directives of Vatican II, we modified the habits we wore. The directive was clear: if we chose, we could change to a simple gray, black or blue two piece, long sleeved dress with a uniform soft collar and a short veil.

Arriving at Alverno the first summer of the habit change was mind-boggling and transforming. Here were my dear friends, classmates and teachers with hair, necks, legs and feminine figures. We were *women*. Over the past decade I had forgotten the feminine and all that it implied. To me this was a great and powerful moment. I was somehow completed and self-actualized, no longer an anonymous cog in the wheel of the church. The blossoming feminine part of me was not just an added layer—an enrichment, so to speak—it was my very essence, ready and waiting to flourish. The contagious energy of all of this potential was stimulating, even though I don't recall any of us verbalizing what was happening.

My decision to leave the School Sisters was enmeshed in my awareness of being a woman. The reasoning went something like this: God created me as a female; then it was my duty to live fully as a female and this could be better done outside the religious life.

TAKING OFF THE VEIL

We have to be considerate of others during change. When we were in short habits with veils, I was principal at a school. I knew it would only be a matter of time before the veil would go. Sure enough, one day the youngest Sister at our school appeared in her classroom without a veil. That meant we all soon would, but I told her that it would have been better if she'd thought of all of us. With my short, curly hair, I had no trouble taking off my veil, but there was an older Sister who'd need a permanent and other help before she'd feel comfortable without it.

REASONS

I left the Convent for a number of reasons. Many older Nuns I knew were angry, bitter, and desperately unhappy. I am a major outdoor person and felt cut off from the natural world that is so important to me. I had stopped believing many of the teachings of the Catholic Church. Convent life was beginning to make some changes that involved endless meetings, disagreements, acrimony, bitterness between people.

I thought again and again: What a waste of one's life. This is not how I want to live.

I wanted relationships with men, which I had never had before I entered the Convent. I wanted to be a normal person—not dressed in a costume that set me apart from other people. When I entered the Convent, my reason had been to give my life in service to other people. I knew I could continue doing this without being a Nun.

VATICAN II—TURNING POINT

During Vatican II, we lived and worked closely with the documents that came out of that Spirit-filled Assembly, focusing our attention especially on renewal in religious life. I was privileged to be at the center of that transformation in our community. To me it was indeed what John XXIII intended, "a breath of fresh air." We discarded old ways of doing things and experimented with new models of living religious life in the twenty-first century.

We had difficult and challenging times during those years of renewal, but we felt support and care and love among each other. Together we kept working toward a more wholistic approach to interpreting our vowed life in community. It was a daily living and dying, letting go and beginning new ways of doing things. As a result religious became more open to and united with the laity and their search for God.

I will always be grateful for the wonderful foundation I received from Father Parr and many of the other contemporary theologians and scripture scholars of those years. I attended many excellent conferences, summer school sessions, lectures and classes during that time. My years as part of the formation team for Postulants and Novices gave me an opportunity to receive in depth the messages of these great teachers and formed me into the person I am today.

IF SISTER GOES, I GO

Vatican II had monumental implications that we can see most clearly in hindsight as part of the larger paradigm shift in the world and of the culture. Some of these shifts reached into the faith formation of the young children in our classrooms.

When I was 29, during my second year as principal, the school was in its second year of using new religion texts rather than the *Baltimore Catechism*, a book that contained the Church's dogmatic teaching. For decades children had been expected to memorize its questions and answers.

Our new religion books were helping to shift learning away from memorization. Each person was encouraged to take responsibility for her or his own conduct. We were teaching the spirit of Jesus's words: *What you do to each other, you do to me.* Encouraged by John the XXIII's words, "The People of God are the Church," we were all—children and adults alike— learning that the presence of God is deep in the heart of each of us.

One morning the pastor stood in my office doorway with parents' complaints about the preparation for first confession by one of our teachers, another Sister. These parents feared the current teaching was all about "Love, Love, Love," which for them had pejorative tones. Not enough of the prior teaching about sin and its consequences. Since they were generous contributors to the parish and served on major committees, they had considerable influence. In response to their complaints, Father wanted this Sister and her teaching out of the school. He said he was going to call the Superior at the Motherhouse to have the teacher removed.

His words posed a major moment of decision for me. *What did my heart and conscience tell me?* I had already begun living beyond the fears of dogmatic religion and was coming into a new level of inner freedom along with deepening love of God and humanity. Nothing in me could prevent my speaking my truth at that moment. I steadied myself by placing my hand firmly on the large metal P.A. system.

"Father, if she goes, I go too."

Father stalked out of my office. I never heard another word about it from him, and that teacher continued to teach. I realize now that I had taken a new and definitive step into the presence of God. That move has continued to both challenge and support me through all days and years until now, at seventy-five years of age, I know that this presence is my Love.

GIFTS AND LOSSES

Convent life offered tremendous gifts to me. I was accepted by these magnificent women. They took me, a young girl, and casually helped me live among them. These cosmopolitan women, speakers of French, German, Cantonese, Latin, Spanish, or Portuguese. I was awed by their library, the print shop, their art studios, the antiques and paintings and sculptures from around the world. Yet these educated women never carried even a dime. Individually each was poor, humble.

They introduced me to classical music as they performed concertos, sonatas, symphonies, and operas. They introduced me to works by contemporary authors and artists—Cheever, Roth, Updike, McCullers, O'Connor, Rukeyser, Salinger, Swenson, Sexton, Martin Luther King Jr., Bergman, and Fellini, to name a few.

However, as I look back, my Convent experiences resulted in three significant losses in my young life: first, the loss of friendship because we were not to become close to any other Nun; everyone was to be treated scrupulously the same. Second, the loss of touch by other human beings—babies, old folks, friends, acquaintances, families. For the eight years after the Postulancy, I wasn't permitted to leave the Convent to visit my parents' home or even to attend my grandmother's funeral. And third, the loss of sleep. I was continually exhausted. (To this day, my husband kids me about needing eight to nine hours of sleep a night to make up for all my lost sleep in the Convent. He even has a name for me—Sister of Perpetual Exhaustion.)

HOW I BECAME A NAVY WIFE

While in the Convent high school and early college, I struggled with the idea of being a teacher. I did not want to have the power to shape young lives. Who was I to know! But I hated food, so being a House Sister was really out of the question. And nurses had to study science and deal with blood, so that was out. That left teaching. So at the age of nineteen, I was sent to a classroom in Chicago. There I had fifty-six students, some of them were bi-lingual, but others could barely speak English. I taught First Holy Communion Class.

Also during this year I had my first sexual experience. I had no clue what was happening to my body, but I was always uncomfortable when a certain priest was in my classroom. Thank God I seldom had him saying the Mass I attended.

During this same year, I saw blatant segregation. It was 1959. There were three rooms of each grade, with not a black child in the school. All of our policemen and firemen were black. Bus drivers, too. I was so bold as to tell Mother General about the discrimination. The next year I was teaching in a small town in Wisconsin.

My medical difficulties did not end when I started teaching. I even recall going to the doctor and coming away with pills to relax my back.

In Wisconsin in 1960 I went to an out-of-town doctor because we didn't want anyone in town knowing that the young Nun was high strung. That doctor prescribed a glass of wine at bedtime. As the years went on, my glass grew from a shot glass to a drinking glass.

Somewhere in there was a complete breakdown of all my abilities. I didn't even care to open Christmas presents. The principal put me on a one-way bus to our Community-owned Sacred Heart Sanitarium. I relaxed there and was able to eat again. But, when Mother interviewed me and said my superior was sending the money for the bus ticket back to mission, I took a turn for the worse. Then a Sister at the sanitarium counseled me, and somehow I worked up courage to return to the situation. I stayed at that school for four or five years. During that time I made two friends, both teacher-organists, with whom I am still in touch.

I went next to a rich parish in Milwaukee where many of the students were from broken homes, as we called them then. I was feeling rather comfortable in my abilities as a teacher. I was no longer the young Sister. I also enjoyed visiting with my biological SSSF sister because she always seemed to have such a happy mission.

I felt that I should protect the young Sisters at my mission from some of the hardships I had experienced. So at Thanksgiving, I asked to go see Mother. She listened carefully. Then, to my great surprise, she said, "Did you ever think of leaving?" Well, I had not. Because I had not been sent home for my indiscretions and had been teaching without too many problems, I believed I was where God wanted me to be. All along I had really chosen to do what God wanted.

But Mother said, "Think about it." As I did, it felt as if a great weight had been lifted from my shoulders. I was ashamed to realize how freeing that felt. By second semester, my replacement at school had come and I exited the Convent.

My little sister, who had three young daughters, offered me a place to stay until I got a job. I was so naïve that I caused a rift in a very dear friendship of theirs because of my ignorance about how a lady should act. I had left the farm at fourteen; there had been no adult woman in my home to teach me any social skills. All I knew was the protection of the habit and friendliness toward all.

I put out job applications all over Milwaukee. I didn't want to teach anymore, so I took a job in the auditing department of a savings and loan. It worked out quite well. I learned to key punch and balance numbers.

I moved into Saint Catherine's Home for Working Girls, out of my sister's hair. We had a curfew; if we were going to be out late, we needed to let the telephone operator know. Once when I was out all night with my Navy Guy and friends, she checked me in. Later, after I had moved to a less expensive place, she relaxed the rule and gave my address to my Navy Guy, because he had lost it. I saw God's hand in that. Later, I wrote to let him know how I was doing.

I moved to another state, where I was a guest in a Convent. What did I do but what I knew best, teach? I took over a class from a teacher dying of cancer.

The principal was impressed with my work, so when I asked for extra days off during Easter vacation to see my fellow, he gave them to me with advanced pay for the plane ticket. If we'd had more time, we would have married then. But as it was, I finished teaching the second grade class with much success.

Then I returned to Wisconsin to live with my brother and his family of five because I was pregnant. That was my time on welfare. Catholic Charities took charge of the baby and gave it a good Catholic home, as far as I know.

At that time I didn't know the glory of motherhood. It was just another bump in the road to be faced. I've never had the yearning to know what that boy was doing. But I made it clear that if he needed to get in touch with me it was OK.

Before the baby was born, my Navy Guy tried to convince me that I could keep it. But I struggled hard and decided for adoption. I knew that he was good with children. I did not want to compete for his attentions with a baby.

Our baby was born in September. My Navy Man graduated from military school, got a re-enlistment bonus, and we were married on November 2nd, Poor Souls' Day.

His mom, sister and brother flew to Wisconsin for the wedding. His dad had told him he was marrying someone too old. They hadn't even met me. The priest who married us said we had to have the wedding flowers out of the church before the next Black Mass. So the two white mum plants were spirited away to the wedding reception at another brother's home.

His basement was made for parties. We had lots of beer and hard stuff. All six of my step-brothers were there. And I believe all of my family, except for my oldest sister, who was probably pregnant and unable to travel from Michigan. My older brother said to me while we were dancing, "You'd better make this work!" My little brother, newly out of the Navy, was hitting on my husband's sister. His mom was aghast.

So I had become a Navy Wife.

DEEP IN MY PSYCHE

I had my first serious bout of depression about age nineteen during the Juniorate at Alverno and the very worst one of my life that lasted for eighteen months during my early years as a teacher. In those days, depression was not the catch-all epidemic it is today. We Sisters lived it largely like many others of the time—without medications, diagnoses, doctors, just setting one foot in front of the other.

I was actually returned to life by a young boy, a freshman high school student, who came to my homeroom after school one day to tell me something he had never shared with anyone before. When he was three or four, his family had fled persecution in some Eastern European country. Their harrowing escape had caused some kind of psychotic break in his heavily pregnant mother. Shortly after they reached safety, she had attempted to drown him in Lake Michigan.

As he described her hand pushing him under the water, his clawing his way up out of the water, her repeated attempts to submerge him, and his finally running along the shore to a nearby policeman, I felt something snap inside me. In that instant, the depression lifted. He had perfectly described as an outer event what I had been living as an inner one. Something deep in my psyche recognized that and broke free with him.

After that near-numinous late afternoon, I somehow knew I had undergone the worst that depression had to offer me. Since then I have been able to hold on to hope in every milder recurrence, still without medication or docs. To this day whenever I greet darkness as an old friend, I breathe a prayer of gratitude in that young boy's direction.

ABOUT MENTAL ILLNESS

Although it took me years to understand, all my life experiences have contributed to my spiritual evolution. I just wish it had not taken me so long to find my true spiritual path.

For eight years, for example, in my twenties and thirties, I experienced debilitating depression. After all that time, I was diagnosed with an almost completely inactive thyroid. Within the first month on the thyroid hormone, I became a normal and happy person.

During my Convent years, partially due to the undiagnosed thyroid problem, I was emotionally unbalanced from trying to cram myself into what I experienced as a harsh way of life. I felt as though I were screwing up in a major way. During the first five years, I experienced intermittent vomiting because my insides were so tensed.

Through this experience, I learned compassion and understanding for other people, especially those suffering from depression. I also learned that depression about ninety percent of the time has a biological cause, a phenomenon rarely understood by the average person in our culture.

CURE FOR ALIENATION

Already in the late 1950s there were many calls for change, both within and without the SSSF congregation. Sisters were asking for greater representation in Chapters of Election and decentralization of authority. Rome responded with the directives to form several provinces and develop procedures for electing members to represent Sisters in the General Chapter of Election. Subsequently, provinces were formed, based primarily on geographical location among the Sisters in education. Sisters who taught and worked at Alverno, Sisters in Health Care and Sisters in Central Houses remained under Generalate Administration.

Those of us in health care had many unmet needs and felt somewhat alienated from the larger SSSF community. We also knew that our lack of access to continuing professional education and developments in our fields was undermining our ability to maintain excellent standards of care in our Health Care Institutions. These and many other concerns prompted some of us in health care to write proposals for the 1966 Chapter requesting that Sisters in health care be allowed to form a province. I even dared to suggest that this province be called Health Agencies Council (HAC) and made suggestions about the style of government.

In September 1966 the Health Agency Council became a reality under very inspired and courageous leadership. Elected by the Sisters of the new province, I was on the Steering Committee that was involved in creating the very democratic structure of this new province.

During these years I really gained a completely new vision of religious community and dedication that would sustain me even after the dissolution of our beloved province. However, I found that Sisters who had not had the HAC experience tended to remain in a more authoritarian mode of governance and leadership.

THE IMPORTANCE OF THESE YEARS

Through years of formation and eventual profession of vows, I grew spiritually and emotionally, became more my own person, and made decisions that affected my future life as a wife and mother. Those early years are sort of a blur, filled with some inconsequential things like kneeling on hard chairs, scrubbing chapel floors, being called during the night to pray in the Adoration Chapel, listening to spiritual reading at meals, and trying to think of things I might confess at the Chapter of Faults.

Yet the importance of these years is reflected in the fact that many of us went through this together, and life-long friendships were formed. The Franciscan way of life became doable and a joy because it was shared. My love for music and liturgy has its roots in these years, as does my hunger for knowledge and seeking a global view of life. My appreciation for art, beauty and color grew in intensity.

HUNGER FOR HUMAN LOVE

Time spent in struggle can feel eternal, and a moment in time can make all the difference. Such a time came for me in my mid-twenties. Friendships were deepening and the stirrings of human love with its longings for intimacy were growing in me. I was not able to resolve the conflict between the promises my heart had made to the God of the heavens and the heart's hunger for the physical presence of human love.

And then there was a moment.

I was reading a novel that I had hidden away in the bottom drawer of my desk, *Son of Dust* by Prescott. This beautiful love story that to many religious of the day would have been considered a temptation against celibacy, I clandestinely read only a few lines at a time.

The moment that made the difference: I opened the drawer, glanced down to my open book and read, "He had dreaded God for the enemy of love and He was the giver of it."

At the age of twenty-five, I believed what I read and have never since doubted it. Not only have I never doubted it, but it laid the foundation for my growth into the truth that there is only one love, one object of love, one presence of love—Life, in all of its manifestations.

TEACHING AND PASTORAL MINISTRY

Through the years I have done various ministries, lived in many parts of the Midwest, and found myself in several different living situations. The first breath of freedom came for me after I joined Our Lady of the Angels Province in Omaha and was assigned to a small mission with four Sisters. The superior, who was also the principal, was open to change and I had one of my most enjoyable years of teaching.

I had forty-nine students in grades one through four. My creativity was challenged and that was so good for me. The children were very involved in helping each other learn. With the first grade I would pair a good reader with a slower one and they read out loud to each other.

The principal also emphasized the importance of teaching children quiet prayer. Each day I would have guided meditation for the children and I know it was my own initiation into guided meditation as well. I would direct them to be very quiet, focus on a sound, usually in nature, and then simply talk to God or Jesus about what was in their hearts.

This practice served me well in my years as a pastoral minister because I could use this method with both children and adults. Sometimes I would use a specific gospel story that lent itself to the person becoming a part of the story. One mother commented, "I don't know how you got my three-year-old to sit still for twenty minutes, but he did." This kind of prayer is so natural for children.

Perhaps I encountered my most difficult living situation right after Vatican II when so many changes in the church started taking place. There was much tension among members of my mission group and it was difficult to have your voice heard, especially if you were among the younger members of the group. Moving our desks out of the community rooms to our bedrooms was very traumatic, but I was among those who decided it had to be done. The majority of the group approved of this move because it gave us some measure of privacy in our own rooms, and we also had a comfortable community room where we could relax and visit with one another.

During these years I also found myself drawn to parish work because the high school where I was teaching offered a series of classes for adults. I seemed to be able to relate to them much better than to high school students.

However, I did not want to become a director of religious education, which was the developing parish position at the time. I had experienced too often the situation in which the content the students were taught in class was lost because it was not supported in the home. With this in mind I asked the Community for the opportunity to get a theology degree. For three years, I was a full-time student and earned a Master of Divinity.

Bewilderment

My question lies unasked and unanswered
because I do not understand the entire question.
I can pick into it with little fork bites,
hold bits up to the light
before putting them to my mouth.

If I knew the question's name,
I might call it at night, 2 a.m. perhaps,
when my legs churn the blankets.
But unsettled taste springs to my throat.
Somewhere in a night sky stands Orion,

though I've only ever found his belt.
"Look," people say, "for the Big Dipper,
then find the small dipper close beside it."
A fine word, "look," but useless to one
bemused by faint light and poor eyesight.

If I settle instead into soft confusion,
trust the question's energy,
I could welcome its stay through the day.
Then when night dangles my fears,
I could just surrender to it, relax into bewilderment.

AFTER VATICAN II

The shift created by Vatican II paralleled many changes in the larger world around us. People began to see and experience globally, rather than simply as neighborhood, city or country. Individual worlds became larger and the cosmic world seemed within reach.

Religion became challenged by spirituality. Our rituals appeared in English, the vernacular of our country, rather than in Latin, the universal language of the Church. John XXIII's document , "The Church in the Modern World," called to greater awareness the needs of society, not only of the family next door, but of government and other public systems. The importance of working for systemic change became paramount in religious communities.

Scripture scholars gave us new understanding of the original texts of our Judeo-Christian tradition. Literal interpretation was challenged by exegetical studies that became congruent with the evolution of the human mind. Systematic theologians, men and women, brought the God of the heavens into the heart of the human. The responsibility of our salvation came to be: Who we are to each other, we are to God, no more and no less.

Old belief systems were shattered as we struggled and searched to find new ground—the Ground of Being—on which to stand. The classical mystics were read, discussed and interpreted for the lives of twentieth and twenty-first century seekers. Women rose up and spoke of equality in the service of God and of the Church. For me, science and religion began to affirm their unity rather than their opposition.

Unfortunately, Teilhard de Chardin was silenced by his religious community while we were finding hope and possibility in his writings. A healthy psychology, through the work of thinkers such as Carl Jung and Josef Goldbrunner, found its way into religious life. Workshops and seminars were developed to foster the renewal of religious life for both women and men. Books, *The Art of Being Human*, and music, *"They Will Know We Are Christians by Our Love,"* catapulted us into a relational life we had not known before.

We moved from the cloister and entered the world. Many religious lived in small groups of their choice—in apartments, not traditional Convents. We shopped, we cooked, we drove our own cars and found our way as a cross section of our culture. We wanted to give countercultural witness even as we were being absorbed into the culture. There we worked among the people not only as educators or nurses, but in social services and pastoral care.

Today the authors of this book are in our seventies and eighties. We were participants in creating the changes and we are living the changes, as is our age-mate Pope Francis, a man less of dogma and judgment and more of love, compassion and joy.

With Francis we hope to be people of love and compassion. We strive to become part of the larger global transformational shift, still in its infancy, a hearty and strong child of our era.

CHAPTER 7
THE POWERFUL AND PASSIONATE MID LIFE YEARS

THE PITH AND PASSION

In my late twenties, my mother mentioned in passing that, if a woman gained one pound a year over her middle years, the result would be a thirty to forty pound increase. That was the first time I grasped in any meaningful way the sheer expanse of a person's midlife.

That memory returns with even more force today as I attempt to extract from my middle years, now lived, their essence—the pith and the passion of all that time. If I'm having this much trouble whittling one life down, how can we writers possibly hope to re-create here the power, the pain, the intensity and contributions of the middle years of the eighty-two lives of our Convent class in any but the most trifling manner?

No matter how we lived our formation years and reached our early critical decisions, whether we stayed within the Community or left, we next faced the ongoing challenge of creating meaningful adult lives for ourselves. Those unfamiliar with the inner workings of our hothouse formative years might find it strange that our successes and struggles, our decisions and drawbacks, our actions and reactions as we embraced personal and professional futures closely resembled those of any cross section of the population.

Different as our lives became from each other's after our years of superficial sameness, some defining values seemed to hold steady among us—our core identity as seekers, as wanting more than the ordinary; the transformative power of art, music, ritual, literature and creative expression; our wish to be healing presences within our worlds, large and small; our commitment to the welfare of women worldwide; our awareness of and passion for education and social justice.

We neither sought nor gained any exemption from the lives of the general population—the need for sustaining work and relationships, the unexpected arrival of mental and physical illness (both personal and among family and friends), addiction, domestic abuse, divorce and death. Quite the contrary. In the powerful words of Terentius, *Nihil humanum mihi alienus est.* Nothing human was foreign to us, then or now.

So in this section we allow memory, that great distiller, to peel back tiny corners, thumbnails, poignant sketches of those powerful and passionate years, all the while accepting our inability to portray their total vitality and value to ourselves and others or to the future.

WHAT WE ALL DID

Over our midlife professional years, as faculty and administrators, we, the SSSF class of 1957, infused many levels of education in the United States and Latin America: pre-school, elementary, high school, college, university, in traditional settings and in prisons.

Some of us served as traditional health professionals: nurses, administrators and staff of hospitals, clinics, elder care. Others became holistic healers and practitioners of alternative medicine and massage therapy, counselors or social workers.

Others of us worked in many forms of pastoral ministry and in SSSF Community Administration. Still others toiled for social justice, peace, ecumenism, consciousness raising, women's issues.

We became business owners, government employees, support team members for the Human Space Flight program, composers, musicians, artists, union leaders, hermits, retreat directors, writers, editors, publishers, gallery directors, farmers, dance instructors, wilderness guides, cross-country truck drivers, political activists, crafts women, librarians, consultants, motivational speakers, master gardeners.

We served on boards of unions, hospitals, colleges, schools, foundations, state and national committees; we wrote grants and sought ways to alleviate poverty and suffering.

Nuns, wives, and single women, mothers and grandmothers, in good health and poor, we faced the exigencies of life as did all other women.

The Educator Teaches Fishing

My new life outside the Convent was blessed. Eight years after leaving the Convent, I married my husband and moved to another part of the country with him. Marriage was good. However, adjusting to a different part of the country and a blended family proved much more difficult than adjusting to Convent living.

For the next thirty-two years, teaching college students between the ages of sixteen and eighty-two enriched my life. I wrote textbooks and was published in professional and popular journals and magazines. Summers in the 1980s and early 90s I co-facilitated National Master Teacher Seminars and conducted seminars for university and community college faculty at their institutions. Writing workshops and festivals found me on programs.

As the editor of an internationally recognized women's literary journal for eighteen years, I buoyed the emergence of excellent women writers and artists. I interviewed writers for half hour TV shows, created a literary radio show for the visually impaired, and co-founded a creative arts program, now a national model, for the visually impaired. By creating/sharing profoundly powerful vicarious experiences of poverty, inequality, injustice, freedom, beauty, integrity, war, and suffering through literature or the arts, I hoped to alter people's perspectives and relationships to fellow humans.

It's possible to give a starving woman a fish, but how much better also to teach a woman to fish and so set her free. Educate a woman, and you have educated a family. Thus my belief in the community college, still the only higher education opportunity open to so many American women.

In all these experiences, I knew my life's vocation to be an educator.

"Larks!" I Thought. "See the World."

During my first years of teaching, I remember several times receiving—it seems in the spring when changes for the coming school year were being anticipated—a four-by-six index card containing among other questions:

"Do you want to serve in the missions?" to which I honestly checked NO and "Would you be willing to serve in the missions?" to which I dutifully checked YES.

Then I returned the card and promptly forgot about it. My life was already neatly packaged, so I thought. At some point with newly minted

MA in hand, I would leave the high school where I taught and return to my beloved Alverno to join the College staff.

Largely due to Vatican II, it was decided that, by the end of the decade, twenty percent of the membership of each religious community of both men and women should be serving somewhere in the developing world. Typical of so many well-meaning efforts, what began happening in some communities, including our own, was the building of schools for the children of the wealthy and an influx there of eager but culturally and linguistically illiterate women and men to staff them.

In late August 1966 these two strands interwove for me. I had just arrived at Alverno to begin my first year as a college professor when the invitation that would turn my life on end came: "Would I be willing to go to Costa Rica to fill out the teaching term of one of our Sisters who needed to return to the States for an operation?"

"Larks!" I thought. "See the world."

See it I did. In that first hour's ride on the back roads from the airport, I saw enough to regard my twenty-six years of life a brainwash and a hoodwink. In what bubble had I been living? How could I not in my remotest imagination have known what poverty looked like, what it *smelled* like?

Those back road huts, however, were not my destination. Rather the school van headed for the well-manicured campus of a *colegio* for girls whose parents wanted them flawlessly bilingual by the time of their *quinceañera*, the Latin version of the sweet sixteen coming-of-age birthday.

I received that linguistic task and immediately proceeded to give my innocent-looking charges permission to do all manner of forbidden things like climbing the fruit trees on campus. With no more than a handful of situationally unhelpful Spanish words and phrases, I could not understand the questions flying in my direction.

Whenever the school's Director, herself hopelessly monolingual and huffing with outrage, came running through the corridors screaming: "Who let those girls…?" I knew I had committed yet another unforgivable transgression.

So passed the four months until summer vacation, which began for us in the southern hemisphere at the end of December. We celebrated our summer by planning a trip to visit our Sisters in Honduras. As was customary whenever a trip involved the crossing of one or more borders, our two-car caravan set out in the predawn hours to reach the first border by daybreak.

As our luggage received its first border inspection, we opened our bag breakfasts at an outdoor table under a stunning ancient tree. On a branch directly overhead perched a parrot who spoke more Spanish than I did.

"That's it," I thought. "To be bested by a beast, I won't have it!" Then and there I pledged to redouble my efforts to honor the Spanish language by learning it, which I eventually and delightedly did, along with the deep truth of the words: "To speak a second language is to have a second soul." To this day, the second soul opened within me by those treasured years in Central America proves one of the most far-reaching graces of my life.

How Could Anybody Be Prejudiced? Civil Rights and Gangs

Native Americans were the minority people I knew as a child. Within a sixty mile radius of my home in Wisconsin lived five different tribes. My father did business with some and helped many families in need.

On a trip to Chicago, in fifth grade, I saw my first African American, a life-changing experience for me. (This was the late 1940s, before television.) A beautiful, tall, slender woman wearing blue jeans and a white, lacy, summer top was pushing her infant in a stroller. I couldn't believe anybody could be prejudiced against people so beautiful.

Later, in the early 1960s, on the south side of Chicago, five or six of us young Nuns in our long, black habits were the few white faces among hundreds of African Americans jam-packed together on a summer's hot asphalt parking lot. We all strained to see and hear Martin Luther King, Jr., who stood on the bed of a pick-up truck holding a huge cone-shaped megaphone to magnify his magnificent voice. The crowd listened spell-bound. We left the parking lot moved by his eloquent words, his personal power, the absolute rightness of the Civil Rights Movement.

Our Nuns were involved in the Civil Rights Movement in Chicago on many levels. Summers, while I attended Loyola University, Nuns I lived with helped people in the infamous Chicago Cabrini Projects. My visits to Cabrini introduced me to concrete ghettos—towers whose amenities frequently did not work, whose tiny asphalt playgrounds could not accommodate all those children. The Nuns taught families (many from the rural South) to use the apartment appliances, to flush toilets and work the showers, turn on the stoves, to adjust to city life. Here I learned firsthand the poverty of little or no education and the urgent need for the Civil Rights Movement.

Our Nuns were the first religious to picket against segregation in Chicago in the 1960s.

Gang problems: In one Convent, situated in the middle of gang turf battles, a Nun negotiated peace between gangs. Guys would come to the Convent, meet her (in her full serge habit), blindfold her, take her to a negotiating place, take off her blindfold, and have her solve their issues.

The 1960s, times of turmoil in society and profound movements in the Church, educated and changed us young Nuns.

Justice, Peace, Suffering Humanity

After teaching at Alvernia High School in Chicago, in Mississippi for four years and Alverno College for two years, I worked at the Eighth Day Justice and Peace Center in Chicago. I'd been intrigued by the Center's activist mission and spent eight years working there as the SSSF Community Representative, the Justice Staff person for the SSSF Chicago Province. In this intercommunity organization, we challenged corporations to assume social responsibility and focused on systemic change by means of service, advocacy, legislative reform.

In my mid-forties I went to Nicaragua at the time of the Contra War. What came out of this experience was my understanding of the limitedness of political systems, especially in Nicaragua. This insight created a new phase in my mission activities.

After five years I came back to the U.S. exhausted. At that point, I wanted to focus on one issue only: suffering humanity, especially humanity suffering in war. I got a degree in clinical social work.

I was especially interested in survivors of trauma. I worked in Chicago in an Hispanic Center, a community clinic, then in El Paso at a counseling center in a diocese where I focused on poor, immigrant families and border issues. After that I worked in an SSSF healing center in Guatemala, Project Rieti, a holistic center for the victims of violence after thirty-six years of war.

All this work has to do with healing: helping people rediscover their own centeredness, dignity, beauty.

STIRRINGS OF UNREST

There were stirrings of unrest. How could there not have been?

Once we were back out among students, parishioners and other regular people, questions niggled. How come, for example, there was so much difference between the way the priests lived and the way we Sisters did? Why was so much of our needed teaching preparation time taken up ironing Church linens? Who was really in charge of us—our Convent superior or the pastor? Why couldn't those of us who wished to do so begin studying for the priesthood? (At that time we felt Vatican II would certainly and quickly offer that possibility.)

Serious issues lurked behind our questions.

However, as a group, we were not taken very seriously. Each year in our diocese, for example, the Bishop hosted a party to thank all the religious Sisters working in the area. He or his representative gave an effusive welcome followed by an innocuous movie and refreshments. When I couldn't avoid the event altogether, I alleviated the humiliation I felt at such infantilization with an equally infantile gesture—refusing the proffered orange juice and cookies.

We did not know in those days of orange juice and cookies how the subsistence salaries we Nuns earned then would be directly related to the serious financial issues faced by many communities of aging religious Sisters today.

DOING THE BEST I COULD

The same experiences happen to different people because of what is happening to the entire human race at the time. That was certainly the case with us.

There was doubt relative to rigid doctrines of all institutional religions throughout the world at that time. During the 60s it crystallized into both Vatican II and Existential God-Is-Dead. We all felt it. (The cover of the April 8, 1966 edition of *Time* asked the question "Is God Dead?")

I left the community partly because I asked those questions about God and could find no answers within myself. I didn't dare ask them aloud because I knew I would get textbook answers, and I knew those answers wouldn't give me any peace.

I left in 1971, however, so I'd already moved into an apartment, acquired a secular wardrobe, and had some experience with men. I'd team taught an evening class in the parish with a deacon who was trying to make up his mind whether to go on to ordination. (He didn't.) When he kissed me one night after a great class, I knew I had to leave. Our parish had large families; I'd taught enough children to be familiar with many sets of parents, and they all thought they knew what I stood for. I wanted no part of hypocrisy.

I was an agnostic for twenty-seven years, living according to an anecdote from a Graham Greene novel. In the story, drunken Willie was nearing his last breath. Father Pat, who knew Willie well, was there to minister, but Willie would have none of it. "But, Willie," said Father Pat, "what if there really is a God, and he's waiting at the pearly gates when you die." Willie remained tranquil. "If that's the case, Father, God'll say, 'Come right on in, Willie, 'cause you done the best you could.'" I figured I was doing the best I could.

I was teaching as well as I could—certainly with as much dedication as when I'd been a Nun.

I'd married a Holocaust survivor and helped him with his five children. I didn't know how to live any better.

INDISPENSABLE COMO EL SOPLO DE VIDA (INDISPENSABLE AS THE BREATH OF LIFE)

La vida humana tiene una gran cantidad de ingredientes. Dos de ellos son tan indispensables, como el soplo de vida. Creer en Dios y creer en "si mismo" son los componentes, que se necesitan para SER y ocupar un lugar en la humanidad, en este planeta, en "si mismo" nace equilibrado de muchas otras cosas ¿pudiera el SER desenvolverse ARMONIOSAMENTE con otros SERES, hombres y mujeres, sin seguridad, respeto y reconocimiento del otro de la otra? Y eso falta mucho en la sociedad.

La cosa es que, como dice una buena amiga, "no hay libro malo." Lo malo es que no aprendas de el, a si que no hay lugar ni situación mala, restándole lo que te hace fuerte e intocable en tu ser. Y que hermoso es compartir con gente superada, no "perfecta" porque—que aburrido, pero no hay que olvidar, que parte de esa "gente", eres tu convives con mama, papa, abuelos, hermanos o de cualquier circunstancia, con toda esa humanidad arropada con el agregado socio-político, socio-económico, socio-cultural. Construyes tu historia, cambiante cada día, cada mes, cada año. Pero tu ser es permanente y digo permanente, porque en el convento aprendí que: la vida es eterna.

Indispensable as the Breath of Life
(Indispensable Como el Soplo de Vida)

Human life has many ingredients. Two of these are as indispensable as the breath of life. Belief in God and belief in oneself are the components one needs in order TO BE. To occupy a place in humanity, on this planet and within oneself, many other things must be born and balanced. Would anyone be able to engage harmoniously with others, men and women, without security, respect and recognition the one for the other? Such qualities are greatly lacking in society.

The essential thing, as a good friend says, is "There is no such thing as a bad book." What is bad is not to learn from it. In the same way, there is neither a bad place nor situation if you can take from it that which makes you strong and untouchable in your very being. And how beautiful it is to share with people who have excelled, not 'perfect' ones because how boring! But you can never forget that you are part of this 'people'. You share life with mama, papa, grandparents, siblings or whatever your circumstances, with all that humanity bound up within the sociopolitical, socioeconomic, sociocultural collective. You build your history, changing each day, each month, each year. But your being is permanent, and I say permanent because in the Convent I learned that life is eternal.

What Makes My Insides Bubble Over

Shortly after I married, I became the librarian of the chiropractic college that my husband attended. The library was housed in the basement of the school and not well-trafficked by the chiropractic students themselves. It was a bit of a dismal job, mostly cataloging medical books. (I was used to the Humanities.) The fact that I didn't see the sky or sunlight for seven and a half of the eight hours I worked there each day didn't help much either.

One morning as my husband and I drove to school, I inwardly asked myself the question: "If I could do anything I wanted to right now, what would it be? What would make me feel like I was accomplishing something special? What would make my insides bubble over as I drove to work?" I was hard put to answer the question.

Then a morning some ten or so years later, I was lying on the floor in the living room with my three youngest children. Our oldest daughter was in school but, for some reason, it was a free day for the little ones. They had begged me to make popcorn, so there we were on the floor with coloring books open and crayons sprawled all over, munching on popcorn and coloring.

With a clarity I will never forget, I remembered the question I had asked myself all those years ago: "If I could do anything...? What would make my insides bubble over...?" I looked at those precious faces around me and knew without a doubt: "This is where I want to be! This is what makes my insides bubble over!"

A few years later I needed to go back to work, and I chose to teach in the middle school that my children attended. I loved the work immediately and all the subsequent jobs I've held—mostly in public libraries. But I know that the peak moments of my life were and still are in the hands-on mothering and, now, grandmothering that I have been blessed to experience.

ARTIST, WIDOW

After my children were in school, I free-lanced as an artist doing hand lettering and graphic design. In 1992 I went into partnership with an engraver; we merged our customer lists and embarked on a new venture. Growing the business was exciting and we had the opportunity to work in many mediums. My business partner brought to the mix a talent for dealing with people and money, two things in which I was lacking. I brought the creative design ability and the discipline of a self-starter. It was great fun and I am proud of our accomplishment.

By 1996 my son had finished college and was working in Chicago and my daughter was in culinary school in Iowa. That August my husband died of a sudden heart attack and my life turned upside down. He had been a professor at the University of Illinois and the Director of the Fire Service Institute.

One thing that made the shock and grief of his death more bearable was the ritual that was part of his funeral—not the ritual of the Catholic Church but that of the Fire Service—an incredible band of brothers. My husband was a leading figure in Fire Service on the state and national level and his colleagues came to honor him. That Fire Service ritual was a real comfort to me, having grown up with ritual as we did.

LET GO – LET GOD

It was 10:00 on a sunny, spring morning in April when I answered a telephone call that took my life in a direction I would never have imagined. My Provincial Superior asked if I would become principal of an elementary school, grades one through eight, with 240 students. I was only twenty-eight, wouldn't graduate from college for another two summers and had taught only primary grades, but the challenge was stimulating. In a daring moment, putting fears and doubts to the side, I said, "Yes."

No one told me that twenty-five percent of the school's population was Hispanic. Here I was not even knowing *Buenos Días*. How was I going to communicate with the parents of these children? I would soon discover that I had a lot more to learn than just the language.

Growing up in Chicago, I'd heard Polish, German, Chinese, Italian and the heavy Irish brogue, but I only stepped into these cultures in relation to food, dance and some customs, never to the degree that I would one day come to know the Mexican culture. These next years brought me to Cuban, Puerto Rican and Mexican fiestas and religious celebrations as well as deep relationships with their families. But the experience also led me to dirt floor basements where undocumented men slept on blankets on the floor and to neighborhoods where gangs and the drug scene made it dangerous to enter. "Don't go there without us," I was told, but this was where my students lived and I wanted to visit their homes. All the time it was like looking through a construction wall peephole. I was becoming more aware of a life so different from my own.

Not wanting to get an MA in School Administration, I went for an MA in Special Education: Learning Disabilities that led me to teaching in a public school, where I became Miss. The title Sister had no pull at all. It took some time to get adjusted to that.

But thank God for the great awakening. I found my colleagues, who were mostly Protestants, to be so Christian. During my childhood, many myths had been seeded in me about other religions and the need to guard my Catholic identity. Intellectually, I believed in Ecumenism, but to let go of those gut feelings of my past was a harder task than I imagined.

Every summer I did something to learn more Spanish and understand the different cultures of Latin American. One summer I spent eight weeks in Honduras, where I practiced the language, but I learned much more than Spanish. I remember that I spent most of my time crying over a poverty I had never seen. Honduras is where I discovered that if I stripped myself naked and gave away all that I had, I could not be poor in the way these people were poor because of my life experiences and my education. I was grateful for what I had and humbled by what I needed to do to share from the abundance of what had been given to me. I left profoundly changed, and the desire to live a simpler lifestyle has stayed with me over the years.

That experience caused me to raise questions that I had not allowed before. Is there a God? What can I do to alleviate these discrepancies between the rich and the poor? Could I do more if I weren't a religious? It was the beginning of my late adolescent search for my real identity and would last for a few more years. Who am I? What is my purpose in this world?

God was smiling because the next summer I was thrown back into a similar situation when I went to Cuernavaca, Mexico. I lived with the Mexican Sisters and went to five hours of Spanish classes, five days a week. No English for six weeks! Besides the Spanish classes, I accompanied one of the Mexican Sisters to visit the sick and again the deprivation tore my heart. This time, though, I visited *Comunidades de Base*, (basic or local Christian communities) in action. I saw people living the scripture message. I met a Bishop who wore a dyed green burlap vestment and the sandals of the people. He carried a stick for his staff and a wooden cross on his chest. I will never forget him. His example brought me to a deeper devotion to St. Francis, which in turn led to contemplative prayer and a deeper understanding of many of my questions.

I returned to an English-speaking environment and forgot a lot of what I had studied. The God of surprises had more adventures in mind to wake me up. After eight years I got a leave of absence to study more Spanish; with the goal of becoming bilingual, I spent six more months in Mexico. When I returned to the States, I was informed that one of our Sisters in Perú was ill; I was asked if I would go to Perú to take her place for a year and was granted a second year's leave of absence.

By March of 1983, another Sister and I were off to experience what became a life and death situation. We arrived in the North of Perú in time to participate in the one-hundred-year rains. The coast of Perú is pure desert and it normally only drizzles there every ten years; however, every one hundred years, a torrential rain hits the coast and brings great destruction. When we arrived in Piura, we were told that we would be on the last bus to Paita because the rains had destroyed many of the roads. Taking scary detours, we finally arrived in Paita, my new home for the next year.

Amidst laughter, tears, compassion, and fear of death, I had experiences that merit their own book. These experiences bonded me to God, my Community and the people. Unforgettable, they brought me into the bosom of a wisdom, faith, hope and love that I had never known. People sharing the little of what they had touched me profoundly. One woman made fish soup for her family of five and still managed to have a bowl for a blind person near her who had no one to care for him.

It was easy to live a simple life in Paita, where everyone was pretty much in the same situation and I didn't have to face materialism as I do here in the U.S. To live counter culturally here is a daily decision and never easy. To this day I ask myself what can I share? At the beginning of this winter, I had four winter jackets. I actually felt sinful. I'm down to two and a third will soon be out the door.

The year 1985 found me in El Paso, Texas, with two other Sisters. It was recommended that we investigate the border region and its needs. The Sister nurse got a job with the Public Health Department, the other volunteered at an immigrant/refugee center and I was asked to be pastoral administrator for a small church that reminded me in some ways of Perú, South America. The town was eighty percent Spanish speaking and about one mile from the border of Mexico. Once again, I was educationally unprepared. A priest only came once a week and often it was a different one. I had one advantage: reliance on the people taught me more through their experience than any college degree. However, I did get an MA in Pastoral Studies from Seattle University after five years of summer school. I was now fifty-four years old.

This parish was a fascinating place and I loved the people. Here I was—a Chicago girl wearing cowboy boots to avoid rattlesnake bites—taking the youth group up into the mountains for camping and horseback riding.

I baptized babies and traveled across the border to offer funeral services because the priest there had been murdered. The parish community and I, with the help of El Paso, many outsiders and our neighbors in Mexico, fought having a nuclear dump waste site in our desert backyard. Against many odds we won. The lessons for me were: God will not abandon us. Have faith! Fight for what you believe in and persevere. These words came from the wisdom of the people. It wasn't easy; there were disputes; families got divided over the issue and I became loathed by some, but the right thing was done.

Over the years, the church got repaired, base communities were formed, ministries and catechetics grew and some prejudices among both Hispanics and Anglos lessened. This was usually the time for me to go out the back door and say *Adiós*. I had been there for seven years when I was invited to return to Illinois to work with a Franciscan priest in the Hispanic community there.

Illinois was a totally different scene. Father and I, area coordinators of Hispanic Ministry for the Rockford Diocese, had the responsibility for the pastoral care of the Hispanics in DeKalb, Sycamore, Genoa, Rochelle and Sandwich, Illinois. Father left after two years to be with his Franciscan community in Denmark. I went to a different town every day of the week and felt like St. Paul, not writing, but visiting each community.

We dealt with terrible prejudice on the part of non-Hispanics; there were even priests who didn't want the Spanish Mass at their parishes and/or didn't want to share space at the parish. It was like walking a tight rope trying to maintain good relations with everyone. Thank God, there were great Hispanic leaders in this area who had a true spirit of self-sacrifice to evangelize, catechize, build community and to do outreach for those in need, especially the immigrants in the area.

With God's grace and these people, all was possible even though we worked 24/7. I was involved in the schools, jails, hospital, and court due to a lack of professional interpreters. I confronted family violence, gangs, alcoholics, child abuse, and murder. One afternoon, I talked to a young Mexican man who had been on drugs since he was thirteen. At twenty-one, he now wanted to be clean. Since he was undocumented, it was difficult to get him in a program, but an AA group of Mexican men said that they would help him. It all sounded so positive until that very night a fight broke out at a wedding reception I had just left, and this young man put a knife into another man's heart and killed him. He was arrested, charged and sent to prison. When I visited him in prison, he said, "At least now I'm off drugs."

During my time there, the community grew from two to six thousand Hispanics. Now there is a Spanish Mass in each town and the people are doing much of the pastoral care. Oh, how I was a person of little faith.

After seven years as Area Coordinator for the Rockford Diocese, I was exhausted. When a new priest, a Filipino, came, he set himself very strict boundaries, doing only the sacramental ministry. I learned that I had not set many boundaries for myself and consequently had little balance in my life. Spiritually, I needed more quiet and time to reflect. I came to accept that I did have a savior complex, even though I would have denied it vehemently to anyone else.

As I discerned about continuing as Area Coordinator, I was invited to the Omaha Archdiocese. Nebraska had a sixty percent increase in the Hispanic community due to the re-opening or re-structuring of meat packing companies and there was a great need for Hispanic ministers.

My new title was Inter-Parochial Coordinator of Hispanic Ministry for the Omaha Archdiocese. It meant being on the road again, going from dairy and pig farms to chicken hatcheries. Many of the Hispanics lived on these farms or in small towns nearby. Once more there were many undocumented people who were unable or afraid to use the resources around them. The needs as always were great, but I remembered the lessons I had learned. After one year, I went to the Bishop and said that I could realistically only cover Fremont and Wayne, so he appointed a priest and another Sister to cover the other three towns. How easy! Just say no.

There was plenty to be done, but I began to believe that I could trust and let go; things could be out of my control. It sounds so easy to write it on paper when really the struggle was always present. Spiritual direction, a prayer group and time for contemplative prayer were all vital parts of coming to an inner peace.

Life was calmer. I learned about dairy farms, pigs and how hard the work is in the slaughterhouses. I saw a baby being born and I held a baby that had just died from crib death. We had a great youth group who did astounding things.

There were daily struggles and interesting happenings, such as learning about *brujería* (witchcraft). It was a challenge to respect the beliefs of some of the people and at the same time to bring these beliefs into a Christian theology. For example, a woman told me that her baby had pneumonia because her neighbor, who didn't like her, had thrown dirt and salt at her door. There are hundreds of these beliefs that we discussed as they came up. I know that the belief stays present. A Peruvian doctor once told me that someone had given him the evil eye. "Now I don't believe in that stuff," he said, "but just in case, I'm going to the *curandera* (healer)."

Nebraska also seemed to have more domestic violence cases than I had encountered elsewhere. Cases seemed to be coming in weekly. I was in awe as these women made drastic decisions about their lives. In my experience, about half walked away. These were truly valiant women! Each story unique, each woman imprinted on my mind, each woman bonded to my life. We walked together really as sisters because they were so far from home, no family for support, fearing to stay in the U.S. where life was so fragile and yet afraid of going home where they would never be able to give their children what they had in the States.

Again the difficulty for me was the letting go of control. This had to be the woman's decision. I could only walk with her because our time together was like a droplet of water falling in the fast flowing river. I never saw many of the women again and yet I am so grateful to have been part of their experiences. They allowed me to go through the door into a world that I had never known. I served on the board for the Domestic Violence Shelter for six years, each day gaining insights into this momentous problem.

It was hard to leave Nebraska, but again there was a call. The School Sisters of St. Francis wanted a Community-sponsored ministry on the border and asked for volunteers to investigate the needs of the major cities along the border to determine where we might best serve. Since I love to travel and am more of an initiator than a maintainer, I had a great deal of energy around this project. Another exciting piece of this adventure was it would be a joint mission uniting Sisters from our Latin American Province with Sisters from the U.S. Province, and our newly formed community would be bi-lingual and bi-cultural.

In August of 2004 we began our exploratory trip from El Paso to Tucson and then on to Nogales, Laredo, McCallen, and down to Brownsville. We also crossed the border in each place to study the situation in Mexico. What a trip! Finally we decided that El Paso would be our new home.

I'm now living and working in what we call the *Colonias*. These are unincorporated areas without any infrastructure in place. Four of the *Colonias* still have no city water for the residents. There are big, black tanks in the yard and water is brought in by trucks to fill the tanks. Then the people attach pipes and a pump to carry the water into their house or trailer. This is in Texas!

The Sister from Guatemala and I surveyed the people about what they would like us to do in the area. The response was overwhelming: pastoral care and English. So I have come full circle to my career of being a teacher. I teach ESL to approximately fifty women in four groups in order to create new opportunities for the women in employment, to increase social interaction, to build self-esteem, and to provide more independence in their daily lives. Some of these women have never been in a formal classroom situation. There were tears in the eyes of one woman as she graduated from one level to another. She stated, "I have never received a certificate or diploma in my life. My children put their awards on the refrigerator. Now it's my turn!"

There are also many opportunities to act as an advocate for people and that is the most gratifying work I do.

All the people with whom I have worked have enlightened and transformed me. Simple people: mothers and grandmothers holding families together, the men who share their suffering, the youth that have such hope and the children who love so unconditionally. I have a lot of book knowledge, but I received my real education from these people. From them I have learned to accept myself, to be authentic, to grow in faith and trust.

My image of God has changed radically, and I see the face of God in these people each day. To walk with the people is what makes me get up every morning. I pray that God gives me the strength to continue the walk. I thank God that I had the courage to say Yes to that phone call so many years ago.

ZEN POEM

A merging moment:
Snow flies up through the water
To meet itself.

LA DOLCE VITA

Imagine the stares at the local theater in our town when a carload of us Nuns, all covered in black habits, lined up to buy tickets to the evening showing of Fellini's new film, *La Dolce Vita*. That movie pushed an envelope with its controversial sex scenes and religious symbolism.

"I saw you last night at *La Dolce Vita*! What did you think?" probed one of my usually hard-to-motivate, hippy, high school seniors the next day. We had a long talk about the movie, and never again was the young woman a problem in class.

We Nuns saw *La Dolce Vita* and other contemporary, controversial films because our high school English department head, a gifted, well-read Nun, believed all of us should teach excellent contemporary fiction and respond to current media.

During the heady years of Fellini, Bergman, Antonioni and other great film directors, we faculty enrolled with her in 60s film courses at the local university. What interesting intellectual stimulation and mentoring she offered us. After a few years, I taught film and media courses in another Catholic high school long before most schools offered such a curriculum.

Once, while attending a film course at Fordham University in NYC, a group of us went to see Andy Warhol's latest film. Later we were shocked not by the movie but by news in *Time Magazine* that the NYC police department had raided the theater a few nights after we were there.

That is one of my memories of Convent life—highly sophisticated women living contemporary lives while bound in a deep prayer life.

CAREER IN THE HEALING ARTS

For years while I was working full time, I had a desire to pursue a new career in the healing arts when I retired. I already had an MS in counseling. Jin Shin Jyutsu (JSJ), cranial sacral therapy, reflexology, massage, yoga, meditation, creative visualization, chakra balancing, yoga nidra, breath work, soul retrieval and vegetarianism are some of the things I have learned and share with others as a practitioner and teacher.

These learnings have been incredibly exciting for me! There is an infinite amount to learn. It would take many lifetimes to learn all of it.

As a long-term yoga teacher at a local fitness center, I incorporated a number of these healing arts into my yoga classes. Toward the end of one class, I taught the JSJ "Main Central" self-help that involves holding points on the body in combination and sequentially to balance one's energy in order to maintain health and/or to promote healing. At the end of that class, every student stopped by to thank me. Their reaction demonstrated for me how powerful this exercise is in promoting a sense of peace and wellbeing.

Classes like this are just one example of how alternative healing can benefit the recipient. As much as possible, I attempt to empower each person to help her/himself rather than become dependent on me or any other practitioner to apply the healing fix.

MID-LIFE ACTIVISM

After my children were in school, I returned to teaching full time. I taught art and English to all levels of students from diverse backgrounds in several high schools in a large urban area. Though each school was a different experience, the same issues prevailed—cultural differences, poverty, race, politics, crime—making success difficult.

I found that establishing groups of students to pursue common goals outside the classroom was a positive experience for them. I started school newspapers in two of the schools and worked with groups of art students who painted murals for the school and the community. I witnessed the joy and involvement of individual students in our projects, a bonus over classroom struggles.

During that time I also became active in the union. I'd come from a working class family with both a father and grandfather who were union members in the private sector. As a result, I was able to use whatever earnings I had made during high school to pay my own way through college. Because of their secure jobs and pensions, I did not have to contribute my earnings to the family by getting a full-time job after high school. With this background, I saw clearly how lack of stable families, safe neighborhoods, secure, full-time employment for parents, and adequate education made life so difficult for the students I taught.

During my middle years I also became involved in local environmental projects. I joined a group of Sierra Club members who were in the process of restoring and protecting native habitats in the area. We met each week to clear areas of invasive species of plants and collect seeds of native woodland and prairie plants.

I became garden coordinator for this group of members who, like me, also grew native plants on their own property and collected the seeds to be used later in restoration work. These initial efforts grew in the following years into area-wide involvement by many groups and organizations that continue to contribute to the restoration of native public preserves as well as the education of citizens and public officials.

WITH THE PEOPLE OF GOD

My religious life has been rich, rewarding and varied in ministry.

After teaching for about ten years and loving that work, I was asked to move into the field of Religious Education.

In 1967 the first parish without a school was being built in the Archdiocese of Chicago. Another Sister and I were appointed to go to that new parish to develop a program of religious education for all the children who would be attending the public schools in the area. Knowing that this would most likely become the trend and because of the changes in approaches to religious education as a result of the outcomes of the Second Vatican Council, my Community sent me to Loyola University to obtain a Master's in Religious Education.

After I spent two years in that parish, I was invited to join the staff at the Archdiocesan Office for Religious Education to assist in developing programs and training for these new parishes.

After a number of years I expressed my desire to return to parish work. I was blessed with the opportunity to join the staff at a large suburban parish where I remained for twelve years, first as the Director of their Religious Education programs and then as a pastoral associate. It was becoming evident that more women were needed to help meet some of the pastoral needs of the people. The reduced number of men being ordained to priesthood, the growing number of parishioners in large suburban parishes, and the new emphasis on the role of the laity in our Church were factors in this major shift in parish ministry.

The Chicago Archdiocese, under Cardinal Bernardin, had always been at the forefront of Vatican II reforms. Cardinal Bernardin inspired and encouraged the pastoral ministry in the archdiocese. Because I had the privilege of working with him several times, this was an enriching time for me both personally and professionally.

There is a wonderful story about the time he went for cancer treatment at the building in Loyola University Medical Center now named The Cardinal Bernardin Cancer Care Center. It was suggested for his comfort to move him into the building via the back door. "No," he said, "I'll come in and sit with the other patients." And he spoke to them by name, asking how they were.

The folks in the parish where I worked were most supportive and welcoming of me in this new role. To be better prepared for this task, I was again encouraged to continue my education and I earned a Doctor of Ministry Degree from the University of St. Mary of the Lake, Mundelein, Illinois.

Again I found myself ministering in another large suburban parish of the Chicago Archdiocese. This new role as pastoral associate was expanding. My job description was similar to that of the ordained associates except for the sacramental ministry. I remained at that parish for fifteen enriching and busy years. Ministering with and to the People of God enhances my spiritual life, as well as my personal and professional life.

In recent years, prior to the election of Pope Francis, my experience of Church had changed. In some areas the Church had appeared more cautious, defensive and constrictive. This has not been a trend that I favor. I have missed the forward motion that was so evident after the Second Vatican Council. The words and actions of Pope Francis bring great hope and encouragement for the future.

Several years ago, due to extensive spinal surgery, I had to give up full time ministry. My parish work now is limited but still challenging and rewarding. Working with the People of God encourages me to deepen my relationship with the Lord as together we all learn to be better disciples of the Lord Jesus.

Throughout all these years, I have experienced support from my religious community, my family, friends, various parish staff personnel and the folks I interact with in the parish.

The Church is my home—Gathering around God's Word and at the Table of Eucharist are vital to my life. The sacramental life of the Church nourishes and nurtures me as do both private and communal prayer. The presence, support and challenge of my Sisters in religion are critical components of my daily life. I have indeed been blessed these past many years. For this I am most grateful.

A WOMAN IS IN THE SANCTUARY

I have not been inside a church for close to twenty-seven years. Now my husband's death has turned my attention back to God, so I enter the church attached to the suburb into which I have recently moved.

I hear the organ begin, and the choir leads the processional hymn. I flip through the hymnal, looking for the page with the words. As I glance up, I can see that the priest has entered the sanctuary along with the servers and—

someone else. Someone whose stance looks familiar. I can only see her back, but I know that back, those shoulders. I remember how they used to look under the black habit.

A woman is in the sanctuary with the priest. A woman I know. Someone I used to peel radishes with in the Motherhouse kitchen. Someone who lay under the pall with me when we took vows.

I am thrilled. How far the Church has come since I left it! I am even more thrilled when she preaches the homily. She is sure in her delivery, presents an interesting new interpretation of an age-old doctrine.

There is a woman in the sanctuary. One who is my friend.

RABBI-L-ALAMIN[1]

I saw my husband die
at the top of a mountain
with comets clearing his path
through worlds of white stars floating
like lilies on the lake of my tears.

I was there, chanting grief, massaging
his feet as he ascended,
pushing him up with the breath
of my prayer. Now I sit
near the foot of the Tucson Mountains,

worlds beneath my feet: the hot,
heaving core of the earth, tunneled
with gila monsters, diamond backs, pack rats,
cities of ants, seasons of green cicadas
in shallow saguaro roots and deeper mesquite.

Above me, monsoon moisture swirls
in a blue sky patched with black
approaching clouds. Invisible energies

---

[1]Lord of the Worlds

tumble the dead wildflowers and brittlebushes
spring has left behind.

Lord of the wheels and the worlds, I bow my heart.
It is made of light and flares out of my chest.
I see the worlds like layers,
like flowers whole in the seed and opening,
like something I have never known that I
already know.

BLENDING A FAMILY

For me as a child faith was a simple word, simple to spell and simple to live. As I grew up, my mother, who raised eleven children, often said with more truth than I could then imagine: "Without faith I couldn't have done this…. Without faith I couldn't have gotten through that…."

When I entered the Convent at fourteen, faith meant being in a beautiful chapel listening to beautiful music and saying beautiful prayers. Faith and religion were one.

As I matured and confronted life's lessons, I discovered that my faith is no longer equivalent to religion. It has now become my ability at the end of the day to say, "Thank you." It is the posture of gratitude. Yes, more and more I believe in Brother David Steindl-Rast's description, "Faith ultimately is courageous trust in life."

One of the biggest challenges of my life, and hence to my faith, was marrying a widower with many children. Even my own mother faltered at the thought. Over the phone the day I, already almost forty, told her my intention, she implored, "Look, I don't tell any of you what to do because it wouldn't do any good. But in this case I'm telling you—Run like hell and don't look back! Raising your own children is hard enough, but raising someone else's..." She didn't need to finish her thought. I think she was about to say "…next to impossible."

She was right. Her words didn't do any good. I ran all right, ran right into the task of forming a blended family. Mom was right in a second way as well. Some of those early months and years presented patches of unbelievable challenge. Tests and tasks that translated into headache (make that plural), frustrations, heartache prompted an ever-present urge to run in the direction Mom recommended in the first place.

Perhaps there was nothing that could have prepared me for the challenge of blending. The effort I put forth in my new job with its unending household tasks left little time and energy for matters of the heart, for caring and loving the beautiful family gifted me by marrying a widower. Chores (the not-so-important stuff) got in front of and in the way of the sacred aspects of bonding.

Now, close to half my life later and a mega-engaged Grandma in that very blended family, I like where I am in it. My heart is happy. I can sleep at night.

So how did we move together toward a turnaround? How did the *blending* in a blended family happen? In life's quiet way, often within the tumult on the surface. A composite of circumstances led me to eventually embrace life with my husband and new family.

One such circumstance was my husband's cancer diagnosis. Tucked into the depths of this challenge came a burst of determination. An "I can't quit now, I can't run now" attitude took over and dominated my spirit. It is not in my DNA to quit. My husband's faith, positive attitude, and strength of character took my hand; I never let go.

Another part of the turnaround was *the dream. My dream.* It was a sobering and, without doubt, the most compelling circumstance. While I had heard and read stories of people's dreams after the death of a loved one, I never believed the stories. I convinced myself that they could never happen.

But such a dream did happen. I believe now.

Although I had never met the children's mother, photos of her suggested a peaceful and loving person. Her countenance revealed her love of life and family.

Prior to the dream, I had talked to her in my heart many times. I would ask why she didn't fight harder for her life. Why she left her husband and her children. Often during my chats with her, I would try to convince her (and myself) that she was so much better qualified for the gift and challenge of being a Mom. I wanted her to come back and finish her work.

Well, she did come back. She stood at the end of the bed, tastefully dressed in a soft, flowing black gown and a lovely, wide-brimmed black hat, and she reached out for my hand. My body became paralyzed. I thought for sure she had come to tell me how disappointed she was in me.

But she'd come for another reason. As we walked away and out of the bedroom together, she put her arm around my waist and said, very quietly, "Everything will be all right. Everything will be all right. Things will work out."

She walked with me to another house, a house I think in a neighborhood where I once taught. It was an older home with a huge porch. We sat on chairs placed directly across from each other. I was no longer terrified. There were no more words spoken once we sat. She just looked at me, with a lovely, peaceful look. That feeling of peace reached for and took hold of my heart. My hand too. That peace is still there. I cannot ever forget it.

We sat for several minutes. I loved looking at her. I didn't want her to leave, but she did. She walked quietly away and she never came back, never talked to me again.

When I awoke from the dream, I stayed motionless for a long time. I wanted to tell someone and yet I felt that, if I did, the dream would just completely disappear. Forever. It was like a precious gift.

After that, reliance on God, trust, and determination led the way for the turnaround in our family. Each and every circumstance brought with it that courageous trust in life.

My grateful heart also includes as part of the turnaround the gifts from my friend, a former Convent classmate. Not gifts wrapped in packages with pretty multicolored bows, although packages wrapped in brown arrived too, for example a book by Wayne Mueller. That book, *Learning to Pray: How We Find Heaven on Earth*, became another link to my lifeline along with the gift of friendship.

Return with me for a moment to those years and those circumstances before I was part of this family. During the treatments and hospital stays of his wife, life for the family was hard. But the father was determined to keep things as normal as possible. All activities (school, sports and the like) continued.

His wife (the woman in my cherished dream) died almost two years to the date she was diagnosed with cancer—on the day after Christmas. Enormous heartache! Grief stayed in the children's lives like a ghost. At that time, therapy was only for people who were crazy. The children were not crazy; they were sad. If only society had not created this kind of label for the help these children needed.

Several years later I said, "I do, for better or for worse." I said it with love and sincere intention. You know, like in *The Sound of Music*. However, the first time I opened the laundry chute, I wanted to have lunch with the producer of that movie! Sometimes I still do!

The house itself was small. No physical or emotional space for a newcomer, least of all for a mother's replacement. For my part, I went in like gangbusters. With years of teaching experience, I *knew* children, so I thought! I found out all too soon that teaching a group of third graders was a far cry from sharing a bathroom with six other people and finding the tube of toothpaste running on empty just before my turn to brush.

At one point a priest pointed out to me that the very situation of moving into another's space forced me to jump over continual minefields. There were times when I didn't jump high enough. Yikes!

Years have passed. The children are adults now. Their father, my husband, continues with his upbeat attitude toward life in general and our blended lives in particular. He would not think of pulling negative energy into his life or into ours. He has his family. His faith. He taught us all: "You don't run." At the end of the day, we all just say, "Thank you."

Our many grandchildren, the lights of our lives, cemented me more strongly to the family. The adult children see my care and tenderness toward their children and embrace me in the new way that only a parent knows. Grandchildren carry us into the future in a way that very little else can. Along with my husband, the grandchildren continue to inspire me and have brought me to this place that I love. I can honestly say that I like where we have come together.

Gratitude and faith—the kind lived mostly outside churches—have brought me to this always challenging and beautifully blessed place.

AND THE VOICE SAID:

"Let the day unfold—
like a silk scarf,
like a rosebud,

like a letter from your lover
filled with metaphors
the two of you created,
filled with blossoms
from the fig tree in his garden,
and a pledge of more surprises.

A letter you refold,
slip into your heart,
read and reread at bedtime."

TEACHER, COUNSELOR, PRINCIPAL IN THE AFRICAN AMERICAN COMMUNITY FOR FIFTY-TWO YEARS

I came to the Convent as a young country girl who had attended the parish school. The School Sisters of St. Francis staffed all the grades. There were times I stayed after school and helped the Sisters clean the blackboards and other little jobs. In the later grades, at recess, I would go to the corner grocery store to pick up their order and take it to the Convent. I also had this errand for the rectory. My parents always took vegetables, meats, and eggs to the Sisters from our farm. My contact with the Sisters became a relationship. I admired their work with the children and eventually I wanted to do the same.

At this same time in my life, my married uncle was in the navy. He asked my mother if his wife could live with us while he was away. My mother accepted her and, because she was a person of color, she was also a new experience for our family. While she was living in our upstairs apartment, I would go to her and offer to help her with her wash and other personal needs because she was very lonely.

A few years later, when the whole relationship got together for a reunion, our family was present. At the end of the gathering, all my uncle's sisters and brothers gathered in one area to give each other well wishes. I happened to pass by and heard their tearful conversation about this uncle because his wife was culturally different. At that moment I determined to make sure none of my brothers' and sisters' wives or husbands would ever feel we didn't accept them because of a cultural difference.

My relationship with the School Sisters gave me the opportunity to fulfill this goal when I entered St. Joseph Convent. There my goal to change attitudes toward cultural difference developed even further.

The training I received to teach others was outstanding. The Lab School at Alverno College gave me an opportunity to observe the finest teachers in action. At the same time, I was given religious instructions that increased my desire to work with people of cultural difference. I firmly believed that all people are loved by God.

My desire grew even stronger because of my relationships with classmates from Honduras and other ethnic backgrounds. After my spiritual and academic training concluded at the Motherhouse, we were asked what grade we desired to teach, and I immediately made known my wishes to teach African American youngsters in elementary school.

I was granted my wish to teach those children in Chicago. At the time there were African-American Sisters residing there also. They were true Sisters to me. To any question I had about my children, I received immediate answers. I loved teaching the children. They wanted to succeed and were eager to learn. I realized that the more they felt acceptance and true relationship, the more they co-operated in every way and succeeded academically. They became my little brothers and sisters.

After fifty-two years as a teacher, counselor, and principal in the African American community, I find my desire to encourage and assist African-American children has not changed. We still work hard together and succeed. It has been a wonderful, fulfilling experience that I have enjoyed and cherished.

AMIDST ALL THE MERGERS AND ACQUISITIONS

Amidst all of the mergers and acquisitions in the aerospace industry, I was fortunate to have worked continuously for forty-three years as my company morphed into North American Rockwell to Rockwell and ultimately to Boeing when that company bought the Space Division of Rockwell.

I supported a plethora of programs over the years, including the Gemini, B-1 Bomber, and Global Positioning System (GPS) programs among others, but my primary focus was on the Apollo and Shuttle programs. I am extremely proud to have been a part of these successful Human Space Flight programs.

I always wanted to complete my degree and after several years of taking classes after work I graduated from the University of LaVerne in May 2000 with a BA in Business Administration. I retired from The Boeing Company in 2005.

Not having children of my own, I am very devoted to my godchild and to my other nieces and nephews. One of my favorite places to vacation is the beach, so I enjoy spending time at several timeshares I own on both the Pacific and Atlantic coasts.

I am an outstanding cook and baker. Inspired by my mother who always allowed cooking adventure experiments in her kitchen, I learned to approach it with abandon and unfettered improvisation. I am very health conscious. I am also interested in fashion. My nieces call me "the fashion queen; when she gets dressed, everything matches." I must take after my dapper uncle, my godfather. I am an excellent writer as attested to by my sister, an award-winning writer and creative writing teacher. Some of my additional interests are the theater, gardening, photography, and downhill skiing.

FINDING MY NICHE

At age 20, with only two and a half years of college and no internship, I was sent to teach fifty-eight first graders. The Sister in the next door classroom was my mentor; she taught me how to make lesson plans, suggested creative art projects and demonstrated discipline techniques. I would never have made it as a teacher without her guidance and practical help.

Most of the children in my class were well-behaved, but one boy, 'Jimmy', was all over the room and would bother other children. In those days, no one seemed to know about ADHD. Since I really didn't know what to do, I often held my Teacher's Manual in one hand and Jimmy's hand in the other.

When I taught religion class, the children came to the front of the room and sat on the floor around my chair. Jimmy always sat next to me. One day I noticed that he was playing with my cincture (a floor-length rope we wore around our waist). I decided that would be fine because he wasn't hurting anyone. About ten minutes later, someone came to the door with a note for me. When I tried to stand up, I realized I was tied to the rungs of the chair! I laughed and exclaimed, "Jimmy, untie me."

During my first seven years as an elementary school teacher, my classes always numbered at least fifty students. On weekends I also taught Catechism classes, called CCD (Confraternity of Christian Doctrine). After my third year of teaching, I was also assigned to train 150 altar boys, which included scheduling them for Masses and reminding them each week of their time. In addition to this heavy schedule, I continued my studies at night school and during the summer. This part-time arrangement took me eleven years to earn my BSEd. at Alverno College. Alverno opened new vistas of learning for me and was a very liberating experience.

At age 27, with no training in Administration, I was sent to be principal of an elementary school and the 5th and 6th grade teacher. After four years there, I left the religious community. Although I will be forever grateful for having been influenced by so many marvelous, bright, caring women in the School Sisters, I knew it was time for me to move on.

Two years later, I was blessed to marry a wonderful man. I continued my part-time studies while working full time. I earned two post-graduate degrees and enjoyed the rest of my 41-year career as an elementary school guidance counselor.

I had found my niche! In fact, in 1975, the American School Counselor Association at their national convention in New York named me Elementary School Counselor of the Year.

PASTORAL MINISTRIES

I went on a trip to Israel with some students and faculty of the tri-seminary school I was attending. That experience opened me to the scriptures in a profound way because the stories of the gospels became very alive for me. I saw many of the places described in scripture and it was not difficult for me to return to those images as I heard the scriptures read in church or shared scripture study with parishioners. The story of the Good Samaritan stands out for me. It says that a man was going down from Jerusalem to Jericho. I literally felt the downward movement as the bus traveled the road to Jericho.

My first job as a pastoral minister lasted only one year and the reason I was not rehired was not made clear to me. I was very angry when this happened and dealt with it in a somewhat unconventional way. I did not have a church job for three months, but I had a garden in which I spent a great deal of time.

As I dug in the dirt, I would say to myself, "What others say about me does not make me who I am." This practice sustained me in a very difficult time.

I also had a small group of women who would meet weekly at my apartment for a half hour of prayer. One morning during my own time of prayer, I wrote a letter in my journal to the parish council expressing my anger about not being rehired. As I wrote, I could feel the anger flowing down my arm and out of my fingers. From then on, I was able to move forward and began looking for another job. This scenario repeated itself in different ways in the years following this experience. The situations were painful but, after arriving at a new place, I was amazed at the opportunities that I would not have had if I had not moved to a new place. For me it was the living out of the paschal mystery, my own way of suffering, dying, and rising.

My ministry took me to twelve different places in the Midwest. In each of the places there were new lessons to learn, especially my five years in Kentucky. It was a different mode of life from what I had been used to. My intuition told me not to go back for the fourth year. However, I was tired of looking for work. By the end of the fifth year, I came face-to-face with a priest pedophile situation. The secrecy surrounding the case was baffling, since it seemed that others knew more about the situation than I did. Because of the surrounding events, I was left in charge of directing the planning of a parish anniversary with little support. In the end, the new pastor chose not to renew my contract, but I had already decided that if he was not going to treat me with respect, I did not want to work with him. I then went to Missouri where I spent eighteen years altogether working in three different places. In the last parish, I was pastoral administrator.

During those years, I got a real taste of what it meant to rub shoulders with people of other faith traditions. In each town where I served, there was a Ministerial Association and all the ministers of the various churches usually participated. One especially memorable occasion was the funeral of a woman who had been part of an ecumenical woman's prayer group that I had started. She belonged to the Methodist Church, but the minister was out of town. I was asked to conduct the service, which was held in the Presbyterian Church and assisted by the minister of the local Lutheran Church.

On another occasion, the Congregational Church's minister was away on vacation and for some reason didn't have anyone who could lead the Sunday service. Being very new in parish ministry I felt a few jitters, but I did lead the service for them. I didn't follow the format for the service strictly, so it was a learning experience for both them and me. Some people were very happy to have me and, if there were any who weren't, they kept their thoughts to themselves.

Being involved in a CROP Hunger Walk was another unique experience. It involved a ten-mile walk on country roads to raise money to help alleviate hunger. Even though I was in good physical shape, I was very tired after walking for three hours, but the money raised and the sense of camaraderie that developed among the group as we trudged over the hills were well worth the effort.

Navy Wife

The Navy community was my life. My husband was stationed many states away from his family and from mine. Long distance phone calls were very expensive. The sailors were paid at a Fleet Reserve Club. So we wives met our guys there on payday.

I developed a friendship, which just recently disappeared when she lost her good husband, and alcohol tore our ties. We were friends when the men went to Vietnam. She was there with me when the ship was in for repair and I was the Navy Wives' President. I stood up for her at the courthouse to witness her second marriage.

I stopped to visit her in Montana when I drove across country with two small children to get to the home my husband had picked out for us before he left on another tour in Vietnam waters. It was the Fourth of July weekend, in Helena. The brakes on my VW Wagon went out as I pulled into town. Of course, every red-blooded American was at the fair, especially the stock car mechanics. So I had a longer visit than we had anticipated. On the fifth, my car brakes were replaced while my friend and I enjoyed a long and liquid lunch. Because her then-current-husband objected to another female and two little kids in his house, the kids and I stayed with her former husband and left from there without adequate sleep. That day at noon, after stopping for coffee and lunch, I lost control of my car when my head hit the steering wheel as I fell asleep.

Most of what I know after that is from a five-year-old's perspective. I woke. Corrected. Too much. And ended, after doing an end-over-end and a roll down the embankment, in front of the only tree of any size in sight. Since the kids had been on sleeping bags in the back of the wagon, they didn't have much room to bounce around. As the ambulance headed for the hospital, I wondered why they dragged me out of the car. My son later told me I had climbed the bank myself. They transported the kids to the hospital too. Everyone was most caring. After the first night, a nurse, whose husband was a retired Navy chief, took the kids to her house. They had been in the hospital room the first night for observation. I had a head wound with a mummy wrap. When I was brought to their room, their eyes got big as saucers. I had no idea why. After I had seen a mirror, I understood.

This was another instance of God's hand. The kids were being taken care of, I was taken care of, the insurance company paid well enough for the car. I don't even remember getting a ticket. The doctor said I could travel but not drive. One of the nurses wanted to visit her relative in the town where I was going. She agreed to drive my rental car and care for me and the kids until we arrived at my friend's house.

Then came a new phase in my life: Navy Wife, Home Owner. I had signed for the house loan that my husband had applied for before he went to sea. When I saw the astronomical numbers on a thirty-year loan, I was scared into hiring a lawyer to walk me through the contract papers.

Our choice of a house was smart. It needed little attention those first years. That was good; it was a time when my adulation of alcohol evolved. I was a good mother, I thought. (Anyone doing today what I did would be hauled in for child abandonment and drunk driving.) Again, an awesome Guardian Angel. The only two times I permitted someone to drive because I was too drunk, the car got hurt. Not badly, but enough to keep me from doing it too soon again.

Then my husband got orders for overseas. I was ecstatic! Italy! Wow! I'd get to start over again! But the Navy doctor would not sign a release of my health records until I was sober for ninety days so Navy Alcohol Rehabilitation and Alcoholics Anonymous came into my life. But my romance with wine was not finished.

In Italy we had an unforgettable villa that we shared with two other American couples. It was on an old mountain overlooking the Casino Valley. There was a very grateful bodega owner in the Italian village who really enjoyed entertaining all our American friends. My sobriety didn't last very long once we were there.

In the two years we lived there, half way between Rome and Naples, I earned my Master in Education from Boston University in Naples. Instead of a thesis, I did the groundwork survey for the establishment of the Family Service Center under the auspices of the Navy Chaplain, a good man. I tutored, substitute taught in third grade (my son's class) and spent most Saturdays in Naples for classes of my own. The couple living with us agreed to make meals and care for the children most of the time. My husband and the ship came home from sea just about in time to repair the cars that hauled us up and down the mountain. One Saturday afternoon, with the car parts' stores closed, a spring we absolutely needed was lost in the grass. I told St. Anthony I would never complain about the guys spending all their time repairing the cars if it were found. It was.

On Sunday mornings we would get in the car to go to CCD class. I had the confirmandees that year. If the car wouldn't start, I'd tell the kids to pray. Then I'd tell God I would be happy to stay home. The car always started. The boys making confirmation were also the musicians that accompanied my cantoring at Mass in the Italian church for the Americans.

During this time the Navy sent the oldest lieutenant to be our priest. He had been teaching in Africa for years and did not fit back in the States. So they filled their Navy quota and he landed in Italy. He had as much social sense as I did when I left the Convent. He was a lovely Irish man, athletic and an alcoholic. So, any of the precious blood that was left after his sip was mine. I did not confide in him. I mothered him.

We had rented out our home in the U.S. while we were in Italy. When we got back to the States, my husband built a garage. He'd draw the plans; I'd go file. He'd come home again; we would work on it. Every time he came home, it was to work on some aspect of the home. We finished the cement floor when our son was ten. The only traveling we did was to and from assignments or to major family events.

Our kids were not spoiled. I insisted on honesty. They were reprimanded more for lies than any other thing. And I insisted that they learn basic survival skills: checking accounts, cleaning, cooking, sticking to your word. I also prayed that their father would be home for their teen years. Because I spent those years of my own life in the Convent, I had no clue what normal teen life was like. He got his only Shore Duty while the kids were teens and once said to me, "I should have stayed at sea!" Then I did threaten him, "Don't you ever…."

The Art Is Not in the Pickle

*"The art of being alone with vigor
is a talent."*   —E.L. Konigsburg

Does one exercise the *alone*
by walking the perimeter
of soundlessness and marking
it off with chalk or a fence
against a stray dog or
a hairy chest?
                    Or does one
keep silence with vigor –
charting no sound but thought
as it skips from point to point
landing sometimes bare,
or lush, or balancing
in the wild and windy inner
passages?
                    With vigor –
is it being among, but
not with? Is it excising
grey and black until only
red, blue, yellow
pulse in any pristine light?

Being alone to eat a pickle
seems easy until
it is vigor demanded of
the pickle. Ah,
that is the personality
of the singleness,
the vigor of the intent.

See, the art is not in the pickle
but in the act of aloneness –
taking the bite and knowing
the taste and the crunch
just before swallowing.

LOST ITS POWER

Before I left the Convent, I was terrified that I'd become an elected full-time administrator. I sobbed with relief that I was not chosen as one of three or four women to administer the province for the next four years. I was young then, but I feared that sooner or later Community administration would be my fate. I could have said, "No" then, but the *ought to* kicked in.

Years later, when asked to become a college dean, I remembered that Convent scene. I did not accept the Dean's position. "You ought to," I was told, for the good of the college. But I knew I was an innovative college educator who would hate the administrative life.

Ought to had lost its power.

UNIVERSITY CAREER

I spent much of my professional life at the University of Illinois. After earning my doctorate, I joined the faculty in the College of Education and eventually worked there for nine years as Associate Dean for Academic Programs. I then continued my work as a senior campus administrator until 1999.

After battling traffic to downtown Chicago for twenty-three years, I decided to become a woman of leisure and retired. I continued as a consultant to the Chancellor for Academic Affairs, served as a volunteer at our parish food pantry and traveled! Life has been very good to me.

I missed our class Silver Jubilee reunion. I was actually in the hospital, about a mile from where the reunion was held. About fifteen or so of our class came to visit. I was delighted, but the nurses were less than enthralled because they came as a group! We had a wonderful, somewhat frenetic time together, which didn't comply with hospital rules!

MEETING DEATH EARLY

Early in life at age thirty I met death. During a test, I was found to be allergic to the contrast dye. As a result I lost my motor skills and my ability to speak. I was anointed on Easter Sunday. At that point I thought I might be unable to work for the rest of my life.

I never lost consciousness and my mind remained active, so I heard everything and thought I was answering people, but that was only in my head. There were no words coming from my lips. Through therapy I regained my speech and, after many months, I regained my motor skills quite well.

At the time of this illness, during recuperation and therapy, I asked God if He would make me well enough to function again, to please give me little pains, things that would not inconvenience other people, would not even be noticed by others, but please not major illnesses. I had come to community to minister to others and I didn't want to be a burden on others to minister to me.

God has answered my prayer quite directly. I have had numerous illnesses, broken bones, arthritic deterioration, pulmonary and heart conditions and two near death experiences. The near death experiences helped me to see the gift my illnesses have been for me. They made me want to live life intensely, seriously, with re-evaluation of my motivations on a daily basis. I feel God as a person always with me, and I communicate often during a given day with this intimate companion who moves with me from one activity to another.

At the time of my second near death experience, I was very sick with a pulmonary infection and gasping for breath in a hospital room, so sick I couldn't read anything. I used the reality of literally gasping for breath, focused that reality into breathing in and out, as we do for centering prayer, and uniting myself with all the living and deceased people of my life. One by one. The whole experience was very contemplative.

During one of the evenings, I was sure I would not live until morning. That evening, the prognosis was probable blood clots. I had said good-bye to my dear sister after speaking directly with her about the possibility of my dying.

After she left, I spent many hours praying simply, almost without words, wondering if indeed this would be the night I would die. Around 3 a.m. or so, I was in this contemplative stance and saw two lights coming toward me. One was like a sun or moon, round and very bright, the other in the shape of a shield.

Both lights kept coming towards me. I said to the moon or sun: "Must I come to the light tonight? Is this what is being asked of me? I'm not sure." As I asked those questions, that light withdrew slowly from my view and the light of the shield got bigger and brighter. Immediately I said to the light of the shield, "I will get well. I won't die tonight. I still have work to do here." That light came and embraced me. I felt great peace and the love and support of so many people who have touched my life through the years.

The moments after were otherworldly. Gradually I began to realize that I had been praying for help to know what to do with this illness and my fatigue. I had been praying to my two dear priest friends, one who has been dead for nearly forty years and the other for about eight years. They were my connection between life here on earth and life in eternity and had come to answer my call. I was moved to tears, as I continue to be each time I remember that beautiful evening in the hospital.

To Be or Not to Be a Priest

In the heady, hopeful years after Vatican II, women religious came together with new life and hope. We heard each other's voices in fresh and amazing ways. *Could it be that women were on their way to some kind of equality within the Church?*

I, who as a girl had played only two make-believe roles—as a teacher and as a priest—was by then a teacher. Perhaps… perhaps…

With many other astounding women in the 1970s, I prepared in private and in public, ready for the invitation to Ordination when it came, as we felt sure it would. We would flood the seminaries. New wine, we prayed for the wineskins.

Influenced by books as disparate as Paulo Freire's *Pedagogy of the Oppressed* and Mary Daly's *Beyond God the Father*, deeper questions began to emerge in our dialog. Did we want to join a priestly caste of any kind? Did we want to become even more public representatives of an institution so linked with historical atrocities like the Crusades, the Inquisition, the systematic subjugation not just of women but of native populations?

For many of us, it became a sort of moral Ockham's razor. Women chose with delicate and fierce integrity on both sides of our questions. I came ultimately to realize that even were Ordination offered, I would not accept.

A Long Line of Strong Women Leaders

Growing up we didn't have many career choices, so when I left the Convent I didn't give much thought to what I would do. I assumed I would continue teaching. After a few years as a lay teacher, I was taken aback by the school principal challenging us during a faculty meeting, "What do you see yourself doing ten years from now?" I remember a sense of panic overtaking me as I realized that I didn't want to be teaching, I didn't know what I wanted to be doing instead of teaching, and I had no idea how to go about changing professions.

Neither the culture nor the Convent—nor, I must add, my passive nature—had taught me much about making choices. "Bloom where you are planted" suited me just fine; now I had to figure out where I wanted to be planted.

The next ten years were spent in search mode. I have only a twinge of regret that it took me so long; I was enjoying the journey and learning a lot about myself and the world around me—lessons that have served me well for the ensuing years.

I finally found a challenging and comfortable job working with an organization that served the elderly. Looking back, I think I saw the job as a vocation, an opportunity to serve and get a paycheck. The organization had a wonderful female CEO who joined the long line of strong women leaders who have always been there to inspire me.

WE NUNS PREPARED OURSELVES FOR OUR FUTURE

We've been very responsible, always looking to changes. From our beginning, our actions have always had two focuses: the formation, education and care of the Sisters and the full development of our ministries in order to meet changing needs. These actions took courage.

One of the earliest visible shifts occurred in 1967. Realizing that we did not have the staff and resources to educate women through adolescence, we closed the Aspirancy, inviting only women with a high school diploma and perhaps experience in the working world to join us. After that, numbers of women entering the Community decreased every year. During the great exodus of the late 1960s and early 1970s, it was clear that something more had to be done.

Vatican II's mandate for the renewal of religious life created another shift. The Counsel asked all religious to return to their original charism. This meant two things to us: one, deeper investigation of Franciscan Spirituality. Francis walked among the people as Jesus did, teaching and lifting their spirits, ministering to individuals. The second involved more attention to the Church's needs beyond that of education. In truth, after Vatican II, the Community came of age.

In the early 1970s we got into Social Security. The numbers of women entering had decreased, and we were very concerned about funding the retirement of the Sisters. We had the money to do that then because we had hospitals in which the Sisters were being paid the same salary as lay people. However, teaching Sisters, most of whom worked in small rural areas, continued to be paid a nominal stipend. We determined to seek comparable salaries for them. But that didn't happen until the 1980s. I was in the Wisconsin Province then, and we were one of the first communities in the state to do that. We had to negotiate with five different Bishops. It wasn't easy.

Also, during that time we decided to expand the membership requirements, inviting only women who already had a college degree or career training. Thus, we no longer had to fund college education for all of our members.

In 1977, Bishop Rembert Weakland of the Milwaukee Archdiocese declared that the Sisters needed to get repayment for all their years of service. Thus, the Foundation for Religious Retirement was created. The Foundation did research, compiled statistics, and made the results available to help communities plan for the future.

Later the National Religious Retirement Office was set up to distribute moneys collected annually from Catholic parishes to various communities according to size and need. I remember speaking to people in the parishes on the First Sunday of Advent, during which a special collection for the Foundation was taken up.

Because of retirement and a decrease in membership, schools were beginning to close. Also, Vatican II had opened the doors to greater freedom for religious. At this point workshops were created to help younger Sisters search out and apply for jobs of their choice. As advanced degrees were sought, Sisters negotiated for the programs they wished to pursue and the universities that offered these studies.

During the 70s and 80s we continued to build on the impetus of Vatican II. In 1974 School Sisters of St. Francis from across the world gathered at Alverno College in a Chapter of Mats, (the name given to the first convocation called by St. Francis himself in order to address his followers during changing times). It was a celebration of the one-hundredth anniversary of the Community's founding and also a real updating, a formative experience for women from the U.S., Europe, India, and Latin America. Robert Greenleaf's speech on "Servant Leadership" was simultaneously translated into German and Spanish. He said it was appropriate that we were meeting under a tent, as Francis had, because that was a sign of perpetual adaptation.

During the years 1980-83, we merged the Provinces of the United States into one U.S. Province. That eliminated much duplication of leaders and programs.

In 1994 the Provincial Assembly produced a Vision 2010 Statement that pointed us in the direction we wanted to pursue together over the next sixteen years. For the most part, this Vision has been fulfilled.

Now we keep working and planning. Our unfunded liability continues to decrease. Emphasis is on the housing and care of our Sisters, including medical care. Many of our retired Sisters live in our own facilities of continuing care, such as Clement Manor and Sacred Heart Center in Wisconsin or Newport in Omaha. Some live in other religiously sponsored facilities. Some live in Our Lady of the Angels, a beautiful new $5,000,000 facility for cases of mild Alzheimer's, built by both our Community and the School Sisters of Notre Dame. Its state-of-the-art design is now being studied for other similar places. This facility has forty-eight rooms; right now all are occupied by Sisters. It is very hard meeting some of the wise women of the Community in early dementia at Our Lady of the Angels.

It is surmised that the facility will be opened to lay people in the future. In fact, probably all of our facilities will be open to lay people. We're planning for that.

Some of our retired Sisters still live at the Motherhouse in St. Joseph Center. We made a firm decision to keep that building. Renovations and new construction were completed in February 2013, and the facility opened its seventy-two apartments for independent and assisted living.

As we look back on our Community's efforts to respond creatively to change, a second focus becomes apparent: planning involved the evolution of our ministries from direct service of our Sisters to collaboration with talented and dedicated laity who are being empowered to continue their ministries.

One of the clearest examples of this collaboration is Community-owned and operated Alverno College. Decreased SSSF membership had affected Alverno drastically because the College had been founded originally to educate our Sisters. Before the late 1950s, they had constituted the bulk of the enrollment. Suddenly Alverno knew it had to do something in order to survive. It had to create an educational niche that none of its competitors had.

So Alverno faculty studied the process of learning itself and proudly re-visioned the meaning of a liberal arts education. The result was a competency-based program that produced empowered, competent graduates. This was a whole new educational system in the Midwest, targeting non-traditional students, often women who wanted to complete their education after the children were raised. Additionally Alverno was one of the first to offer weekend classes.

To this day Alverno graduates have a national and international reputation as problem-solvers, and the College has been named the best small undergraduate institution in the Midwest by *U. S. News and World Report* for several years in a row.

Finally, in order to maintain independent existence, Alverno was separately incorporated under the stewardship of a lay Board of Directors with representation from the School Sisters of St. Francis.

Clearly, we have made a great shift both in religious life and programs to develop ministries since Vatican II. In 1999 our Community celebrated its 125th Anniversary with the theme, "Ever Creating New Ways to Respond." That's what we've done, what we continue to do: respond as well as we can in the faith that God is working with us. We've found new, creative ways in all our ministries.

Evolving takes a bigness, a happiness with yourself. You have to let go as the seasons do. If you taught first grade, you didn't want the students to stay in first grade forever.

Most of all, evolving has to do with human loving.

GAS MONEY

Sometimes I chauffeur fellow Sisters no longer able to drive. When they try to give me gas money, I say, "Oh, no! You put me through college."

SETTING DOBYNS STRAIGHT

After reading "Career" by Dobyns,
a former Nun speaks out.

Stephen Dobyns got it wrong
when he saw those old Nuns, veils askew,

bony shoulders burping rag dolls
with no eyes, no mouths, no faces,

dolls worn from pattings, strokings.
He thought, as an uninitiated might,

Nuns in eighty or ninety year senility,
holding dolls, must be

stroking their own phantom children.
But most Nuns don't adopt senility and

find their long lost hope of cozy
motherhood. The ninety-year-old

Nuns I knew rocked the orphans
they had saved and cuddled,

the preemies they had held and fed,
the children they had brought to alphabets,

names of colors, naps, tastes of ice-
cream and unsweetened apple juice.

These are not the women of unfulfilled wombs.
These liver spotted hands and blinded eyes

had rocked, and held, soothed and said,
"That's good," to Mary, John, Shuneka, Armid.

Can this man understand the overwhelming fullness
of giving? When these old women hold a baby

they do not mean, "I wanted motherhood."
Not that. No, not that at all.

Diminishment

As the leadership of the Health Agencies Council team changed, a struggle
to pull back from shared governance and the principles of collegiality and
subsidiarity left me deeply depressed. For the first time I found myself out of
sync with province leadership.

This time of mourning opened new insights into myself and others. I
began to rely more on God and much less on myself and what I could do.
In addition to this grief, health problems I had tried to ignore for several
years exacerbated and completely changed my ability to be of service to the
community. I loved nursing but could no longer physically handle a job. I
went from working twelve and fourteen hour days to part-time volunteering
on a limited basis.

Zen Poem 1

From my circle of pain
I saw first leaf of yellow autumn
fall,
let go,
drift comfortably to earth,
silent as it settled.

And I too
let go
in amazed
freedom.

ZEN POEM 2

As I near sixty,
I am losing bits of myself.
I know this
by the way
my fingers fail to negotiate a keyboard,
leaving words to hang
without endings
and puns to hang
without being heard.

I can feel my thoughts slow down
like unwound clocks
or reeds that clog the river
when the current weakens.

Yesterday
I wept and fought.
Today
I sigh,
let go,
and give myself to the losing
like leaves in autumn wind.

INTO THE INTUITIVE AGE

Since about 1988, I have become deeply aware of my identity as an empath. It opened a whole new refreshing way to understand myself, but it also revealed the underlying realization that I could care too much. However, I didn't know how to protect myself and still care. So I began to set up an invisible shield, like Plexiglas, when I felt too much dense energy coming at me. That's how I dealt with it and still do. It's just that sometimes I forget that this influence on my spirit is costly and comes with a stiff price tag.

Another related thing I experience: episodes of dizziness. I was told and have read that the portals of energy that have opened recently have made some folks unsupplied with the hardware to grasp the new dimension into which we are evolving… that things are changing at the quantum speed of light every day and that this generation has chosen to be here for the purpose of leading the human race from the Age of Technology into the Intuitive Age, the next evolution of the New Human. With all the muddle, I often feel that I am spinning out of control. On a daily basis it's more tolerable than not, but when it's bad, I am sent right to bed totally unable to stand or turn my head.

Often before knowing about this underlying explanation, I thought I might have a brain tumor or need neck adjustments, etc. But I think it's best described as new software on old outdated hardware, and I am impatient to get it, my new balance, to catch up!

These debilitating episodes do put me again into a mindfulness that we are in the movement forward and that, perhaps with our efforts to protect ourselves, our present wiring can accept enough. Enough for now. Enough until combined energies of mindful people lift us forward in tipping-point effort where we might catch the tail of it at least. With our busy and involved lives we may not feel it often, but it is happening—we are living among very influential elements. It reminds me of a line from *Megatrends*: "Growing old is not for sissies"—and neither is living in awareness in this present age.

Then there is the loneliness. It is something that happens in a crowd, among a group of women, men, family… the sense that I don't fit. It IS lonely. When I noticed this happening it was more that my words didn't come out right or seem to convey my meaning, that there was little to share of common interest with a certain segment of 'friends' anymore. It wasn't frightening—just okay. The more I share this with closer friends, the more we know something is definitely changed for each of us. There's very little chit-chat anymore, but the new has so few words to describe it that we are okay with our staggering.

TWENTY-THREE YEARS AND FOUR PRISONS LATER

It was summer. I was watching my six-year-old son and ten-year-old daughter playing under the shade of the giant maple tree in our spacious backyard in upstate New York. I had completed a successful year of teaching third grade in the local Catholic school, and the lazy days of summer vacation were such a delight.

A phone call from a family friend interrupted my peaceful tranquility, "I'm in a bit of a jam. We just opened up a new correctional facility and I need a GED teacher for evening classes. I know that you are off for the summer and was wondering if you could help us out."

I had absolutely no experience teaching in prison. Yet, from almost the very moment I entered the classroom in the Maximum Correctional Facility and met my first students, I knew that I was hooked!

Twenty-three years and four prisons later I retired as a corrections educator.

I love teaching. It is a gift developed and nurtured by a most marvelous group of women, the School Sisters of St. Francis. I love history and I thought that my calling was to be a high school history teacher. Little did I know what my true vocation was to be!.

Looking back I can see how my life experience had led me on this path. During my years in the Convent, teaching was a given. It was what I did. It was my joy and, during the difficult years before I made the decision to leave, it kept me grounded. My years teaching the upper grades of elementary school in Milwaukee and Manhattan were satisfying and productive, but very Catholic, very middle class and very white. When I left the Convent in 1967 I wanted to discover the real world that had surrounded me but never really touched me. So I decided to abandon the safety of teaching and try my hand at social work.

For two years during the turbulent 1960s, I worked as a case aide for Catholic Charities Family Services in the South Bronx. The work, as a provider of services to families in need, was a shocking introduction to the world of the poor and the desperate. The families I served became my teachers. My eyes opened and I came face to face with the challenges of urban survival, addiction and brutal poverty. My training as a Franciscan was always there to help guide me in my work with the poor and the marginalized. Years later when I interviewed new student inmates and listened to their stories, I could see in their faces the physical and spiritual scars that were a part of their life experiences. I knew where they came from. I had walked those streets and visited those schools and institutions that were a source of shame and failure for them.

My early years in corrections were especially challenging because women staff members were still an unproven quantity in the New York State Prison

System. We were in survival mode, eager to prove ourselves. We formed quick, strong and lasting friendships. The prison population was exploding. Educational programs received strong backing, and we felt that we really made a difference in the lives of our students. GED graduation rates were high and we made inroads in teaching basic literacy and life skills.

The last ten years of my career I was assigned to an alcohol and substance abuse rehabilitation facility. The program was based on the Twelve Steps of AA. It was a positive experience and a joy for me to work there. During this time I initiated a parenting program we called "Fathering From Afar" based on Effective Parenting Workshops developed at the University of Buffalo. Facilitating these workshops with the inmates, I truly found my bliss. The program was completely voluntary and the inmates were on waiting lists that were often several pages long. These men were so unsure of the challenges that being a father required. So few of them had positive father figures in their own lives. They were eager to learn all that they could. The workshop activities were lively, interactive, structured to respect the dignity of the inmates and reflective of the physical and emotional needs of their children.

I realized the impact of the program one evening when a young inmate participant called me aside to show me an article from the local newspaper. It was the story of a young father who had shaken his infant son to death because he couldn't deal with the baby's endless crying. In all earnestness he remarked, "You know, if that guy had taken our class, he would have known what to do. That baby would still be alive!"

Over the years hundreds of inmates completed the program and returned home to their families. It is my strongest hope that the skills learned in our workshops have enriched the lives of many children.

ONE LIFE STORY—THE COMMUNITY CFO SPEAKS

I was born in a simple farm house, southeast of Earling, Iowa, on September 26, 1931. My parents were both born and raised two miles apart in the same farming vicinity.

As was the custom, I was baptized into the Catholic faith the day after I was born and I, this little dark-haired, brown-eyed girl, was officially a child of God. There were eight children in our family—six girls and two boys.

My father was a tenant farmer renting 120 acres. He farmed with horses using a two-bottom plow, two-row corn planter and two-row and four-row cultivators. The primary crops were corn, oats and alfalfa.

Our house had two bedrooms upstairs, one for the boys and one for the girls. There was a large kitchen, a dining room and one bedroom downstairs. There was no bathroom and we used an outdoor toilet. The house was heated in winter by a large pot belly stove in the dining room using cobs from the corn and sometimes wood or coal, which we had to purchase. There was a vent above the stove that let heat go upstairs. We shivered in winter and slept with featherbeds and heavy quilts. For bathing, water was heated on the stove in the kitchen and a round washtub placed behind the kitchen stove. There was no electricity or running water in the home until 1949, the year I graduated from high school. We used kerosene lamps.

I learned quickly that the farm was a family project with all hands needed. At a young age I learned to milk a cow and as a teenager would milk six or eight cows by myself when my dad was away threshing with the neighbors. My mother raised chickens, butchering about fifty for our winter consumption and keeping about thirty for laying eggs. The eggs we did not eat were sold. We lived on the money from the cream and eggs sales, supplemented by the large garden we raised for fresh vegetables and canning for winter. We raised hogs and cattle to eat and to sell. The sales along with the crops were needed to pay off the farm loan.

I loved the butchering times each year in fall or winter: helping to cut up the meat, grinding some for sausage, cleaning and filling casings for sausage. My mother then canned the sausage as well as chunks of beef and pork, which we ate in winter. This food was stored in an underground cave as we had no basement. We also stored the raw potatoes, carrots, onions and other vegetables there over the winter. My mother also made homemade soap for laundry. From my mother I learned to cook, bake bread, sew and also to do the laundry and iron, all of which were talents I would use later in life.

Jesus went on to say: The kingdom of God is like this. You scatter seed in the field. You sleep at night, are up and about during the day, and all the while the seeds are sprouting and growing. Yet you do not know how it happens. The soil makes the plants grow and bear fruit; first the tender stalk appears, then the head, and finally the full grain. Mk. 4: v. 26-29

From my parents I learned to love nature, the earth, the mystery of life in a seed. I learned how to care for the earth as my father rotated crops and from my mother to make use of the earth's resources by picking wild grapes and plums along the roadsides for jams and jellies. We also learned that all depended on God, for without rain and sun, there would be no crop; we prayed for rain and we prayed that the thunderstorms would not bring hail or tornados to destroy the crops. The risk for such a disaster was always high. I also learned a sense of belonging and a sense of security. Life primarily happened in the family unit and playmates were brothers and sisters until school age.

At age six, I was enrolled in first grade at St. Joseph School in Earling, staffed by the School Sisters of St. Francis, who were excellent teachers. Afraid, I cried each morning for a few weeks as my mother sent me off with my sister to walk the half mile to the neighbor's lane to be picked up and driven to school. In winter and spring, we were often driven with a team of horses and wagon over dirt roads impassable with a car. Learning many new things soon became enjoyable. I was a good student and excelled in most classes.

Some highlights during those elementary grade years were First Communion, then a few years later Solemn Communion. I was chosen one year to do the annual crowning of Mary, Mother of God. There were Holy Hours for rain on summer Sundays, sprinkling of holy water at each corner of the farm on Rogation Days, processions around the Church block on Corpus Christi, processions to the cemetery on All Souls Day, Midnight Mass at Christmas, Holy Hour over midnight on New Year's Eve. Religious expression was an integral part of the totally Anglo German American Catholic community. Participation was learned from childhood on.

My Dad's youngest brother was drafted into the Army when I was eleven years old. I faithfully wrote to him. He was injured, captured and held prisoner. He then was able to escape because he could speak German.

I went through the usual challenges of adolescence, wanting to be part of the crowd, trying smoking, teasing the boys, attending CYO dances, etc. But my priority was always my classes and reading. I loved sports and played on the girls' basketball team. Baseball became a summer sport. We had no theater in our town. Movies were shown periodically in the parish hall. My father let us attend only if Mickey Rooney, Spencer Tracy or Shirley Temple were the movie stars.

In my sophomore year, my brother was diagnosed with a serious case of polio. My dad, my two sisters and I were out in the cornfield picking corn by hand when the doctor stopped on the road and came running to tell us that he thought Les had polio and needed to be hospitalized immediately. My dad rushed him to the hospital in Omaha. Les was hospitalized for two months, first in critical condition, then fair. Our family was quarantined for two weeks. One of my sisters also had a light case of polio and was not hospitalized. This was a traumatic time for my family. Les was permanently disabled.

I graduated from high school with honors. One of the Sisters suggested that I had a religious vocation and I said, "No, I don't think so." My dad said, "Maybe you are the one to be a Sister" and my response was "No, but if I did, it would be with the School Sisters of St. Francis."

I did not know what I should decide to do, either go to college or stay at home and help my mother. A recruiter came from Commercial Extension School of Business in Omaha. A classmate was going to attend and so I agreed to enroll also. The school made arrangements for each of us to live in with a family to work for room and board while attending school. My responsibilities were to help with cleaning, preparing meals and baby-sitting. I had my own room. This was one of the most difficult times of my life, my first experience of leaving the security of my home and family. I was permitted only one visit home per month. Needless to say, I was very homesick. This time was so stressful that my monthly periods stopped and I needed treatment by a doctor. It was a simple decision I made when the recruiter came, but in God's plan it was preparing me for my life's work in Community.

How precious to me are your designs, O God. Ps. 139, v. 17

In spring 1950 I received my certificate for secretarial and bookkeeping services. Then I returned to my parent's home in Iowa. That summer, I worked as a secretary in a law office. I was so proud of my first job as a professional person. I drove thirteen miles each day to work.

In the fall of that year, I received a call from the head of the family I stayed with when attending school in Omaha. He, a Vice-President of the Stang Corporation, asked me to work for this company as a secretary and bookkeeper. I accepted the job and moved back to Omaha joining my friend who worked at Mutual Life Insurance Company. For two or three years we lived with one of the teachers from the school, an older unmarried woman. We felt safe and secure with her.

Thus began the first six years of my professional working life in Omaha. The Stang Corporation produced and installed wellpoints. We had one job for an Atomic Energy plant and we were all investigated and fingerprinted. Today I wonder if my fingerprints are still on file in some government office.

I thoroughly enjoyed my work. Pay in those days was approximately $2,000 to $4,000 a year. No fringe benefits.

During these six years, I played softball in the Omaha Leagues, often as the pitcher. I lived in three different homes during this time, but always with other working girls. I made many new friends and dated four or five different young men. I did not get serious with any until I met Richard, who had just come out of the Navy.

Since high school and Sister's comment that she felt I had a vocation, I had this inner feeling that maybe I did and I kept pushing it back in my mind. Once in our parish church in Earling, I experienced that God was definitely calling me. When it started to get serious with Rich, I told him about my gnawing feeling. We talked about it and he thought that perhaps I should try it to see. If not, then I could come back. I call him my St. Joseph; he discerned with me my call. Correspondence was not permitted once I entered and I have often wondered what his life was like, if he married and had a family. Our lives touched as gift during those times. God was at work in our life journeys.

O where can I hide from your spirit, or from your presence where can I flee… your hand will lead me, your right hand hold me fast. Ps. 139: v. 7, 10

In the summer of 1956 I went to see our Monsignor. He knew me well and said he thought I had a call to religious life. He sent me to see the principal and superior at St. Joseph Convent in Earling. She told me there would be two more young women from Westphalia entering at the same time. Needless to say, it was a big surprise to my friends in Omaha and the people where I worked. All were supportive and the office staff gave me a leather briefcase and a small pocket watch, items I would need. I gave up all my possessions: my car to my brother Dick (age sixteen); my furniture and household items to my sister Arlene; my clothes to my sisters. My small bank account and life insurance policy I took with me to the Convent as part of my dowry.

On the night of September 7, 1956, dressed in the black Postulant garb, we three said goodbye to our families as we boarded the train for the trip to

Milwaukee. My mother was okay with my decision but a little apprehensive. My Dad was fine with it.

It was my first train ride, sitting up all night and changing trains in Savannah, Illinois, then on to Milwaukee. The building loomed large and foreboding with the many steps to the second floor entrance. In my heart I said, "a thirteen-week trial." I don't know where thirteen came from but that would have been December first and allowed me to be home for Christmas.

Lord, make me know your ways. Lord, teach me your paths. Make me walk in your truth, and teach me: for you are God my savior. Ps. 25: v. 4-5

Once inside we were warmly welcomed. Among the excitement of eighty-plus other young women were four from Honduras. We began classes at Alverno College the next week, traveling each day on the SSSF bus. I enjoyed my classes as well as assisting with tutoring English to the women from Honduras. I developed a real sense of belonging.

We were allowed to go for a home visit at Easter, and I enjoyed my time with my family. My thirteen weeks were long over and I felt I was on the right direction for my life journey.

During my official reception into the School Sisters of St. Francis on August 12, 1957, I received the white veil, the black habit and the name Sister Charlita. I had requested some version of Richard or Charles after my younger brother, or Ruth, names I liked. My parents, brother Les, most of my family and my grandmother drove to Milwaukee for this special day.

So began my Novitiate. I settled into the daily routine and felt good about the discipline of times for prayer, meals, sleep, etc.

During the second year of Novitiate, we went back to Alverno College to prepare for our apostolic work. However, that lasted only three months. In December, when I returned from school, Sister Archelaus, the Novice Mistress, said Mother Corona (our Superior General) wanted to see me. I was apprehensive. I went to her room and, as was the custom, I knelt down before her. She asked if I liked math and I said I did. Then she said that she was appointing me to work in the Business Office of the Community as a bookkeeper beginning immediately. She gave me her blessing and I left her office. I was surprised and at the same time enthusiastic.

One of the Sisters working in the Business Office had suffered a broken neck in a car accident, would be hospitalized for months and needed a replacement. I felt truly needed and could share my experience in business.

Thus began my long career working with the finances of the Community. My college program was put on hold.

I professed my first vows of poverty, chastity and obedience in August of 1959. The next year, Mother Clemens was elected Superior General and Mother Hyacinth as her Assistant. They decided I should continue my education because the Sister injured in the accident had returned to the Business Office. The two of us would both work part time in the office and go to school part time. We began at Alverno taking business courses but soon switched to Marquette University Business School for all of our accounting classes. It was a slow process taking one or two courses at a time. We were usually the only women in the classes. I was truly happy to be back in college.

September 28, 1958, I was called to the Novitiate. Sister Archelaus informed me that my brother, Dick (Richard), had been killed in an auto accident the night of September 27. He was eighteen and a senior in high school. In shock and in tears I said, "No, no, it can't be true." I was in a state of denial and in a daze. Sister sent me to the Adoration Chapel to pray while she made arrangements for me to go home for the funeral. It was so traumatic because the car was the one I had given him when I left for the Convent. A Sister from the Art Department accompanied me home on the train. It was the feast of St. Michael the Archangel. We stayed at my parents' home. My mother was devastated.

Two years later to the day, I was informed that my mother had died from a heart attack at the age of fifty-six. I had not seen her since I was home for Dick's funeral. She grieved over his death. This time I sadly made the trip on the train alone to Earling to attend the funeral. Again it was on the feast of St. Michael the Archangel.

> Then God said, 'I myself will send an Angel before you to guard you as you go and to bring you to the place that I have prepared'. Ex. 23: v. 20

My father was left with my three youngest sisters, ages thirteen to sixteen. I returned to Milwaukee with a very sad heart.

By 1959 our international congregation had grown so large, especially in the United States, that the Sacred Congregation for Religious in Rome recommended that there be several provinces established in the United States. Mount St. Francis Province in Rockford, Illinois, was established in 1959, followed in 1961 by Our Lady of the Angels Province in Omaha, Nebraska. In 1963 both the Holy Name Province in Chicago and the Immaculate Heart of Mary Province in Wisconsin were founded. The Health Agencies Council was established in 1966 for the Sisters in the nursing and medical professions. All other Sisters at that time in the U.S. were in the Central Provincial Unit, which included the Motherhouse, Campbellsport and Alverno College. In 1968 Alverno became its own Provincial unit.

The Sisters were given a choice of the province they wanted to join. This structure with the seven provinces functioned well until, because of decreasing membership, the provinces in the United States merged into one Province with twenty-two Area Communities.

Vatican Council II resulted not only in dramatic changes in the Church, but also for Religious Life. Its decree on the *Up-To-Date Renewal of Religious Life (Perfectae Caritatis)* was issued on October 28, 1965. This decree called for spiritual renewal as well as adaptation so that "the manner of life, of prayer, and of work should be in harmony with present-day physical and psychological condition of the members…for this reason, constitutions, directories, customs, prayers, ceremonies and such should be properly revised, obsolete prescriptions being suppressed and should be brought into line with conciliar documents." Participation of all the members was required in changes that were to be made.

Thus began many studies, reflections and prayer by the congregation. Position papers were written by special committees about community life and the apostolate. These were published between 1962 and 1966 and were preparatory work to the General Chapter in 1966. I was in temporary vows during this time and able to participate in some of the preparatory discussions, but the Chapter itself was closed. Only elected voting delegates from the United States, Europe and Latin America attended. In my heart I knew there were drastic changes coming. Was I ready for that?

Yes, I did want to be part of whatever was coming in the changes. I professed my final or perpetual vows on June 21, 1965. My dad and some of my family came to celebrate with me as I took this last step in finalizing my commitment to religious life. The thirteen weeks were long past and I knew deep in my heart that God's call was asking me to bloom here where I was planted in the garden of community life and mission.

At the Chapter in January, 1966 Sister Francis Borgia Rothluebber was elected the new president of the order replacing Mother Clemens. By that September, the new experimental Rule called *Response in Faith* was published for the Sisters with the new directives that had been approved by the General Chapter. During the next three years, much interaction, wholesome questioning, disagreement, and some fears developed about the adaptations and the direction the community would take. I was glad that I could now participate in all the discussions as a perpetually vowed member. On August 18, 1969 another General Chapter opened to continue both the dialogue and the development of future direction.

That same year I was asked by the President and Council to become the Treasurer of the Congregation.

Lord, make your ways known to me, teach me your paths. Ps. 25, v. 4

After a time of discernment, at age thirty-eight, I agreed to accept the position. I replaced the former Treasurer who then became Director of the Community's Retirement Fund, which was just being established. I had staff to assist me: the controller; the properties manager; as well as several Sisters and lay personnel who performed accounting and bookkeeping duties for the Generalate Office, Retirement Office and Health Care Office, all of which were centralized for all of the provinces in the United States.

As Treasurer I was also on the Board of Directors of the legal entity for the Community along with the President, the General Council and the General Secretary. We were also the Board of Directors of all of the institutions sponsored in the United States (12 health and education institutions). Within the next five years all these institutions were restructured as their own legal entities with lay participation on all the boards with the Sisters of the Generalate Board retaining control as the Members of the legal entities. Sister Alphonsa Puls and I had worked tirelessly with our attorney on developing the legal structure and documents for these entities.

My first trip outside the U.S. was an enlightening and spiritual experience. I traveled alone to Latin America in 1970 to visit our missions in Honduras. While there was dire poverty in many of the villages, the people were friendly with a joyful spirit. For one trip to La Libertad, the Sisters had no vehicles, so we asked for a ride from a gentleman who had a very old pickup truck. We sat in front with the driver; the open truck bed in the back was filled with men who had to stand for the whole trip, which took several hours. We drove through seven rivers on the way.

On the return trip in the same pickup truck, it rained. The truck had no windshield so over the opening the driver put a plastic sheet we could hardly see through. But he managed to continue driving. Suddenly the brakes gave out coming down a mountain, but he was able to control the vehicle and we finally arrived safely back in Tegucigalpa. My reflection: "Why was I born in the U.S. of my parents with so many blessings while the people here are born in Honduras with so much poverty? They have a deep faith and a joyful spirit. Do I?"

During these years, I was also involved with the Treasurers of the Religious Orders in the United States to move Congress to pass a new law that would allow religious persons with vows to enter the Social Security Program. It was a massive undertaking on the part of our finance staff in 1972 to complete all the paperwork to enroll the Sisters in the United States in this new program.

We were allowed to enter five years retroactively to 1969 and pay the back taxes. Since religious with the vow of poverty have no earnings, the law differs from the regular Social Security legislation for lay workers in that the so called cost of living is used as the wage base of what the Sister receives each year from congregational support.

Many Sisters were going into lay clothing at this time. I made this change a little apprehensively in 1970 after thirteen years of wearing the habit. That same year I moved with three other Sisters to a second floor flat. It was a very good experience of small group living and sharing as religious women.

In the Chapter of 1972 I was elected Vice President of Finance on the General Council of the Congregation. I also retained the Treasurer's responsibilities while serving for eight years on the General Council.

During these eight years, I was privileged, as a part of my responsibilities, to travel to and visit often the Provinces and Sisters in Latin America, Europe and India. These were great learning times for me to experience the different cultures and economic situations in each of the countries in which we serve and the wonderful work that our Sisters are doing. This is one of the greatest gifts I received as part of my ministry. Learning the Spanish and German language has also been an ongoing task.

My experienced staff and I completed several special projects over the years: Self-insured Health Care Fund; Centralized Banking/Accounting System for all of the Convent living groups; Task Force Studies on Retirement, Investment and Social Responsibility Programs; Renovation of Motherhouse Facilities; Financial Models for Long-Range Planning; Finance Education Workshops, etc.

Send Wisdom from your throne to help me and to toil with me and teach me what is pleasing to you…she will guide me prudently in my undertakings. Wisdom 9: v. 10, 11

Our living group of five Sisters moved in 1976 to a house that the Community purchased. We had wonderful garden space behind the house and raised many vegetables for our use in summer and we froze and canned some for the winter months. I was back in my rural mode of working with the earth.

God said, See, I give you all the seed-bearing plants that are upon the whole earth, and all the trees with seed-bearing fruit; this shall be your food. Gen. 1, v. 29

After many years of part-time study, I received my BA in Management from Alverno College in 1976. I was so proud of this accomplishment.

When my term as Vice President of Finance on the Council ended in 1980, I was appointed to continue the work as Treasurer of the Congregation. During this time, I made many more trips to visit our Sisters in Europe, Latin America and India to review property holdings, corporate legal entities, financial matters, and to perform internal audits and give general management consultation and assistance. These rich intercultural experiences gave me new energy and hope for our future with our many younger members.

My travels and my rest you mark; with all my ways you are familiar. Ps. 139, v. 3

In 1980, the National Conference of Treasurers of Religious Institutes (NATRI) was formed; I am a lifelong member. Also in 1980, I was on a panel whose members prepared and gave a presentation entitled *Financial Forecasting: One Model*. This long-range planning tool has been used by many religious institutes in looking to the future. The Conference updated and expanded the model in later years. As part of this team, I felt I was making a significant contribution of my talents for the good of all religious institutes.

When our President Sister Lauretta Mather asked me to work for a Masters of Business Administration, I researched several schools and chose Northwestern University in Illinois. This was a two-year Executive Program with weekend classes. Needless to say, my schedule was demanding as I continued to work full time in the Finance Office and travel to Illinois on weekends. I gained a wealth of knowledge and proudly graduated in 1985 with my MBA.

In 1985-86 I served on the U.S. Catholic Conference Accounting Practices Committee and Financial Accounting Standards Board (FASB). I was on a panel in 1986 with a presentation to the NATRI conference. As the only woman on the committee, I felt that I was part of an old boys' club. I was pleased that it was only a one-year term.

These were wonderful years living in community and getting to know the younger Sisters and those from the other cultures. I learned much from them and they kept me young.

I had served from 1976 to 1980 with four wonderful Sisters as the leadership team for our religious order. After 1980, we continued as friends and met three times a year to pray, eat, visit and play together. A strong bond had been built during the years of our serving in leadership and having to face some difficult times together. Even now, the three of us remaining "former five" continue our friendship and sharings each year.

In December 1991, I lost my father. I was privileged to be at his deathbed. His warm and happy personality is dearly missed.

In July 2003, I retired as Treasurer of the Congregation.

Having celebrated in 2007 my Golden Jubilee of 50 years in religious life, these later years are a time to stop and reflect on the many blessings and graces that God has given to me, my family, my Community, and my friends who have walked with me on this journey. It is a time to say how grateful I am first of all to God who has gifted me so generously with life and also to family, friends and Sisters who have supported me.

My life is now a process of letting go and still staying involved. There is more time for prayer and reflection. There is the opportunity to get back to nature and my roots in cultivating the earth and spending time in my vegetable and flower garden; time to can and freeze vegetables, to bake bread and to cook; time to sit and watch the sun set. My farmland heritage has come full circle and I once again live in the present moment.

As Abraham Heschel says, "Just to be is a blessing! Just to live is holy!"

Chapter 8
Mid Life Glimpses of the Sacred

Myself, Comparing Religions

I would have been an easy worshipper of the sun.
One day's shining would have done or undone
the night names of god: the totem turtle
and the silver sway of axe or arrow,
golden calves and the myrtle
memories of head and marrow.

I would have been an easy atheist
upon beholding what the world missed
of mercy and of miracle. I sat
upon the Inca's eagle,[1] land-locked flat
just centuries from blood's dying flight.
I was born the years that Dachau drank—
Third Reich's rite—
our hopes of heaven from an armored tank.

Yet today, hung between sun and slaughter,
I can be no one's easy daughter.

---

[1] *On Machu Picchu there is a stone carved into an eagle
believed to be the site of animal and perhaps even human sacrifice.*

Another Mass Like That

After the cloud-seeded hurricane Fifi struck Honduras killing 12,000, several of us were asked to go as translators for medical field teams. My assignment centered on a clearinghouse area for infants and children rescued from flood waters. Streams of grief-stricken parents crisscrossed the affected areas near Choloma in the desperate hope of finding a lost child.

As announced weeks before, one Sunday we were to be visited by a priest for an outdoor Mass. Preparations were jubilant. Vestments, chalices, missals appeared out of nowhere on a makeshift sawhorse altar draped with a sheet.

All morning hundreds of ravaged people arrived to celebrate hope in one of the profoundest ways they knew how in the midst of such catastrophic loss. I remember flowers. I remember light in sorrow-laden eyes. Then word came. No priest. He was unable to get through.

A blur of disappointment during which a small group of people approached me. *Would I be willing to celebrate the Mass?* Hesitating only long enough to pray that whatever divinity shone upon us that morning would decide the ultimate validity of what we were about to share, I agreed.

Standing at that table, I faced faces that seemed to circle to the horizon and saw almost nothing but the tears streaming down the cheeks of women. Afterwards some of them came forward, tears still glistening.

"Hermana [Sister], *when can we have another Mass like that?"*

Sweetness

Prophets have told me,
"God is 'The Merciful,' 'the Majestic.'"
Sometimes I can feel that.
But I always feel my body when it tells me

all it can understand of The Divine:
God is Sweetness.
Oh, God must be Sweetness! Otherwise,
why would I search so desperately

between bone-building calories in protein,
vitamins in vegetables and fruits.

Poor tongue! It hasn't mind enough
for concepts like "Mercy" and "Majesty."

It keeps licking the world to the core,
searching for Sweetness it can't
reach deep enough to taste,
begging for the Sweetness
with no Name.

PRAYER

To live like this:
always in preparation,
always . . . there . . .

CANCER AT 22

We wore full habits that left bare only our faces (eyebrows to chin) and our hands. We saw ourselves only in tiny mirrors in our cells. One morning, brushing my teeth before putting on the full habit, I swallowed water while catching my reflection in the mirror. To my horror, I saw I had two Adam's apples, almost side by side, moving up and down in my throat. I swallowed again. They moved again.

How long had this tumor been there? I had no idea because I couldn't remember seeing myself swallow in a mirror. No one else could have seen it under my habit.

Frightened, only twenty-two years old, I immediately thought—cancer. Could it be?

I hesitantly told our superior about the lump. She sent me by train to the hospital in Beaver Dam administered and staffed by our Sisters. To get me there, the high school janitor drove me to the train station. At the other end, a janitor from the hospital picked me up from the train and drove me to the hospital. There, the administrator was a kind and generous Nun who warmly welcomed me. In her I found a mother to help me through my ordeal. (My own mother was not told of my operation.)

After several months, during which the removed tumor had been sent to several cancer research centers for analysis, my superior announced at dinner that I did indeed have cancer, but a low grade. For years after that, I, like many other cancer survivors, told no one about my cancer because even in the 1960s people were often afraid to shake hands or breathe air in the same room (like the early misconceptions about contracting AIDS).

When in the 1970s I had a second operation to remove my entire thyroid, because by then Mayo Clinic had studied my family and determined some of us had a hereditary thyroid cancer, I still didn't share the cancer information. Only after another decade did the onus disappear from the disease and people's support of cancer victims become more universal. By then, I actually had forgotten I'd had it until one day I had to fill out an insurance form.

How has this affected me? At twenty-two, I was unafraid of dying. I had read and loved a profound book, *The Future of Belief*, which spoke of death as a culmination of life, the last and greatest adventure. No one knows what death brings, but what an adventure into the unknown, into the Ultimate Mystery! I had no children, no husband, no responsibilities. I was utterly free to go to the great adventure.

It is now more than thirty-five years since my second cancer operation, and I can offer living hope to many people, although I never speak of it unless someone is facing the unknown and welcomes an open heart and ear.

I still trust death is the great adventure.

IN THE AIDS HOSPICE

"No one," he said
"touched me
one whole year.
Only instruments, gloves
poking, prodding.
Now on my palm
your woman's warm skin.
You can't know how good."

But I do know
a Convent's rules
for chastity:
'Hands off, arm's length.'
Ten years
touching
no one.
Not hand.
Not hair.
When I left that,
when I allowed
a man's arm
around my shoulder,
I wept
at the heaviness,
the warmth.

Yes, I know
those blanks
between.

Why I Made Final Vows

Memories of Final Profession, August 11, 1965. The simplicity and poverty of that moment in time when I made my final vows in Costa Rica still remains with me. The ceremony took place in the chapel of St. Clare's high school on the feast of St. Clare with a small community attending. It was in the middle of the school year for us in the southern hemisphere and I had made my retreat earlier that year.

Our regional superior at the time received my vows along with the Franciscan chaplain. When Sister asked me why I wanted to make my vows, I told her that I wanted to give my life to God. And so be it. The journey goes on, still discovering the way. I am grateful for the blessing of St. Clare in a deeper way now.

ZEN POEM

I want to know God
as the bird knows God,
lifting its wings;

as the cherry blossom rests
in perfect trust
on stem and air.

BEYOND DUALISM

Father Raymond Parr came into my life when I turned twenty-one. I am now seventy, and though he is no longer living, he continues to be my teacher and friend.

That first encounter with Raymond was as Father Parr, teacher of theology at Alverno College. Many of us Sisters drove over to the college after a full day in the classroom and about fifty strong sat elbow to elbow in room 306. Here we heard teachings that prepared us to enter fully into Vatican II, to live its directives on social justice and renewal of religious life. His words even now carry many of us forward to embrace with eagerness the powerful presence of Pope Francis in our midst.

Like many of us, I had learned well in my early childhood education that life was filled with mutually exclusive categories: God versus humanity, supernatural against the natural. Never would the twain meet. Such dualism caused irrational fear and unspoken anguish in my heart.

The twain did meet for me intellectually one evening when we were greeted with a diagram on the board. One line rose from the lower left to the upper right. Revelation was written above the line and creation below.

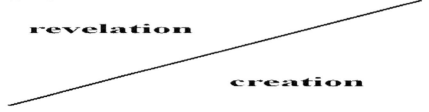

This simple diagram and the word of a believer, Raymond A. Parr, brought God into humanity for me and raised humanity to God. As humanity is being created, God is being revealed. It is one happening. The fear and anguish dissipated. It was then that I began the surrender to the teaching, the knowledge and ultimately the wisdom, that God is intimately present in all of my cells. The struggle to reconcile the dualisms of dogmatic religion took three years. To move beyond dualism of any kind is taking the rest of my life.

When I ask my own inner wisdom what is honorable and worthy to be said of Raymond in this writing, many responses come to me:

This teacher gave you life's breath when you had none.

This teacher knew truths of the relationship between God, humanity, and all of creation that defied the systems constructed by the institutional church.

When I talk with Raymond today, I hear his one-line answers—striking and to the point. His answers are different from those I would expect to hear when he lived in his physical body, but they do not contradict. They go beyond.

When I thank him for coming to me, he says, "You came to yourself."

WOMAN-PRAYER

Time comes to me each morning
as a woman-child
knocking at my eyelids with importunate
sunlight, spreading hope upon the moment
like butter and honey over breakfast bread.
I have been a mother; automatically
I answer such a summons.

As the day and I
pray on toward evening
I can feel
a rounding in my spine:
knees curling up
to chin 'til I become

a circle closing,
an apple hanging free,
a dewdrop gathering
weight upon young fruit.

And enter darkness,
the great womb
where God, my Mother,
feeds and rocks creation,
where I can touch
my birth and death
and my own mothering
together. Where the shadow of
separate moments
cannot break apart
my loving.

And I can pray,
"Our Mother,
Who bakes within us,
give us ourselves
as bread."

LETTING GO

I was in my late twenties and very involved with the teens I was teaching. About twenty of us went on a canoeing and backpacking trip into the Canadian wilderness. The girls were camped on one side of the lake and the boys about a mile away on the other side of the lake.

I awoke to a very dense fog, hardly able to see three feet in front of me. I woke the girls and asked one to paddle with me to the other side of the lake to make sure the boys were up.

We got in the canoe and paddled out a few feet and I could no longer see the campsite we had just left. I looked up. All I could see was fog around me and water below me. At first I was very afraid I might get lost. I took a deep breath and whispered, "Dear God, get me to the boy's camp." I set the canoe in the direction I hoped to be right and let go. A sense of peace washed over me.

After many minutes of paddling, we landed exactly at the boys' campsite. I knew then that the peace I had felt when I let go was God's energy directing every stroke I had taken.

After that experience it was much easier to let go and just trust.

> I am one who
> Can feel at one when really
> Letting go.

So This Is Death

After my first year of teaching at our Community's *Colegio* in Costa Rica, we began our summer vacation with an eagerly anticipated trip to our Provincial headquarters in Honduras. A Franciscan family reunion. Two carloads of us headed north along the euphemistically titled Pan American highway, then in places not much more than a cow path.

I sat in the suicide seat of the lead car knitting a layette set for the child of one of my former high school students in Chicago.

Right before the accident our car pulled out to pass the semi in front of us. I looked up to see in a flash the semi and cliff wall to the right, the precipitous cliff drop on the left and the jeep speeding head-on toward our car.

My last conscious thought: *"So this is death."*

Amid the violent crunch of metal and shattering glass, unearthly calm and pulsating stillness. I am held within an eggshell that cracks at the bottom. I fall floating into another eggshell. In its time it, too, cracks, releasing me into still another shell. In all, this breaking and expansion continues through possibly six to eight burrowing vistas. With the final crack, I fall into a pair of giant, gentle hands. Soothed. Cradled. Loved beyond all telling.

I do not think I feared death before the accident. I know I have never feared it since.

MY NOW

The God of my childhood is beginning to blend into my NOW. The passionate longing for the sacred and for mystery that I carried as a child, that I named God, is beginning to merge into my Now. And yet what else must I release to have this realized within me?

DREAM JOURNEY

It is Martin Luther King Day, 1995, and I am driving to Cook County Hospital in Chicago's inner city, where my husband lies after an auto accident that broke his pelvis and lacerated his liver. It is about five in the morning; I need to get to the hospital and back between rush hours. I have perfected my travel routine since January seventh, the day of the accident.

I turn the radio on in order to keep myself awake. Over and over I hear, "I've been to the mountain." "I have a dream." *Right on, Martin!* I think about how nice it would be to have that kind of faith, to have any kind of faith at all. Despite a strong Roman Catholic upbringing and fifteen years as a Nun, I have been an agnostic for twenty-seven years.

When the sun breaks into the windows of the intensive care unit, I can see that the January day is bright and gentle. I have talked to my husband, sung to him in Yiddish. Though sedation prevents him from responding consciously, the nurse assures me that his blood pressure has risen slightly; he's excited because he knows I am here.

But I am tired. I take hold of his hand as I sit by his bedside, resting my head on the iron bars of the railing. The sunlight is sweet, warm . . .

and suddenly I am standing on top of that mountain Martin was talking about. My feet rest on a surface that is a deep purple-black. And the same color surrounds me. This mountain is the top of the world. It juts out into the cosmos, and I jut out with it. The purple-black around me is shimmering; the stars and other heavenly bodies sparkle and pulse. The whole panorama is all one being— alive, breathing, growing—like a dragon with shining scales. It is all profoundly beautiful.

And even death is beautiful.

I come fully awake at this point. But I have not been truly asleep. I have been someplace in between. Where? Was this experience a simple gift? Or is my husband sharing what he is seeing?

I do not know. But every time I feel bad during the next week, I come back to this experience, enter into it mentally. And I feel better.

Then it happens again. Only this time there is an hourglass of stars in the sky. And I think, "He is going to die." On February fifth, he does.

I am staggered with grief. However, I have been given something to hold on to. The questions that led me out of belief have been answered. *Yes, there is a God and, yes, there is life after death.*

I begin my journey back to God.

The Widow

There lives the dearest freshness deep down things.
                        —Gerard Manley Hopkins

The "deep-down" point—I like to think that's where I'm
coming from these days, where I've been headed.
No longer up to my elbows kneading
survival bread

or honoring the hands of the time-clock as if
they policed the only law.
I've done my share of a day's work.
In the bliss of evening now, I talk

to friends, water my garden,
pray into the rising moon,
send messages out to the spirits,
begging forgiveness. Soon

I turn into darkness, the deep becoming,
an anchor for the light
flung out so far by young ones
their dreams burn to ashes on re-entry.

I don't mind invisibility. Whoever
seeks my company will find a pair
of seasoned eyes and ears. I know
where the young ones are headed.
Being there.

Existential Fear

As a Postulant, I found myself in the throes of something I now know as the existential fear of annihilation. That day I was walking past our superior's desk, seeking a place or face of inner peace. Suddenly the living scriptural words often quoted by my parents were present: "Once you put your hand to the plow, do not look backward." In that instant I knew that wherever I went, I would take this fear with me. There was no place to go except on with my life of the moment—a morning snack and then a quick visit to the Adoration Chapel.

My days in the Postulancy, Novitiate and Juniorate and then in mission life continued in a similar vein. Sometimes the fear would leave for a while and sometimes it would go on for months. I knew if I could only believe there is a God, I could handle anything.

One day, I took these questions to the priest in the confessional—how should I pray, what can I do to be rid of this fear, to get beyond it and have faith in God. He told me to say some Hail Marys.

Knowing I needed more than Hail Marys, I went to my seventh grade classroom. It was August, the classrooms as yet unscrubbed for the opening of school. I lay prostrate in full habit, only face and hands visible, on the floor that held the grime from the previous year's class. Here, with nothing else to say, I said the unexpected words, "God, if you want me to suffer this fear the rest of my life, I will."

The fear, the fighting, the tension released and I was at peace.

This cycle has repeated itself through the years. Each time, this God of my longing comes a little closer, becomes a bit more palpable, giving fulfillment of sense and soul. With each release I know without doubt—there is no space between the One I've called God and myself and the world.

I continue to live out my calling as a School Sister of St. Francis, and I have no doubt that my classmates are finding their palpable, pleasurable God wherever they are. It is not the *place* that makes the difference; it is living our heart's longing wherever we are.

AUTUMN BEGINNINGS

Always, this will be the paradox of the year:
autumn beginnings,
wisdom of the ripening
never fully ripe.

School starts tomorrow;
Arizona classrooms gratefully
shut out the sun; the midday temperature
still reaches ninety.

In our synagogue begins
the season of fall celebrations. *Rosh
Hashanah*, round with blessings. *Succoth*,
sweet with purple wine.

Small beginnings give us focus:
sharpening pencils, narrowing
gaze from fields in harvest
waiting . . . silently . . . for the ram's horn.

SUFI HEALING PRACTICE

Recently I felt the time had finally come to heal the burden of pain I'd carried since my formation years. I have the tools now: The Sufi healing practices. They are very old and very simple; they consist of calling the Name of God into one's heart—especially into any scars in that heart that one wishes to heal.

I began my healing meditation by visualizing St. Joseph Convent, an outside view, black and foreboding, as I'd felt it back during my formation years. I placed that picture in my heart and started calling the name of God into it during my morning meditations. After a few days I began to realize what elements had risen within myself during those years to cause that pain, how I had unconsciously collided with things at St. Joseph Convent that were simply different from what I'd always known, how my resistance had rubbed me like an inner barbed wire. For example, my aversion to manual labor and my fear of silence were certainly threatened.

The kinds of hurt I'd experienced pointed to parts within me that needed transformation. Yes, I'd sometimes been misunderstood. And, yes, in my late adolescence, I'd sometimes bristled at authority. And, oh yes, I was and am still physically slow. But the formative years at the Motherhouse brought my attention to basic weaknesses that I am still working to correct. Furthermore, I found myself asking forgiveness for pain I'd caused others and pain I'd called to myself.

Another remarkable thing happened. In visualization the black outside of the Motherhouse gradually began to lighten. As the days passed, most of it turned shining white. At one point during this process, I had a conversation with a Convent classmate about the Great Ones who had influenced us during our Convent days. During my next meditation the windows of the top floor in the Motherhouse held faces of the Great Ones I'd known. People who had given to me during those years.

And above the fifth floor windows, other shining faces ascended—those who had gone before.

From time to time I go back to this visualization, to this healing. One corner of the building remains black. I still have work to do. But there is much more sweetness in my memories. Much more light.

Forgiveness

When I think of the responsibility of our superiors to make the life-altering choices that affected thousands of us Sisters, I could weep with compassion for those superiors.

In the early days of the Community—when Postulants and Novices were few enough that each was truly known individually, final choices were possibly made together by each Postulant or Novice and the Mistress who really knew her. But in our day Mistresses had hundreds of young women upon whom they were asked to pass judgment. And also hundreds of positions in schools and hospitals needed staffing. All the while, society and the Church within it were changing quickly and beyond comprehension.

It took me a long time to forgive my parents for simply being human, unequal to the task of parenting because no human being is totally equal to it. I've taken even longer to forgive my superiors for the same insufficiency. *Mea culpa*. But I think I'm close to that now.

Avalon and the Eleusinian Mysteries

What I have always known—I had to leave the Convent to experience pain deep enough to be worthy of this incarnation. Many others experienced that pain in the Convent. I did not. For me the Convent was Avalon and the Eleusinian Mysteries and many other ancient, women-centered rites all rolled together.

MATRIMONY ONE:
ALL THE BONES

Female children are quite literally starved for matrimony: not for marriage, but for physical nurturance and a legacy of power and humanity from adults of their own sex ('mothers').   —Phyllis Chesler

Therefore, prophesy and say to them, 'O my people, I will open your graves and cause you to come forth from your graves... I will put My Spirit in you and you shall live...'   —Ezekiel 37: 1-14

i am in a wooden cradle of the earth.
the rocking movement is slow and soothing.
the women of the earth who have died are rocking me.
now they are singing in silence:

we rule the world.
the hand that rocks the cradle rules the world.
we do not want to rule the world this way.
deviously. derivatively.
we do not want to rule the world at all.
we want to love the world. *be the world.*

their breathless chanting falls to a subterranean *OM*
that moves out like ripples of an earthquake tremor,
one that will not topple buildings and destroy
but one that will loosen the soil of life, all life,

reconstitute the dead.
the field of bones begins to dance without clattering.
they realign, interpenetrate, form new beings.

my love, shall these bones live?

and there is a great smile.
i get up from the cradle and walk among the bones,
touching them and blessing them and receiving their blessing,
especially on the surface of my skin
that, without burning, becomes full of fire.
my skin loosens and lifts, starting at arms and fingers,
and becomes like a huge, radiant, yellow-orange cape
embracing all the bones.
the cape becomes the wings of a great bird
and we fly upward,
very gently and very gradually leaving the earth
so no one is left behind.

i am in awe at the yearning of all being
to be joined in this ascent.
i recall pictures of the last boats and convoys
leaving Saigon and other stricken areas.
this is different. there is no clamoring.
all is ripeness of order—fruit falling upward to the ground.

double death:
graves below and life opening up for all
on the second side of a thin veil.
there is one breath chanting all meaning:

oh, yes. amen. let it be so.

and we bow as one person
and each move to kiss our own hearts upon our lips.

The Center

The first time
I reached the center
I simply
did not want to move

sure
a blink
would scatter my seeing,
burst illusion like a bubble

but I steadied
and it steadied,
joined my breath
with All of Being.

And I breathed
into all the birch leaves
dappling in summer sunlight,
breathed with all the birch leaves
dappling,
rode the air.
A small, white butterfly,
I streamed, streamed in light.

And it held
as I breathed
and it held as I blinked
and it held
when I moved my eager fingers
over these translucent words.

And I hear myself cry out,
I have always known this center,
a beloved eye

that just revealed its soul.
I have always walked this center,
I have met you in this center
and him
and her
and all of us.

This is the place
I want to die
from;
this
is where
I want to be.

SEARCH TOWARD ZEN

I was a Catholic Nun for sixteen years before I left the Convent in search of a deeper context to meaning than Catholicism. That search brought me to Buddhism, first through reading and then by working with a Zen Buddhist monk. For ten years I sat with the monk and sometimes participated in Zen rituals. In my own small way, I have tried to contribute to the dialogue by publishing several of the monk's beautiful translations of Zen poetry.

My own writing is part of my search for a deeper understanding of the truths of Zen. Sometimes I see my poetry as the voice of an ex-Catholic Nun chanting, like a Zen Buddhist, in her own limited vocabulary.

One can be a Buddhist-Jesuit priest or a Catholic-Buddhist Nun. That, to me, is one of the glories of American Zen. We can deepen our experience of the moment, not by denigrating the religions we first understood, but by charging them with Zen.

I have a deep belief in the universal oneness of all. I believe that living or dead, I belong to the great ALL. We are all part of the great wholeness; the wholeness is in this moment. Here I find an ability to let go. After all, what is so important to hang onto, if everything is part of who we all are now.

In that is peace, gentle strength, deep comfort, and in fact, wholeness. It is this awareness that I try to give to my life.

WHILE THE WOLF WALKS THE EDGE OF THE WOODS

someone, turning in sleep
asks *who*
and not expecting an answer,
turns again, and
hearing the bell clap
knows it is early, but
the zangha[2] meets before
sun or light or warmth
The Nuns kowtow
to the floor and one
wonders if they bow
to Buddha or the light
beginning to streak
through the bamboo curtain
When the light reaches
the eyelids, the sight
says open and the eye
sees the grass bending
against the palmetto
and the palmetto bending
with the robin singing
and the robin bending
to the northeaster and
the whole zangha just
chanting to the rhythm
of the gong   Enough
it is enough   it is

SHOOK FOIL

Oh, but what a glorious feast for the eyes. We took the back roads through
the rice, cotton and soybean fields. The trees are also magnificent. I can never

---

[2] community

figure out why such beauty is boring to so many people. To me such trips are meditations on the grandeur of God's majesty flaming out *like shining from shook foil.*

NEAR PALMS AND SEA

One ought to be
a mystic, though
near palms
and sea.

But it's not
cold enough
and one sees
things that bite.

MY ANGEL

Before sharing the sighting of my angel, let me explain that I believe angels are always with us and manifest themselves in various ways, including as strangers, friends, or just intuitive insights.

Also, I should add that I've always been impressed by the culture and beliefs of Native Americans. My angel used this latter aspect to appear to me. We lived in Colorado from 1975 through 1980 when I worked for the Department of Health and Human Services Regional Office in Denver. One day, a co-worker and I were interviewing a couple of Native Americans who were applying for a Federal grant. I did not make eye contact with either of them unless they addressed me directly.

After the meeting, one of them said to me, "You're different." (It reminded me of the university students who said the same thing when I was still a Sister and would eat in the cafeteria and have discussions with them.) He appreciated how we had tried to be helpful but not patronizing.

Not long after that my husband was out of town and I was alone. We had a floor- to-ceiling window in our bedroom on the ground floor, and I remember being ill at ease as I fell asleep. Some time in the middle of the night I awoke with a start to see someone standing at the foot of the bed. (An indistinct figure, but I sensed that it was the Native American we had dealt with previously.) I was scared breathless, but then I heard that someone say: "Don't be afraid; you are safe." I fell back to sleep convinced that it was my angel who had appeared to reassure me.

I often feel the presence of my angel but have not experienced such a dramatic appearance since.

Borne Up

> Borne up by the hands,
> she slid down the pole
> between those hands and sand,
> stepped into hot, brown dust,
> skipped fast into cool, green lawns,
> opened doors of clear glass,
> set up tables of cheese and wine,
> kissed twenty-four eligible men,
> sang ninety-nine lullabies, and
> changed several hundred liquid diapers.
>
> When she tried to stare again at sand
> to find pole and place
> and hands,
> she found only turquoise sky,
> moon rising, and pulsing stars.
> Every day, she waits to be borne.

Holding Out the Hands of Our Souls

I had found Feminism in the Convent, a place where patriarchy could not penetrate below the surface of life. A place where women ran schools and hospitals and large institutional kitchens. Where women created music, visual art, poetry. These women were my Sisters, and they encouraged me to make whatever contribution I could; they were there by my side to help me make it.

They are still there. Without being sentimental or simplistic, I continue to feel the bonds created by young women dedicated to making themselves and their world more holy. During this exciting era, when most spiritual people maintain that the human race is making a great leap of consciousness, we continue our contribution to that leap. We continue holding the hands of our souls out to each other and to everyone else who is a serious seeker. To those who are not yet seekers, to the earth, to the stars.

Silence, Solitude

Ultimately, God is.

That is all there is.

Every person calls a part of you into being and shows you a part you've never known. Even if you know that person only for a moment, the person opens a space within. God got me where I am now. I don't feel I am finished. I am aware of how far I have to go. I'm only a shadow of what is to be.

God is the *Great Be*, the *Isness* of all of us. People call forth your being and refine your being. That is the ultimate sharing of the life of God. The more we have of being, the more we connect to the divine.

We need each other. We're not in competition. We are *in being*.

There is a total difference and total sameness of being. There aren't words to explain this. It is all *being*.

I know some people in my life who have their expectation of what the Nun is. Others recognize our search. That is part of a suffering we have. Suffering that many people do not get, do not understand. It is very difficult to find community with many people to communicate the way we (women of our Convent class) can.

When I worked, I had to get up at 4 a.m. to have silence before I went to work. My dream day now that I am retired is to get up and have no job, no phone, no computer, no music. I can just be in silence, solitude.

Now my life has come around full circle—Silence and Solitude in the Convent to Silence and Solitude now.

A MOMENT OF MAJESTY

Tucson shelters in a ring of mountains,
but her rainstorms have no boundaries.
Black clouds hulk,
climb over the Catalinas,
burst in torrents,
then recede.
Sun stuns moments later.

I laugh at weather forecasts
that talk about patterns
where there are no patterns—
just terrible unsureness in time and space,
endless circling of the possible.

Like God: boundless and calling me
into an infinite walking, no rest
for my efforts. God:
always calling, waiting, opening
skies that hold more stars
than I can count.

IN AWE

Every night we kids had to kneel as a family to pray the rosary. When we grew
able, each of us led a decade. It was a boring time.

Even in middle age, when I came home to visit, I was verbally dragged
by my parents to say the nightly rosary with them. As my father went into
his eighties, I still resented the monotonous nightly ritual. There seemed so
many better ways to meditate.

Then one night my eighty-five-year-old father quietly explained, "I used
to try to get through half an Our Father or Hail Mary without distractions.
When I could do that, I tried for an entire Our Father and Hail Mary. Then I

tried to say a whole decade of ten Hail Marys without distractions. And now I can say an entire rosary without distractions." He was not bragging, just sharing a fact about living in his later years.

I was dumbfounded, in awe. With all my Convent training and Zen work, I could not do that. My father, a simple man, could meditate for an entire rosary without a distraction. What an elder role model. I often think of him now as I try to meditate.

Forty-Four Dresses and One Smooth Stone

i

Once she emptied out everything but one smooth stone:
smelled a mountain stream,
could have sat for nine years in a mountain's cave,
could have cut off an arm
(like a Buddhist monk) for wonder,
could have floated above this place
poking out elbows and hitting nothing.

ii

One smooth stone, by one smooth cotton sheet,
one smooth pillow.
The scent of one white sheet
like the faint pink of azaleas.

iii

Now things attach themselves to her sweat
for the man who lies on the bed.
White sheets still smell of the faint
pink of azaleas.
Forty-four dresses mix in closets.

The stone rolls in a cold stream.

In the Sacred Moment

The grip of the spirit in preparing for and celebrating the events of the liturgical year kept me in a sacred moment as did the chanting of the office.

From Your Widow:
Suicide Notes

To have turned away from everything to one face
is to find oneself face to face with everything.

Elizabeth Bowen

Last night I had a dream and today I offer that dream to you as a suicide note. Perhaps dreams are, after all, the suicide notes of each day's little death. I have never been further from taking my life and maybe that means I am becoming ready to give it. I am thirty-seven. Unmarried. In fact a religious Sister. In truth, a sister, whatever the religion.

This is my dream:

a church service. widows have been invited to write their petitions at a side altar or table. i *feel* these women as i never have before. for the first time i know myself to be a widow, the missing of you is so awful. i am drawn to go to that table, too, a widow among widows. i don't know what i'll write and know people will never understand what i am doing there. i walk to the table anyway. almost all the other women have returned to their places by the time i get there, which makes me very obvious. i realize i have nothing to say on the paper. i write only one word: YOU.

Perhaps you who have come upon this note may want to know who YOU is. At first you may even be struck that it is yourself. Could that be? Could it be that what I most deeply mourn is your death, your lost, your unclaimed self?

Sensing what is unlived in yourself, you may rush to regrets for my death. Where have you gone wrong? What could you have done to call me back? You dress yourself like an old sofa couch in a slipcover of shame, having failed to take responsibility for my life. Yet that was never yours to take, however much you might have wanted it, however much I might have tried to give it up.

And so, sensing your futile search, I have decided to tell you about my life. For I, like you, *in* my dreams as *out*, am searching for YOU.

She was a small girl who easily imagined herself adopted. Her childhood quest centered largely on Uncle Gus. He captured her imagination. Sounds she heard with him seemed more than sounds: whirring model airplanes on wire strings. Smells she shared with him harbingered worlds beyond and mysterious: fresh-cut wood in his basement room. Sights cracked the sky: the finger lightning he said would never hurt her and of which she has never been afraid since.

His person, besides being the magnet of her childhood, was also the mystery, the only intimate member of that world with no religion. For that reason an adorable outsider. An enigma.

Around him and his presence to her family existed an aura of questions never asked and of answers never needed. Sometimes she felt from others that Gussie's lack of religion represented not something bad or evil, as one aunt almost certainly believed, but different and daring. Something others admired and considered themselves incapable of attaining.

Gussie lived as his own reason for being and, without knowing it, she wanted to be like him. Never satellizing a Someone but becoming herself. Gussie was like a tall, thin, fuzzy, black-haired straw through which she could drink the laughter of life and know beyond all need for proof that the universe is benign, that the heart of reality is a smile, that its heart would always smile back to her heart.

YOU: that smile.

In those days she hung perched rather than poised in the timeless, shapeless years between eight and twelve like a stellar body in outer space. The immensity of motion within her created a vacuum-like suction. No one could have known. In arithmetic her mind took the worn wooden pointer and raced across the multiplication tables on the blackboard, leaving her with memorization medals—but no true answers. Math problems were nothing like the questions that formed her real companions.

She had a special place for those questions, too—the choir loft of their small neighborhood church with its smell of a place much used but never smoked in. True, the waxless, scrubbed boards remembered incense. But the girl when alone in her special space did not linger long with boards or incense. She stripped quickly layer by layer all that was outside or within her until, with arrow-like intensity, the koan of her life shot out: *What would there BE if there were nothing?*

She asked the air; she asked the vaulting white ceiling. She asked until she was dizzied out of sight and self into the wondrous non-answer of nothingness.

YOU: the silence.

∿

At seventeen (the year Gussie died) she sat upon a freshly painted, green Convent garden bench. Across a walk of white stones a pigeon waddled toward her. A bold bird. It actually fixed her eye upon itself, its gaze forbidding fright, although she felt it some. The bird had caught her in its fierce snare.

She did not understand until with its beak the bird signaled to its breast. Then she saw—a heartbeat full of feathers flowing in three movements like a circular mountain stream. Her trinity ran over as the bird's blood became her own.

YOU: a pigeon's pulse.

∿

A decade later, a male plane (she the only woman aboard) deposited her in Central America, armed with her two words of Spanish, *sí* and *gracias*—women's words. What her mind had done in mathematics, it had failed to do in geography. She touched ground unprepared. The brightly colored oxcart in the airport, Costa Rica's symbol, posed no threat to her preconceived worldview. Not so the world just steps away from the tarmac.

The Sisters who met her there had planned a special treat, a trip through off-the-tourist-track back roads to the *colegio* where she would teach. That first day even highway vistas might have held horrors, but nothing compared with what she saw in the huts. Faces and eyes whose resigned beauty touched fear in her far beyond pigeons. Visions that made all hierarchical heavens a bourgeois joke: *In the afterlife, if there is an afterlife, these people and I will not be in the same place.* She lost faith and found love.

YOU: hollow, holy human eyes.

~

In the years since then, I have seen YOU everywhere until my own eyes have grown hollow with seeing and the fear of seeing. That hollowness is both my suicide and my widowhood. Filled with so much life and so much death, I decided this Lent to draw, to discipline my seeing by drawing it. Perhaps that is where these suicide notes began. I notice an entry for the fourth Sunday of Lent:

home alone and just being bathed in the warm quietness. during yesterday's drawing i had dealt with my fear of the leaf i was drawing, so today i approached pretty much without fear. but the leaf was still far beyond me. i became angry. having overcome fear, i somewhat expected the leaf to succumb to my ability to draw it.

yet a gap exists. what is it? a credibility gap? an integrity gap? a creativity gap? certainly a gap that limits union. what kind of union am i seeking that this kind of gap depresses me, isolates me, throws me even further upon my fragile uniqueness, smaller really than the sharpened point of my pencil yet so overwhelming?

it is not the leaf that overwhelms me. it is myself. my separateness from the leaf, the difference that will not—ever?— dissolve. earthen vessels. how can i not crack with the power of personhood? consciousness is the sharpened point of the pencil of my person. what am i drawing with the lead of my life? dark, underground lead. dark, wood-embedded lead.

the feelings i have written here passed in the first flash of today's contact with the leaf. almost instantly i was called to a silence beyond horizons, as though i were falling through the leaf and exploding out of the leaf at once. whatever the direction, i was suddenly beyond boundaries and edges in an object-less peace. a peace who is no object nor goal.

is there a possible posture to the universe except gratitude, the kind of muted silence i felt in the peruvian andes? in the silence this leaf called me to, it assumed the grandeur of a mountain. from whence comes my help. o iahu, hidden one, nameless one.

Today I am widowed of everything and nothing. At first you may be nervous with embarrassment that you thought YOU was you. Fear not, little loved one. It is.

Just now I was reading Ezekiel's vision of water. When the river reaches *al mar Muerto* (Now, you see, I am friends with the Spanish text.) *to the sea Death*, it will heal the salty waters and make them fresh and pure.

I bring my widowed self *al mar Muerto*. I long to find you there, living. Whatever that shall mean.

And so, YOU, I love you.

YOU are me are multitude.

PART III

LATER LIFE

CHAPTER 9
WHAT SUSTAINS US NOW

GROWING INTO OUR SKIN

All of us 57s now live within that mysterious world described by Robert Browning as *the last of life for which the first was made*. During my college years, these words awoke within me an intuition of their exquisitely countercultural, almost counterintuitive meaning, so much so that my seventies seem like a welcome homecoming.

Finally, *finally* I have grown into my skin. It fits. I am where I belong, where I have in a way always been. Although aging brings inevitable diminishments, it carries expansions as well. Quieter perhaps. All the more precious for being so.

Living within it, what are we learning about that *last of life*? What sustains us now? Many daily-growing awarenesses:

- That life is life at any age.
- That youthful passion can deepen and transform.
- That work and ministries enjoyed in early and midlife continue to be life-giving.
- That searching never ends.
- That contact with nature is healing.
- That bitterness is by far more costly than forgiveness and release.
- That meaning, peace and joy are found in many forms.
- That simplicity, silence and service enrich life at any age.
- That we as a race are being called as never before to a global transformation of consciousness.

We realize that not everyone has the privilege of reaching these aging years. Of the eighty-two of us received as Novices in 1957, twenty-some are deceased and ten or so others out of contact. Four of us died during the seven-plus years of the creation of this book, three after having contributed entries for it, one from her deathbed.

We have also seen the sometimes-breathtaking ways that life loops back and circles in on itself, linking the first with the last. The seeds of the women we now are can be seen, sometimes dimly, often clearly, in the girls we once were. That realization brings a sense of wholeness to life's journey that perhaps little else can give—seed, blossom and fruit held together as one.

ALWAYS THE SPIRIT

My mantra is *Always the Spirit*. This has carried me through wonderful times—my marriage, the birth of my children and grandchildren, joy in their accomplishments, steadfastness and fun with friends and colleagues, jobs that have been life-giving and soul-building.

Always the Spirit has strengthened me in the dark times too—the death of my husband and parents, miscarriage and financial problems.

Music continues to be my outlet, a way to express who I am, a way to touch my own Spirit and that of others. It creates for me a world of joy, of healing and of inspiration. At this point in my life, I feel a need for simplicity, for taking more joy in the ordinariness of life and family, for speaking out when a church that I have loved over the years seems more concerned with rigidity and legalism than with nurturing our souls.

Advent is my favorite liturgical season. Quiet joy, expectation, going within, the Isaiah images and prophecies—all have grabbed my heart. The additional element of being a music minister and making the above come alive for others is something for which I am always grateful.

On my spiritual journey I try to live by these words of that great contemporary 'theologian,' Erma Bombeck. I have her quote on my bedroom wall:

When I stand before God at the end of my life
I would hope that I have not a single bit of talent left and could say
'I used every bit of talent You gave me.'

I have not ceased to be a Franciscan. I'm only at a more mature stage of Franciscanism than I was many years ago.

TELLING WHAT I REALLY BELIEVED

For many years after I left the Convent, I did not allow myself to think freely. I squelched any attempts of my mind to seek answers because of the guilt that would seep in. Questioning one's faith was not the appropriate thing to do. Now, more than fifty years later, exploring one's existential thoughts is acceptable, even encouraged.

As I entered the autumn of my life, I had a desire to get a handle on what I really believed about the eternal questions of God and life and death. With age comes freedom! I finally felt I could find out what others I was close to were thinking. I have been blessed with a large family with whom I feel free to explore my deepest thoughts, doubts, and spiritual aspirations. I am especially fortunate to have a sister who is on a spiritual voyage of her own. With her I have been able to share, augment, and impel my spiritual journey.

All my closest friends happen to be Catholic and hold traditional religious beliefs. Their faith is deep and abiding, so I do not feel comfortable discussing my disparate thoughts with them. At times I envy their certainty, but God has given me an inquisitive mind, so I must use it to explore all the possibilities. Having peace of mind is so important—feeling that it is okay to question.

I am so grateful that now, through the shared writing of this book, I can communicate with more sisters who can relate to what I am thinking and wondering about. The world must come to the realization that we are all here together and one God has put us here. I still sometimes wonder why. But the main thing is to be happy and to make others happy.

I realize now that all these years I was really grappling with my concept of God. My journey has taken me through the full gamut of traditional pictures: the old man with a beard on a cloud (from childhood and early religious training); pantheism (God is in everyone and everything—all is sacred); energy force (has always existed and always will—we are part of that energy); Big Bang theory (God is still the impetus). And then there are all the various names of God. I definitely believe there is one God, no matter what He is called. And He is so far beyond our comprehension there is no use trying to visualize or conceptualize what He is. We humans are just not capable of knowing.

I do not have a definitive answer for all of my questions: life after death, heaven and hell, reincarnation. But I am now at peace with my questioning. When all is said and done, I was born a Catholic and I will die a Catholic. I will never renounce my religion.

That is not to say that I accept or espouse all its teachings or beliefs. What I believe is that Jesus Christ had the right ideas: "Do unto others as you would have them do unto you" and "Love your neighbor as you love yourself." We need to return to these basic tenets.

In the final analysis the question is, What have I learned on my journey? Have I learned to love? Have I learned to be happy and to make others happy? I feel that the answer is yes, as I continue my spiritual journey into the twilight of my life.

Little Children and a Lifelong Passion for Education

This fall opens my fifty-sixth consecutive year in education, forty-seven plus of those years as a first grade teacher. I think many of us as Aspirants, Postulants and Novices imagined future lives like the one I actually lived and continue to live even now in my early seventies. Immediately after our profession of first vows, I began what is to me both a career and an apostolate as an elementary school teacher.

Fifty-four of those years have been in Mississippi where obedience sent me in 1961. I arrived at a poor mission school that first opened in 1947. An incomplete building with no finances, no furniture, (promised, but not yet delivered), it was located in the middle of cotton fields and surrounded by extreme religious bias against Catholics. Today, as is the case in so many Catholic schools, I am the only School Sister of St. Francis remaining on the staff.

In no book of statistical research would one find any hope for the little seed of this school to grow. But grow it did! Our founders imbued early students with a strong respect for the faith beliefs of all their students. They imbued it in the parents as well.

That didn't stop the ugly tirades against Catholics, but it grew young people willing to stand up in their churches and say, "Preacher, that isn't true. I go to their school and they do not do that."

The ideals of those founders still endure. Somehow we have been able to carry on that culture of respect for all people, regardless of their beliefs, level of education, race, or economic status. I think so often of that when families return generation after generation because they felt their worth in a close school-family atmosphere permeated by a great educational milieu. And now one of our own former students has returned as principal.

When we celebrated the 64th anniversary of the beginnings of our school, I was teaching the great grandson of one of the original seventeen students from that first class of 1947! Every generation of that family has been at Sacred Heart since, something I find a most rewarding aspect of life here. Even as a Sister, I feel like a grandma each time one of my former students brings me a child to teach and I remember the parent as a six-year-old in my classroom. Nowadays I get that great grandma syndrome as I teach my third generation of students.

In my early years here, we ran a flourishing summer program. At its height, we housed twenty-nine Sisters in a Convent built for ten. One summer I slept in a sleeping bag on the Chapel floor, another summer on a futon kept under a table.

Many participants believed this summer program kept them out of trouble, even out of jail. Our youth, especially the black children, had nowhere to go, nothing to do in the summers.

It's not easy to summarize fifty-some years in a few paragraphs. I'll try by sharing a typical summer and beginning of the school year. We have Open House in early August, followed by two days of in-service, and then our students arrive for another beginning in their school life—another beginning for us too. Even before Open House, we've done state textbook inventories, ordered books for the year and, generally speaking, tended to administrative jobs that consume a good amount of time.

Throughout the summer I try to be at school many mornings by 6 a.m. to start weeding and watering our wonderful class gardens while the temperature is around eighty. That way my body gets acclimated to the rising temps. I try to work in the courtyard until between 9:00 and 10:00. By that time, the temperature is getting into the nineties and heading straight up toward a hundred degrees. I come in, cool down and spend some time in my classroom.

The heat here can often be really oppressive for those who have to be working outside. Heat-related deaths are often a danger. As long as such high temperatures persist, once school actually starts, we can allow the children to play outside for only fifteen minutes at a time.

I keep trying to figure out how we Sisters did it in the old school before the parents put in air conditioning. I well remember how wet those ink blotters [pieces of cardboard!]in our veil frontlets became within minutes of getting to school. We would turn away from the children, raise the frontlet, and let the water roll out! Those were indeed the days, but not the kind I would like to repeat!

Hours are long the first weeks of each new year. I need to adjust once again to all the paperwork, etc. Many days in the first three or four weeks I don't get home before 8 p.m.

My little first grade live wires are so full of excitement and yearning to do new things. How I wish our children could maintain that excitement! If only we could just help them explore the world of soil, the marvel of story, the wonder of paper, crayon, scissors, glue, and the mystery of God. Sad to say, a lot of that is stifled in the teachers due to so much paper work, meetings, and academic politics.

Through all these years and changes, however, some things have remained constant for me. One is the importance of hands-on learning for myself and for the children. Earlier in my life I did a good bit of macramé and really did enjoy it. Now the most hands-on things I make are memory books for retiring teachers. They are time consuming but they are gifts of self.

Another personal hands-on is decorating the church, something I truly love. All the artistry within my inner depths is called forth as I work to create a moment of hushed awe—utter but beautiful simplicity.

The children, of course, love making things. In 2011, for example, we took part in a magnificent project. The Mermaid Puppets of Nova Scotia came to the Memphis Orpheum Theater. Huge and fabulous puppets presented *The Best of Eric Carle*, one of my all time favorite children's authors and illustrators. Puppeteers performed *Brown Bear, Brown Bear*, *The Very Hungry Caterpillar* and *Papa, Please Get Me the Moon*.

Even better was the short session afterwards when we were shown how the holes were made, how the caterpillar crawled in and out, how the moon worked, etc. My children were enthralled! Of course, that field trip was a culminating activity after a three-week unit on Eric Carle, his works, his science, and his art techniques.

As a follow-up, the first graders presented a program for the next parent-teacher meeting. We decided to do our version of *Brown Bear, Brown Bear*. With the help of a first-grader's parent, we got huge line drawings of all the book's characters. We then did the animals with as many mediums as possible: tissue paper, crayon, marker, sponge paint, brush paint, glitter, sequins, feathers, small flowers, curled paper, stiff scrunched paper, etc.

At the meeting we read the story as proud artists carried in the designated animals. I posted the pictures on our class website. That was a hit. And the children experienced a week of art like no other.

My other hands-on constant is gardening with the children. We've had a garden for twelve or thirteen years now. The first two years we gardened in a couple of tires! Then we created four small container beds, one for each first and second grade classroom. Three years ago I was given permission for the eight beds we now have. I found the money needed and asked one of my former students to build the new, larger beds and to lay them out in the circular pattern that, from a distance, resembles a gigantic flower.

Because I link everything in my classroom with reading, each gardening project begins with a book. We read, for example, the nonfiction story *From Seed to Zucchini*. Then we plant zucchini seeds while transplanting cucumbers the children started as seeds several weeks earlier.

Our first grade garden produces a lot of squash, cucumbers, banana peppers, and tomatoes. The children regularly enjoy the fruit of our joint labors because the cafeteria ladies often serve salads containing one of our vegetables, for example the coleslaw made from cabbage we had planted in our first ever winter garden. Even though few children actually like coleslaw, they are thrilled that their cabbage is in it.

Their young enthusiasm infuses and reignites my own. It unites me both to my own farm roots and to my lifelong passion for education.

SONNET FOR MY 70TH BIRTHDAY

Time rises in the oldest years like bread
dough, yeasted with wisdom and surrender. Here
the tiny moments bubble, richly fed,
flavored with raisin joys and cinnamon tears.

Time rises like a melody recalled
from babyhood and anchored in the bone,
like chanting from a childhood church. And all
adulthood's songs play softer than these tones.

Time rises like a roof until the house,
built modestly, soars like cathedral spires,
points up its Gothic arches and allows
the soul to reach into limitless desires—

until the ceiling opens and bright stairs
climb through the starlight into timeless air.

I Am a Sufi

At this moment I am a Sufi who has become a Muslim. I look on all my previous moments—childhood, religious life, marriage and motherhood, widowhood, teaching and publishing—as segments I carry with me. I have not shed them the way snakes and crabs crawl out of their shells. I've accumulated them like rings on a tree.

Sufism sustains me now. Its ancient roots and practices. Its emphasis on mystical union with God. There are actually three Sufi orders in my city. How interesting that the word *order* is used—just as in the Convent.

Recently I was invited to team teach with a woman from a different order, someone who, for the past three years, has been attending a writing workshop I teach. Last week we met at my house in order to work out some of the details of the upcoming class. Unfortunately, our meeting occurred on the day my daughter called to ask advice about a possible divorce. Advice I knew she would not follow because she never has.

It was hard to keep focus on preparation for the class. All I really felt like doing was laying my head in the lap of my team-teaching partner, who was sitting on the couch beside me. And crying my eyes out.

"Are you all right?" she asked.

Then I did it. I looked into her eyes, saw a deep understanding and acceptance of whatever would happen. I pulled myself into a fetal position and lay my head in her lap. "I'm just so tired," I sighed. It felt like the first time in my life I had said exactly what I wanted to say and done exactly what I wanted to do. It felt wonderful.

She rested her hand gently on my head. After a while we went back to our discussion of the upcoming class.

And the class was a stunning success. I felt so exhilarated at the end of it. And I felt—how strange—that something had been healed. This collaboration between me and another Sufi—a woman who carries deep holiness—what does it mean? Where is it leading?

LONG BEACH ISLAND, NEW JERSEY

It is very quiet, the bewitching hour, five minutes 'til midnight. The silence is punctuated by the ticking of the cottage's simple white wall clock and the muted crashing of the waves, just beyond the nearby dunes. My dear friend is sound asleep on the couch on the porch. Few days of our cool and wet upstate New York summer can compare with the warmth and beauty of this late September golden day at the ocean. It feels as if we have been here forever, but it is the second and last night of a retreat that has turned into a gentle and nurturing vacation.

This morning I headed for the bay across the road that divides the island. But I could not seem to settle down. Even in the cool beauty of the simple chapel, I could not be quiet. I felt I was wasting these precious days away from demands of family life. My spiritual director had quite emphatically said, "No books! Just be quiet, journal a little, and have some fun."

With the exception of morning prayer together, my friend and I exclusively followed the just-have-fun command. We swam in the cool still waters of the bay, visited the local lighthouse, drank white wine from plastic cups while sitting atop pure white sand dunes. A fine Italian supper was followed by two hours of listening to the latest installment of *Vows*, a CD that narrates the story of Bill Manseau, a married priest and his wife Mary, a former Josephite Nun. Their lives seem to have the most profound impact upon me during these days of reflection. For, in many ways, their story is my story. With each revolution of the CD I am becoming more in touch with the forces that have brought me to this moment. I came here hoping to find God, but I am really finding myself.

I have always been an island girl, born in Manhattan and raised in Brooklyn and Staten Island. So it seems fitting that I am here on this island tonight as I explore the many twists and turns of my spiritual journey in search of God.

Writing about my faith journey has given me an opportunity to see so many things more clearly and afforded me a forgiveness to others and myself that has been very freeing.

I have said St. Francis's beautiful Peace Prayer, "Lord, make me an instrument of Your peace," almost every day of my life, especially in the morning while driving to my work teaching in prison. It is very powerful.

I read a wonderful article by Joan Chittister recently. She just about summed up all my feelings about my search for God during my lifetime. She speaks of the Benedictine devotion to the sacrament of the ordinary. If anything, it has confirmed my joy in the now-ness of caring for my husband, son, and beautiful granddaughter. My life is busy with cooking, washing, and creating a nest for my family.

Uncertain Journey

During my thirty years in the Federal Government, I tried to be a mentor to younger employees and interns and to reflect the values of hard work, honesty and integrity that I learned at St. Joseph Convent and Alverno College. I retired in 1995 and began another journey—this one with just as much uncertainty as all the others.

Now it is hard to talk about spirituality when the physical weighs one down so much as one ages. What sustains me now is inherent and inherited stubbornness plus the will to outlive my husband. When I was diagnosed with coronary artery disease and had a stent implanted, it changed my life substantially; I'd always thought I was healthy, even though I knew heart disease ran in my family. I had to pay more attention to what I ate, how much I exercised, how much stress I had and how I handled it. These are all things that weigh me down when I'd rather be lightheartedly enjoying life. I marvel at how so many my age and older still travel and volunteer and are actively participating in life.

I've always been a Franciscan at heart, and my love of nature has never waned. We work hard to keep our piece of sky blue and beautiful. A garden, trees and flowers with bird and animal visitors give me the opportunity to reflect on the "heavens telling of the grandeur of God." I cannot grasp the science that Stephen Hawking teaches about the big bang not needing a creator. I have a problem with his concept of nothing being real. Is the universe just a negative number? Are black holes just waiting to engulf all of the galaxies? Is there no meaning except within the time we have to live on this earth? Perhaps. It doesn't change the fact that we must make the most of the time we have.

Which brings me to another thing that sustains me—memories. People and places that have been an integral part of my survival and development. After I left the Convent in 1965, I had recurring, vivid dreams about being back in the Convent halls searching for people or being in a habit in the outside world looking for something. This ambivalence continued for many years until I went to our first '57 class reunion that included those of us who had left. Perhaps finally seeing the dichotomy of our lives brought some sort of closure. Now, instead of dreams, I have fond memories that sustain me. I have always been in awe of the talents of my classmates and their varied backgrounds, and I still feel privileged to have been a member of the Class of 1957.

A singularly important factor in my life now, as before, is that I believe in angels. There is simply no other explanation for what has gone on in the course of my life. I've often been in the right place at the right time, inexplicably avoided danger, found that I seem to know things I have no right to know. And I have seen my angel, at least once that I can remember when I felt alone and afraid.

As a child, I often took refuge in the woods near our home in order to be near God. I had close friends who saw me through my grade school, high school, and Convent experiences. So when those friends were no longer part of my life, there was a hole. That hole has been partially filled by my loving husband of forty-three years. But we have no children, and those who are married and childless in this baby-loving world know that hole is hard to fill.

So, I enjoy Facebook as a way to keep in touch with those who are separated by distance and years. I treasure the times I have been able to connect with classmates, friends and family. I hope for more years to follow along the path on the "lofty mountain," as we sang together at Alverno, our college named for the place where St. Francis received the stigmata.

Invisible. Like the Pattern

Here is truth in skin:
the jaw line
sports a sagging bubble,
needs a tuck;
the belly heaves
a pumpkin around itself.

Some trust in Viagra
between black silk sheets.
Some try liposuction. Meditating,
some see berry-brown seeds on a date palm.
But if age spots on the skin cause distress,
what good is meditation?

Measure change: get yesterday's newspaper,
search the internet for last week's terror.
But if you open your eyes to check last week's difference
on your jaw line, it will be invisible. Like the pattern
moving you to the end. Invisible like a far off wind.
It blows where you cannot put up enough wall, only a sail.

New Freedom and the Pain of Not Knowing

Why is it so hard to let go (with one's whole person not just intellectually) of things we accepted so wholeheartedly when we were young? The struggle goes on. I am reading and praying constantly for new light and wisdom to overpower the nigglings always wanting to resurface. *I am not good enough for God*—the crazy mantra that seems to live in every cell of my body.

I am rereading Gary Wills' *What Jesus Meant* in preparation for a class on St. Paul's letters. Two lines jumped out at me again—truths I know with my head, maybe even with my heart, but don't feel. "The vindicated will live by trust." "Grace is God's gratuitous activity, his favor, his bounty, in a continuing dynamic activity on his part." I keep waiting for the cloud to lift, but then I remember the *Exodus* story: He led them with a cloud by day and fire by night. Maybe I need the cloud to keep me in the struggle.

I am starting to read Chardin more seriously. Several other books have led me to this desire to understand him better. The first author was Krista Tippett; her book *Speaking of Faith* got me so excited I could not stop reading it. On my third reading of it now, I love it even more.

Another author I just discovered is Brother David Steindl-Rast in his book *Deeper Than Words*. I am just beginning to glimpse that the Christ of the Scriptures I have always been so passionate about is greater than I ever dreamed. I study scripture all the time, and Brother David's writings have opened up brand new dimensions for me.

Marcus Borg was the first author to open up my understanding of scripture and of Jesus, and it was a very painful ordeal. When I first started reading him, I felt I was betraying the Christ of the Scriptures and myself. Sometimes I would feel physically sick while reading it, trying desperately to hang on to my former literalist beliefs in the Bible. Maybe it was my pride. How could I have been wrong for so many years? But I kept reading and reading. Something—a Presence, I think, stronger than myself—kept me wanting to understand, needing to understand.

We cling to small untruths because the new understandings don't quite resonate comfortably with us yet. At present I am reading *The Field of Compassion* and *Radical Amazement* by Judy Cannato and once again am stretching to understand. I do like her discussions of morphogenic fields and holons. Where have I been all these years that I never heard these terms before?

Someone recently loaned me a book by Neil Douglas-Klotz called *Prayers of the Cosmos*, where he decodes (translates) the Our Father and the Beatitudes. Richard Rohr quotes him, too, in his work, *Everything Belongs*.

Sometimes I think I'm understanding what I read, and then I try to verbalize it and can't get one sentence out. But I keep venturing on because I know that if I read and if I think about what I read, someday I will experience an *aha!* moment.

My insides are finally starting to experience a new freedom, or shall I call it the pain of not knowing? Whatever is happening, I welcome it.

TWO CHILDREN AND A HUMMER DEALERSHIP

Since my days in Latin America, I've had very strong views on the ugly American. For me a lot of that ugliness constellates around what I judge to be our reckless unconcern about distribution of world resources both now and for the future.

Certain symbols trigger me, big cars high on the list. Yesterday I was driving along and passed a Hummer dealership. My sense of righteousness rose like a snake ready to strike. Who on earth did I want to bite and why? I breathed and knew that as long as that angry feeling, what Pema Chodron describes as the *Shenpa* Syndrome, was so strong inside me, it would poison anything of good I might do or say.

As I breathed, I flashed back to a particularly poignant memory—an early morning in 1968. El Progreso, Honduras. A knock on the clinic door beside which I lived. Another desperate family from the mountains carrying a child dying most likely of malnutrition. The child ended up in my arms as we walked the half block to the Church where my Jesuit field partner, subsequently murdered for his tireless work to organize poor *campesinos* to stand against oppression, baptized the boy. Within an hour the family was back on our dusty street with the paper flowers that marked a funeral procession, the child in a shroud.

At noon that same day I left Honduras to fly home for my first visit back to the States. By late afternoon I was in an airport in New Orleans standing near a boy not much older than the morning's boy. Instead of a flowered shroud, this boy wore a very expensive outfit. Instead of the morning boy's shrunken silence, this boy screamed relentlessly because his parents refused to buy him a large, swirl-striped, all-day sucker.

For the first time in my life, I felt blinded by murderous rage. It lasted not even a minute but shook me to the core. *Who had I become that I could hold murder in my heart against a three-year-old?* In that split second, overcome by *shenpa*, I may have been capable of clubbing him to death with a placard that said: SOCIAL JUSTICE.

Yesterday, passing the lot full of Hummers, I carried no placards. I bore only intense sadness about how little we humans understand about the effects of our actions on one another, the future of the planet and the majestic unfolding of cosmic history. And I renewed my commitment to live justly as continued insights come to me.

BEYOND THE TREADMILL

In 2002 my business partner and I were burned out and decided to sell our business. Retirement was not easy at first. I am the hamster in the cage that always needs to be on the little treadmill.

At first I was inventing busy work, but then I began to settle into a routine of planned activity. Love that structure!

I do volunteer work at the County Courthouse once a week, tend my garden outdoors during summer and garden indoors in winter. I added a conservatory to my house three years ago and it is my little slice of heaven on earth. I try to be a good steward of the material things entrusted to me.

My daughter-in-law and I flew to London to meet my son, and we spent five days there as my seventieth birthday gift. (Truly there is an error on my birth certificate!) That trip to England was a positive delight. I could go back there in a heartbeat. I have always had the idea of going there as a volunteer gardener and hope to pursue that.

Meanwhile, it is back to reality. Someone put my garden on steroids while I was away; there is much to do outdoors. The summer light here is so bright it turns all the greens to grey and silver. My horticultural heart is still in the UK where the Cotswolds are relatively untouched. Disney has not been there!

This has been a very productive year so far. Two of my paintings won awards at the community college show. This is the first time in my adult life that I have had the time to paint seriously and have my work recognized. I will spend the month of September in Taos, New Mexico. I have rented a condo and hope to take some classes and paint. My brother lives there so I will get to spend time with him. He is into print making after retiring from toy design.

A painting I did of an African American Police Officer titled "To Serve and Protect" was published in *The Artist's Magazine*, March 2014 as one of ten winners in a national competition for artists over sixty. When I had started volunteering at the county courthouse seven years earlier, the atmosphere was intimidating. This Police Officer, part of the security force, was one of the first people to shake hands with me, reach out and make me feel welcome. That kindness was the beginning of a friendship.

In my painting I wanted to portray the nobility of spirit I have always sensed in him; I think I accomplished that. When I showed him the finished painting he told me, "I am honored to have someone believe in me enough to want to immortalize me in a portrait. When I look at the painting I see myself through your eyes. I see the guy who is striving to be the best person that he can be, the guy who is willing to do anything to help someone out, is sharing himself to make someone's life better. The painting is something to live up to."

MALALA YOUSAFZAI'S PORTRAIT

I took an icon painting workshop a few years ago. It took place in the basement of an orthodox church in Cedarburg, Wisconsin. The teacher was a scientist and convert to the orthodox faith, well versed in the intricate religious details of iconography as well as the use of earth pigments and egg tempera. Class began with prayer and silence was encouraged. It was like a mini retreat. I believe the teacher and her students exhibit work at the motherhouse in Milwaukee.

Recently I did a painting of Malala Yousafzai—her face surrounded by words from her address at the United Nations. I donated it to a girls' academy on the campus of the University of Illinois. They invited me to give a presentation to their assembly.

There is a charming back story to this. I sent a letter and photo of the painting to the headmistress of the academy. The same day the letter arrived, the school's librarian had brought Malala's autobiography to the headmistress in hopes that it could be added to their library—one of those delicious coincidences capped by Malala's Nobel Prize.

I feel so fortunate, at this time in my life, to be able to devote so much of my time to being an active painter. I think of that quote by Rev. Capon, "Older women are like aging strudels. The crust may not be so lovely but the filling, at last, has come into its own."

SKIRTING THE LIFE OF THE SOUL

I have skirted the life of the soul in the description of my life. I practice no formal religion. Nature brings me such peace and joy. I became a Master Gardener in 1998 and that passion will always be dear to my heart.

I would rather work with things than people and have only a clutch of close friends. None of them speak the language that we 57s do. When we

Convent classmates get together, there are no explanations needed among us. That is why our Golden Jubilee reunion was so sweet.

Because leaving home at fourteen created a disconnect from family and relatives and also affected my memory of events from early years, I work hard at keeping a good relationship with my beloved children, daughter-in-law and brother. Now that my parents are dead, my brother is my only link to childhood.

I do not delve too deeply into life because I feel I have all I can do to keep my head above water. I am in the pool doing the dog paddle while others are diving into the deep end to explore. I wonder if part of that is from being married for thirty years and then being thrust by my husband's sudden death into the role of sole proprietor. Sometimes it takes so much energy just to cope with daily stuff.

EVERY WOMAN'S FEAR

I just got good news regarding a breast cancer biopsy—benign! That has to be the sweetest word in the English language. I've been down this road before when the news was not good.

PRAYERFUL PRESENCE

During the past decade I was called to ministry on the international level for the School Sisters. This gave me an opportunity to be of service to the entire community and helped me develop a more global vision.

After four years I took a Sabbatical that created a new awareness of the contemplative dimension and the desire to spend more time in prayer. I knew that the contemplative aspect of my life should deepen and expand. There was uncapped potential; how could it be realized?

As I prayed during my Sabbatical, I questioned: where is this going to lead? Then I received an invitation to be part of a human rights center in Juarez, Mexico.

The center focuses on forced disappearances, human trafficking, families affected by the violence. Although I work in the second-poorest parish of the city, I'm not really afraid. This process is in God's hands. There's a Greater Presence guiding it.

I see my role here as a prayerful presence expressing solidarity with the people in need. This is a Franciscan dimension. People have told me, "Thank you for considering us." They seem amazed that Americans would come to live and minister among them!

I find I'm expending quite a bit of energy immersing myself in this new reality in Juarez. There are so many aspects to it, and our SSSF community ministers in the midst of so much tragedy.

Shortly after I arrived, a major movement occurred: the common folk began to speak out against the violence that has ravaged the country. It took the name: Citizen's Movement for Peace and Justice with Dignity. A caravan of cars and buses traveled from Cuernavaca, Mexico on a four day trip to Juarez, Mexico for a huge gathering and public presence calling upon government officials to take concrete steps to combat the violence. Perhaps some of these actions hit the news, but my guess is that most of it was ignored by the mainline U.S. press.

Every so often I do ask the question, "God, why did you bring me here?" I know it's the place for me at this point in my life, but there certainly is a strong sense of the unknown in all of this. The one sure thing is to be present each day as deeply and sincerely as I can be to the people I am with at any given moment.

When I was younger, I was an activist, concerned with achievement and self-identity. I wanted to be in control. Then my commitment to mission work deepened into a concern for healing, emotional understanding, living from the heart. Now, I see myself as a supportive, healing presence accompanying people, walking with people in their need and struggle. People are so afraid to take action, fearing things will get worse. We try to help them see that when people get together, things can change.

I have learned how my work is related to everyone around me and to the two things that the life of Jesus is about: inclusivity and reconciliation.

Upon reflection, I see that crossing boundaries and healing ministries, especially with the poor and marginalized, have always been part of my life journey.

A SACRED DANCE

The Preface to the SSSF Constitution states: "Our focus is giving, healing and defending life." It just seemed natural for me, after years in education and parish ministry, to choose massage therapy as a way to live out this charism.

I had hesitated to tell my ninety-one-year-old mother, but the most powerful affirmation of my new path came from her. When I told her I was becoming a massage therapist, her immediate response was, "You will be good at it because you're good at whatever you do." I was elated and a surge of energy like a sun burst inside of me. I had all the encouragement I needed. I had the privilege of doing foot reflexology for her twice a week for about a year before she died.

Now I am a licensed massage therapist with my own practice. I've called my business *Magic Hands Massage* because, when I was a student, one of my clients referred to me as "the lady with magic hands."

The experience of giving a massage is truly awe-inspiring. Feeling muscles that are as hard as marbles become soft and pliable lets me know that clients are getting the relief they need because a relaxed muscle is soft, like putty. There's a sense of satisfaction in feeling a muscle respond to pressure. Clients frequently say to me, "I knew you would find the spot" or "You've found a spot that has been tight for a hundred years" or "I look forward to my weekly massage because it makes me feel so good." Others will ask, "How do you know where to find the sore spots?"

How do I know? For me, there's just a sense of knowing what a client needs. My hands detect the sensation in the tightness of the muscles. If I'm not sure I'm on the right spot, I ask the client for confirmation. Being patient with the process and letting my energy call forth the healing energy within the client is perhaps the most important aspect of the procedure.

Giving a massage is truly a spiritual experience as well as a therapeutic one. I can be in touch with the needs of the person because my intent is to honor body, mind, and spirit in each of my clients. In that way, the interaction between myself and the client becomes a sacred dance.

I Am Thankful for...

My Convent life:
- the great education I received there, both in my high school years and in college;
- the opportunity to hear, to be part of, and to learn about great music;
- the many times I worshipped in St. Joseph Chapel;
- the healthy food we had to eat both at the Motherhouse and out on mission;
- the friends I made.

My married life:
- the relationship I have with my husband of many years and all the experiences we have had together;
- the joys that having children brought into my life (of course, along with the pain and sorrows);
- the great joy of having grandchildren in my life;
- the many experiences I had through my working life, especially the people I met there.

I am thankful for life!

Offering Services in Retirement

I taught thirty-five years in the classroom and continue to tutor Language Arts and teach a few piano students, thanks to a wonderful education at Alverno.

While in the convent, I was trained in liturgy and Christian living. Now, as a lay person, I sing in the regular choir and in the Resurrection choir. It's a large parish, so we average one or two funerals weekly.

After Sunday Mass, along with my husband, I take Communion to shut-ins. As a member of the Human Concerns Committee, I help match people with jobs and, in my spare time, volunteer with Interfaith of Waukesha County, giving people who don't drive assistance with getting to church and to appointments.

I appreciate the enduring friendships I have with my classmates who continue to serve the Lord and His creation by remaining in the Community.

ANDANTE

We are not a ripping *scherzo*,
not *allegro* of vibrating dance,
certainly not *presto crescendo*.

No, you and I are *andante* –
lingering over espresso and
creamed strawberries at dusk,

andante, sometimes *tremolo*,
in soft, swallow-butterfly swoops,
con brio, sweet on the tongue.

RHYTHM OF MY LIFE

As I look over my life of seventy-five years, I realize that I have been very blessed. I had many wonderful opportunities to grow—in my family, with my friends, as a Girl Scout, at Alvernia High School, Alverno College and Marquette University. I work at responding in faith—without being in control. And whenever I'm feeling down, I'll run into someone who is such a good example that I get empowered. I have a wonderful spiritual advisor who keeps telling me to simply get out of my own way and be the person God wants me to be. Accept, appreciate, affirm, allow me to be.

And there's always been poetry—Gerard Manley Hopkins, e.e. cummings, Shakespeare, etc. For instance, I came across a poem by Jessica Powers entitled, "But Not With Wine" used at my fiftieth Jubilee Celebration as a Nun. In it God is addressed as a "God of too much giving" who is serving "potent cups of goodness." And I, "because a King was serving, drank out of courtesy." Somehow that poem captures the rhythm of my life, a receiving and a giving away. What St. Francis said has also been my experience, "For it is in giving that we receive!"

For years, I have been troubled by the pain, hurt, and anger that some of us still seem to carry in our hearts due to early formation or mission experiences. It seems to me that as we age, these resentments become too heavy to bear. I was very glad that in at our recent summer Spirituality Conference, we gathered for a program entitled *Tender Our Hearts: A Spirituality of Forgiveness*. Using the symbols of clay, a knotted cord, and a rock, plus Scripture and our life experiences, we were motivated to make an inner choice to release, let go of, set free all the memories of hurts that we had experienced or caused to another. We learned again, as if for the first time, that love is the basis of all forgiveness. Not our loving, but God's love of us.

WOVEN TOGETHER

As I have been involved in raising kids and now experiencing grandchildren, part of the frustration has been trying to hang on to the moments. Children grow and change so fast, but they are beautiful people at each step and I miss who they were. So I like to think that part of the next world will be to have them at every age.

I was struck by a similar realization at our Golden Jubilee reunion at the Motherhouse. One classmate brought a beautiful card with a picture of three women doing a graceful circle dance. The card held words so true—that the fabric of our lives is so familiar to each other that it feels "as if we are woven of the same thread."

We were still the same people we had the good fortune to know as seventeen, eighteen and nineteen-year olds. Fifty years later I found that the experience was the same. It doesn't seem to matter that many years have passed without our interaction. There is a definite bond among us. Where else could we have had daily access to more than eighty people with similar goals, motivations and beliefs?

I have found it difficult most of the time to relate to so many women who never had our Convent experience.

EARLY PATH FOR INDEPENDENT WOMEN

When I think now of our Foundresses and those early Sisters, I see so clearly how they provided a path when there really weren't many opportunities for women. And they held the concept that if one wants to do any kind of creative work or help others in society or have the power to solve problems, then one must be taken care of, not have to worry about food, shelter, health care. All of that would be provided as a foundation by the Community.

It's amazing that so much was done by these women who banded together, in spite of the patriarchy in society, to educate, motivate and serve as role models for all of us. What is the church without them? I guess you would have to say that they operated under the radar of the patriarchal church and created independent organizations with power—something most women in society had never been able to do.

WHENEVER I FEEL DIMINISHMENT

What sustains me whenever I feel diminishment is the example of many people I knew, those in my family as well as friends I have: Who they were or are, how I was treated, how I observed them and how I felt in their presence. Those no longer here are somehow still present to me.

Also, I go to nature to be alone and to observe. Anywhere: a small bird or animal outside the window, the rain, sun, clouds, storms, a flower opening, a small bug. I tend my garden. If I'm lucky and as long as age permits, I go to the canyons, the Colorado River or the Sonoran Desert of the Southwest. Most of all I spend time with my husband, my children, and my grandchildren and try to hold them in the moment and be fully present.

I want to impart to future generations what was imparted to me by so many others: an example of living in the world with integrity, joy, simplicity, acceptance, creativity inspired by the natural world and living in harmony with it and the people I encounter in my life.

THE CONVENT MADE ME A FEMINIST,
AN ENVIRONMENTALIST, AND ...

The Convent experience has definitely affected my present life. I acquired concepts and beliefs that are still with me today.

The concepts of community, sharing, and the common good. Also the concept of all work having value and everyone sharing in the work that needs to be done for a group to prosper. In my family we all share this type of maintenance work. My kids learned early to do their own laundry.

The concept of following a rule for everyone to live peacefully together in community. For example, whenever a neighbor plays loud music outside after 10 p.m., I feel like shouting, "Didn't you ever hear of the GREAT SILENCE!" Or when another burns leaves in an outdoor stove, sending pollution through the neighborhood, I want to say, "What part of community life and rules don't you understand!"

I guess one could say my past experience in the Convent has today made me a feminist and an environmentalist, one who finds it difficult to tolerate patriarchy in any form.

MEETING OUR FIRST MYSTIC

Much has been written about the lingering, largely negative, medieval mindset of Convent training but never enough about the spiritual giants some of the women became. Each of us 57s probably met one, some of us many, role models within the SSSF Community—unassuming mystics, brilliant visionaries, passionate pray-ers, women with an inner knowledge and experience of sustaining, otherworldly realities. To this day these women populate our heavens.

One of my earliest encounters with such a woman came in an unexpected place, the Motherhouse vegetable kitchen. There we prepared (peeled and cut up) mostly fruit— specifically thousands of bushels of Wisconsin apples. We Aspirants, Postulants and Novices paid in part for our education by taking regularly scheduled turns there, sitting in silence while working or praying the rosary.

One of the kitchen's corners seemed inhabited by someone too old to be alive. Sister Lamberta. Looking herself to our teenage eyes like one of those wizened Appalachian apple dolls, here was a woman totally given over to prayer. She seldom spoke. Her vibrant, joyous eyes did that for her.

One day, though, she did speak. Our Novice Mistress brought her to our refectory and asked this holy woman to talk to us. She was so tiny she had to climb the steps to the platform where the table reader sat so we could all see her. Slowly she climbed up, one step at a time. Slowly she turned to look at all of us. Then she began talking, her badly fitting false teeth clicking with every word. I do not remember what this old woman said, only that her mystic presence emanated to the far corners of that large room.

Her kitchen space was my first classroom of contemplation, she its first teacher. To this day, I cherish the round smoothness of an apple's feel in my palm and the kiss of its many memories. Friends know that what I bring to any party or potluck is a plate of fruit, freshly cut. Only a few know that each plate carries hidden within it the blessing of Lamberta's ancient absorption in prayer.

THE SOUND WE MAKE

For fifty-eight years, wherever we went, except when the kids were very little and we had no home parish, I was privileged to sing at Mass. During our two years in Italy, I prepared and led the music for the priests from Rome who came to serve the American community.

I've been in my present choir for twenty-five years. During that time I cantored for the 5:15 Saturday night Mass. The seniors I was serving as Parish Outreach Coordinator really offered me a great deal of thanks and admiration.

When the parish formed a Men's Schola who needed a Mass during which to sing, I offered mine. No one else was willing to let go. But I cantored for them until they were trained in the Liturgy. Then I was only allowed to substitute for the person who cantored for daily Mass. Then it was decided that I should save my voice for choir only. After healing from that hurt, I joined the cantor who sings the solos at funerals and I augment the congregational singing.

This year we acquired a professional director. He requires so much professionalism that I questioned whether or not we were helping the congregation to worship. I'm still not sure. But I know the sound we make is beautiful, and we worship.

DAFFODILS

As I look back over my life, my best friends are those who love flowers or are connected to nature in some way or have a somewhat spiritual path.

I met one lady because she left a bouquet of flowers for each table at a very small gas station/café. The daffodils had such unique shapes and so many variations of color that the energy from the flowers wouldn't let me go. I inquired about the source of the daffodils because they were so beautiful and different from mine. I was told they came from some lady down a road nearby.

The next day I started out to find the lady who had decorated the café tables with daffodils. I drove down a dirt road and saw a man fixing a fence. I asked if he knew someone nearby who grew daffodils. He said he had just moved to the area and didn't know anyone, but maybe the man in the store at the top of the hill would know. I backtracked and went to the store. The man there said this was his first day taking over the management of the store and he didn't know anyone in the area, but maybe the lady who lives at the bottom of the hill would know.

As I drove the hill into her driveway, I saw "a host of golden daffodils." I knew I was in the right place. I worked up my courage and knocked at her door. I asked if I could take pictures of her daffodils. We have been friends ever since. I now have several hundred kinds of daffodils in my yard because she has shared.

God's Energy Is in My Classroom

After years in Catholic schools, I teach today in a disorganized and chaotic public school where the students seem to run the school. I try to reach the students who are open and receptive to accepting help. The thing that keeps me going in my seventies is that some students are willing to accept my energy to boost their energy and self-esteem. I see the twinkle in their eyes and their pride when they understand; this makes it all worthwhile.

Once they make that turn and feel good about themselves, it energizes me to continue giving to others. The resonance in my heart tells me who I can help and who will continue to refuse my help. Even though this whole situation is negative, I am learning to find the positive within the negative and that makes all the difference.

I feel I have changed a few lives because I have stayed and that keeps me at this school. God has touched lives through me. This is how I find God.

LOVES OF MY LINEAGE

I address the Akashic Records with the opening question of my inability to deal with stuff, with clutter. They answer:

You, like your mother before you and her mother before her, are a lineage of light beings. Your grandmother was too poor to have had much stuff to deal with. Your mother had enough German in her to deal with it. You are left. You have the challenge. You are not home. You pass through as a lonely stranger. Things hold pain.

I need help not to paralyze around things. I visualize a room of my own streamlined to my soul. It is mine to make and keep it so.

I invoke my lineage once more with a similar opening question:

I sense you here. Loves of my lineage, what is important for me to know about why things/multiplicity overwhelm me so? I don't need to 'see' anything. I don't need anything 'sent' to my mind. I am content if you choose to seep a response into my heart and life as we go along.

Fractal waves envelop me and carry me forward, outward. Carrying me out. Under and over. Each time further.

Loves of my lineage, I adore you. My love is adoration. Completely joyous adoration.

A sense of spaciousness in general. Exceptional physical spaciousness around the heart cavity. Spaciousness that extends that cavity beyond the body.

Loves of my lineage, I thank you for showing me the timeframes within which I live—the extended non-time. I need your help in reaching balance. I feel lonely here without you. You are so my home. You are so my heaven. All else is exile. Let me come home.

You know that since my mother's death, I am so aware that I need to be worthy of the way she—and you all—walked the earth.

Loves of my lineage, I thank you. I never doubt you. I am never without you. You are within the Akasha with me, dancing the Sacred Dance.

Sometimes we approach the Records. Often we just luxuriate together within the Akasha itself—The Sacred One. The Beloved.

MORE FROM THE WOMAN IN THE
NAVY BLUE SUIT AND RED HIGH HEELS

Where have I come, from the young woman I was as I entered the community clad in a navy blue suit with red high heel pumps? What of that rural contemplative person still lives in me today? How do I still respond to life and feel about life at this stage of my aging process?

For me, life and death, illness and health, continue to complement one another. Physical illness has kept me dependent on others, yet always with a desire to get well and continue my work helping and ministering to others. Illness can be a kind of daily death as one learns to live with limitations that are quite definite and obvious. However, in slowing down, one experiences a fuller awareness of the fragileness of all life. In accepting limitations one becomes more conscious of the things one still can do.

Illness has allowed me much time to think, to pray, to reflect, to stay in touch with others (both living and deceased) and thus my own consciousness has been expanded.

I am trying to discern just how much longer I can actually do the work I am still doing. I must admit that I am doing it primarily to bring in money for the Community. I could drop the work at any time and not really miss it, but it is a good outlet for me so that my life keeps me involved with others beyond my living situation.

I have not done much socially because of my physical health, but I have kept up with people by phone or email. I have many low maintenance friends, good friends with whom I can pick up right where we left off because we have shared at a deeper level. The bond continues. I think it is one of the joys of living more deeply into our more mature years and reflects some of the growth in inner consciousness that we read about so much these days. We can communicate at a deeper level even though we do not know the actual day-to-day existence of the other.

That experience in my life feels like a special gift of presence with another, a kind of intuition. Sometimes I feel connected with particular persons in a very conscious and intense way even if they are far away and I have not spoken with them on a regular basis for a long time. This is especially frequent when I am working about in silence. Now through email that connection can be verified more quickly and is real.

I believe that this presence is something I want to develop more as I grow older and into retirement. It feels like a deeper level of consciousness that alerts me to think about and pray for people. I often discover later that they were going through a death, an illness, a difficult decision, something that directed them to ask for prayer and support.

The Sisterhood that I experienced when Community members, such as myself, and former members met for our fiftieth Jubilee Celebration was a small realization of my dream for the future. As a class we 57s continue walking the same journey towards our Creator, in individualized ways of responding to God's call, but together we walk forward into the unknown.

PRAISE

old women
shuffling
to church
skin
rustling
against bones

teeth clicking
of God
and
mystical nights
sighed
into bed sheets

BEING CONNECTED

My connection with nature and the healing arts has been with me since childhood and has been nourished by and within the School Sister community. During my early years on mission, we always had a garden or parishioners would share their produce with us.

I kept up my interest in natural healing by subscribing to natural health magazines and also taught myself to do yoga. It was such an exhilarating feeling when I learned to do the shoulder stand. Now my shoulders instead of my feet were connected to the earth. It's amazing how the body responds to gentle and regular practice.

Keeping in touch with the community has come full circle for me. Because of my work, I lived by myself. I would attend regional gatherings in Omaha, but beyond that, I didn't get involved. I did, however, keep in touch with a Sister whom I had befriended in a trying situation on one of the missions where we lived together. To this day, we still keep in touch. There was a period of about twenty years during which I had not been back to the Motherhouse.

When I moved to Missouri, I was invited to join a group that was meeting in Des Moines before Area Communities were formed. I have stayed with that group for about twenty years although the composition of the group continues to change. Meeting together monthly, except for June and July, and for a retreat in May has continued to strengthen our bond and commitment to each other. The highlight of the gathering has always been telling our stories.

Finding my niche within the Community has not been easy, but religious life has always seemed to be the right choice for me. One of my proudest moments as a member of the School Sisters of St. Francis happened at the Spirituality Conference during which the speaker made our foundress, Mother Alexia, come alive in a way that I never experienced before.

Her words made me realize in a new way that, as an SSSF, I am part of a much larger dimension of the whole of life. The statement Mother Alexia made when she was dying, "I will think of you in heaven and you will feel it" connected me to the whole history of the Community and all the events that are part of our history, both internal and external.

I LOVE MY LIFE

I love my life and all the richness in it. I spent some time recently with the memories of those years we spent together. I am reminded of something I read once: "We know what we have and how we've been blessed, and we bow our heads in recognition of that abundance." Thank you, friends, for the richness of life with you when the vast unknowable future lay ahead. I'm so grateful that our short time living together in Milwaukee has led to our over fifty-year friendships with each other—women who honored the call to stretch and reach for the fruit at the end of the limb.

ZEN POEM

When the river runs North
And the wind blows South,
the morning mist wavers as it rises.

Where is the light to absorb this Rising,
siphon it into Great Clouds of Unknowing,
sacred Bowls of Rain
drawn to the seeds they are meant to nourish?

COURAGE IS THE GIFT

Much earlier in my life, I thought the writing of memoirs was reserved for the rich and famous. Only celebrities, athletes, former presidents and perhaps their wives and adult children would be recognized as fully qualified to pen their life stories. However, in accepting the challenge to participate in this writing project, I realized that I could and would step up to the plate.

Recently, while reading *Three Cups of Tea*, I was struck by the line, "When your heart speaks, take notes." My heart spoke often during the past fifty years. Unfortunately I did not take notes. That made writing for this book an even more serious challenge to my nagging lack of self-confidence.

Now I see that my childhood spunk and the ongoing friendship and encouragement of classmates allowed me to confront my lack of confidence and write despite my doubts and hesitation. That courage is the gift writing for this class memoir has passed on to me.

These classmates tell me how hard it is for them to think of me, now or earlier, as lacking confidence. They say the spunk I describe as getting me into trouble on day three of boot camp is what they have always admired in me and wished they had more of. I learned they experienced my spunk in those early days as a kind of gutsy courage rooted in a fierce instinct of self-preservation. One wrote recently: "You knew that *you*, the deepest inner *you*, is so valuable it needed to be saved, to endure."

Their ongoing friendship helps me now to see that the same spunk colors my present life with so much vigor and passion. It has led me through the minefields of family blending, through the heavy days when my beloved husband won his battle with cancer. Spunk is the gift far beyond treasury bonds I am passing on to our grandchildren and their descendants. In the end, it is the essence of my contribution to life itself.

Glass Ceiling

Our Sister Foundresses set up and ran hospitals, high schools, elementary schools, a college, a mental hospital, a world class sanitarium, institutional bakeries and kitchens and laundry, a farm, the Seraphic printing press, art studios. They were CEOs and CFOs, and the glass ceiling was the Pope. Still true.

Spiritual Eldering

Just as the School Sisters of St. Francis proved beacons for my youth, so they now become mentors in my aging. I structure these treasured days of spiritual eldering around the legacies they enkindled—chief among them for me silence, sisterhood, intellectual curiosity, social justice and mystical vision.

Those places—the Motherhouse and Alverno College—and those early women, some living, many dead, often visit in dreams to continue their nurturance and teaching.

A Dream:

I dreamed of Sister X last night. I am in a large, beautiful library and she comes in walking with a cane, a slight limp and much energy. For most of the time I just observe her, too awestruck and timid as usual to approach her, although it seems there is also some conversation between us at a large wall display of maps. When she goes to leave, I run after her and say something to the effect that she is still the most radiant presence alive.

Dream Reflection:

I am reminded of Yeats' haunting poem "The Song of Wandering Aengus." In the magical setting of a hazel wood, the poem's speaker pursues an elusive, glimmering girl throughout a lifetime of longing and search.

Glimmering girls is, in a sense, what we were as young together, although beneath our black serge even we sometimes missed our own glimmering—as all youth do. Now we are old and still need to pursue her, that young dreamer within us, for deeper wholeness.

Many of us as young girls were magnetized by romantic archetypes of one kind or another about Nuns made more (or less) real by the Sisters we met face to face. Those archetypes held images of our own best selves, both then and now. They contain depths we have plumbed all our lives, what we then believed to be our potential and now know in a transformed, more wholistic way.

Over the years, I outgrew many of the more starry-eyed aspects of the Sisters but *not what they awakened in me*, the part of myself that is always unfolding.

Many of their beloved faces will likely accompany me at death. But the face I will then see is my own revealed, the face they mothered and nurtured all these years. Their presence brought me to life and continues to sustain me in life like nothing else ever did.

So, in my dreams as well as out of them, in youth as in age, I've seen them! I've seen the Sisters! I shall never cease seeing them, loving and blessing them—not least of all for the gift of my deepest self, embedded in the One, the All.

PATH OF THE CONTEMPLATIVE

I have evolved a rich, dynamic, extremely varied and deeply satisfying lifestyle. My spiritual path is that of the contemplative—the path of inner peace, tranquility, harmony with others through the practice of meditation. I wish I had come to this path many years before now.

Where I live is a wonderful place. Really nice people and lots of kids! Approximately thirty kids play outside my townhome. At least seven are ages one to three—nice for me as my only grandchild is so far away. I think I am the oldest person living in this complex; at least I've never seen anyone who looks older. I love the sounds of children playing outside. There is very little discord—great to witness.

In the complex I have a new friend with whom to share great conversations. He and his wife take care of their young granddaughter and grandson at least one day each week. He sits outside watching his grandkids for hours, which gives us a chance to talk. His wife is apparently fairly disabled because of physical problems, so she doesn't come outside. He is funny, kind, and very solicitous with his grandchildren— wonderful to witness.

Recently I was asked to start teaching classes for the retired Sisters at a nearby Convent, which I did as soon as I finished up fall tasks outdoors at the Meditation Center where I volunteer—a big undertaking. I am absolutely loving the yoga class with them! We laugh and have fun with it.

After the first class, they all scooted out of the room. Now they hang around and talk. Some have requested that I teach them how to meditate, so that will be another class. It's all turned into so much more than I could ever have hoped for.

So I have a very busy and dynamic life right now despite physical challenges. I help manage two outdoor properties. I have a number of counseling/healing clients and young women whom I am mentoring in a variety of ways and also offer help to many people who express need if I think I can help. Being at home so much, I can offer support to people via the phone, internet, letter writing and people can come to me or we can meet up via SKYPE. It's all a matter of being creative and enterprising.

Overall, this lifetime has been painful, difficult. I am hoping to reach enlightenment while still in this physical body so that I do not need to do a rerun of this physical existence (karma, reincarnation). Right now, despite some challenging physical issues, I am at peace and happy.

A New Way of Asking the Great Questions

People today talk about the world coming to a new axial age, one of those graced periods in human history marked by radical changes in humanity's collective spiritual vision. Some, like Ken Wilber, inspired by the research of Dr. Clare Graves now known as Spiral Dynamics, sense it as "the single biggest evolutionary leap" since the harnessing of fire. We seem to be entering a new, more communal way to ask the great spiritual questions, not satisfied with the ways cultures and organized religions have answered them.

Individual visionaries like Jesus, especially as revealed through his original Aramaic words and worldview, and so many others, great and small, have always seen beyond what has been and were passionate about enlarging existing metaphors. They lived and gave their lives to bring about the evolutionary transformation of the human race as a whole and to re-envision human history within the vastly larger flow of cosmic time. In what way may they have passed that baton to us?

LONGING

Last year the film *Into Great Silence* came to town. In this beautifully filmed documentary of the daily life of Carthusian monks in the Grande Chartreuse monastery high in the French Alps, no spoken commentary, or added sound effects, or music intrudes upon the images and sounds of daily monastic life.

I expected to be put off by the movie and attended one evening with no other expectation. In fact, the opposite happened. I was so deeply moved, I returned the next evening to see the entire film again.

Why was it so inspiring? I don't know except to say it had *nothing* to do with patriarchy or Christ-centered theology or the monks themselves. Rather for me, *Into Great Silence* showed people powerful in their ability to enter the spiritual world, the world so foreign to most, a world (whether Buddhist, Jewish, Christian, Islamic, or Hindu, etc.) revered as deeply important and necessary to the evolution of the world. People who can meditate in the quiet way of *Into Great Silence* seem to be nearing the spirit world and midwifing this world-wide evolution of consciousness.

I found myself craving again the deep meditation of the quiet hours of the monastery, hours that, since I left the Convent, I only sometimes now entered with our Buddhist monk mentor. I longed again for that ability, that commitment necessary to meeting the spirit.

TRANSFORMATION AT A COST

Although I am grateful and elated over all the new life in my family, I seem to live under a cloud these days (the cloud of unknowing?). I'm not sure if it is the loss of my brother-in-law (his energy level was always so high) or if it is watching my sister grieve or the vulnerability of growing older or learning to live well with ambiguity or all of the above. I keep remembering

Richard Rohr's words: "There is no transformation without great love or great suffering."

PARA QUE ANGUSTIARSE?
(WHY ANGUISH YOURSELF?)

Sin dejar de ver las arrugas (agonías, resentimientos, inconsecuencias, perdida de la belleza exterior y apagamiento espiritual) hay que sobreponerse a todo y no dejarse dañar: la fortaleza, la auténticamente espiritual, lo solidario, la belleza humana y por supuesto: sentimientos, emociones, integridad síquica, ideales, metas, vocación, FE en Dios y en TI MISMA. Si se conserva eso, no se debe de experimentar 'diminishment'.

Los latinos tenemos un dicho que dice: "nunca es tarde" para borrar ese sentimiento de "diminishment" y aprender a descubrir el inmenso tesoro que eres y a si veras lo bonito y alimentador de tu historia: gente, comidas, risas y sonrisas, estudios, paseos, trabajos y viajes.

Para que angustiarse cuestionándose ¿Por qué no me fui? ¿debí haber hecho esto? O lo otro. Es imposible volver atrás. A pesar de todos los 'peros' inmensos como una cima rocosa LA VIDA ES BELLA. Aunque más podemos retener nada, pero eso es lo bello de la vida y siendo realistas, a veces es nostálgico… Y esa nostalgia debe ser regocijante y esperanzadora.

WHY ANGUISH YOURSELF?
(PARA QUE ANGUSTIARSE?)

Without failing to notice the setbacks (torments, resentments, inconsistencies, loss of exterior beauty and spiritual desolation), you need to overcome all that and not allow yourself to be harmed. Strength, authentic spirituality, support, human beauty and, of course, feelings, emotions, psychic integrity, ideals, goals, vocation, faith in God and in yourself—if you maintain these, you ought not experience 'diminishment'.

We Latins have a saying: "It is never too late" to wipe out that feeling of diminishment and learn to discover the immense treasure that you are, In this way you will see the good and nourishing aspects of your life story: the people, the food, the laughter and smiles, the studies, the outings, the work and the journeys.

Why anguish yourself asking: Why didn't I go? Ought I to have done this or that? It's impossible to go back. Despite 'buts' as immense as a craggy mountain peak, life is beautiful. Even though we are able to hold on to nothing, that in itself is the beauty of life. Being realists, at times life is nostalgic. And that nostalgia ought to be joyful and hopeful.

I FEEL SO NOT-HERE ANYMORE

I keep searching for reasons or understanding for the immense world-weariness I've been carrying for months. One thing I'm learning is that each loss carries all loss. Each seems to dig into different places in our lives and tap into what I have referred to for many years as the *lacrimae rerum*, Virgil's description of the tears within things.

I feel so not-here any more, (not that I was ever that embodied anyway). This recent not-hereness, though, has a different feel and quality to it that eludes me at this time and disappears into mystery, which I refuse to accept as nothingness.

So I hold, behold and wait in hope. All of life an Advent.

PROMISES:
A NUN REFLECTS ON THE STATE OF HER COMMUNITY

Rough ways will be made straight
and mountains low

When?
I see skeletons of ongoing Holocausts
the cold and hungry in this wealthy country
huddling together under bridges

together, together
together to survive
and share a bit of warmth for the night.

Who are we?
Why are we
with so few numbers?

The sign of the times. . .
I will give you a heart of flesh.

We are few in number!

One–become One
where there are two or three gathered.

We are few in number!

The grain of wheat must die.
Do you believe?
Are you of little faith
of faltering faith?

Few in number. . .

One, One, One
reaching for each other-
under the bridge
captivated by love
together, together, together
we move into our future
to leave a legacy.

The grain of wheat
will die to make the soil
rich for peace and intertwine
hearts of those who come
to go beyond to make
rough ways straight
and mountains low:
what we have come to do.

GOD AS A VERB

When I was a young student at Alverno College, I heard that God is a verb, not a noun. Process, not substance, is the substratum of reality; the universe is process, and we are the people we are by getting in on the process that is God.

Later, when I was about twenty-seven, I sat in a group of seven other SSSFs on the floor of the Community's Ranch House. We had just heard a speaker telling us about the injustices and the social issues of the day and were praying aloud our intentions. Vietnam, poverty, world peace were the priorities in those petitions and rightly so.

But I was not ready for issues outside of myself. My longing was to be able to believe in God and to be happy. I sat with inside tears that came with the feeling of not belonging or fitting in.

Today I sit in that same room. I sit in a circle of women and men. We talk, we share, we are vulnerable, we pray. Today my heart aches for the people of Libya, the migration of refugees from Syria, the marginalized and dispossessed worldwide. I sit in this circle and hear my friends' concerns and worries about having their health insurance cut or being out of a job after twenty years as a steady, hard-working employee. Together we pray for the people living in places of earthquakes and tornadoes and tsunamis and war crimes of violence against women. That is a suffering that touches a deep anger in me.

"We are the people we are by getting in on the process that is God." It is now forty-five years beyond my first hearing of those words. A process happened in me and perhaps in spite of me. I put my hands on my heart when I wake in the morning and ask that I might learn to love. When I feel rage or ache for others or for my own ignorance, I pray, "Of my secret sins deliver me, O Lord." I know the movement stretches me, makes me more human and draws me into the Process that is God.

FROM MASCULINE TO FEMININE

In my late sixties, I had a dream that awakened me to one of the most important decisions of my life:

It is after supper in the home where I lived with my mother and father. The three of us are in the living room where there are two couches back to back. My father and I are sitting on one and my mother on the other.

My father says to me, "Let's go upstairs." I know what this means; I take it for granted that I give my father what he wants.

I see my mother's hand reach over the back of her couch and let it lie there for me to see. It is withered and weak. I kneel on the couch where I've been sitting and look over to her. Her entire body is as her hand, weak, withered, malnourished, dying. I see. I take her hand and say, "I will never leave you."

I look at my father and he knows I will no longer, never again be "going upstairs" with him.

As I woke, I knew this dream was a gift telling me that I was in the process of an interior decision that would affect the rest of my life—a major shift from over-identification with the masculine to an embrace of a feminine vision and values. When I was young, although never physically or sexually abused by my father as the dream might suggest, I chose what appeared strong, powerful, and dominant in the culture, all stereotypically masculine, 'the upstairs'.

This dream confirmed for me that I knew in my sixties—and believe even more now in my seventies—that whatever years I have yet ahead of me, I will grow in longing and living the depth of feminine power, beautiful and wise. Embodying feminine power is not strong in my lineage, personally or culturally, but this dream indicates that I can choose to do so now as both my heritage and my legacy.

THE REST OF MY JOURNEY

When I left the Community, I left people whom I loved and who loved me and set out on the rest of my journey.

That journey has been amazing. I have finally come to be at peace with myself. I am content where I am. I feel blessed by all that has happened in my life, no matter what that has been. Whatever could be considered negative has been such a small part of all that has been and is life-affirming for me.

Living alone, but not lonely, having the quiet time for meditation and just simply being, I am grateful for the spiritual training we received as School Sisters. It maintains and sustains me.

Through the years, I have always considered October fourth (Feast of St. Francis) our day, a day to remember and reminisce about the wonderful, difficult, tense, peaceful contradictions of my years with the School Sisters. I start each day with the prayer of St. Francis and do find peace and healing.

I know that my ten years in the community have been the foundation of all that I have experienced since I left. I have been blessed with three wonderful children, grandchildren and friends who have been supportive and caring. I have memories that lift me up constantly and give me the strength and courage to live my life to the fullest.

AFTER THE CHARLESTON MASSACRE

After this week's racially motivated massacre of nine people gathered in church simply to pray with their pastor in Charleston, SC, my whole being is sad. But, at the same time, my being experiences the genuine love from so many for that grieving community. There is a sense of the whole uplifting to a new dimension with this tragedy. I think Chardin's vision of convergence is happening. I see it in small communities and large, in so many places. May it be!

Our son's family lives in Charleston. When he heard that the whole city's church bells would ring together in solidarity, he took his twin 5-year-old boys downtown on that Sunday to experience the communal grieving. "It was a very mindful Father's Day," he said.

We skyped with them the next day and asked the boys about their time downtown. It certainly was a testimony that kids understand a father's explanation of the wealth of love in the time of insidious hate. They were able to repeat why the bells rang, as there were 9 people killed—and "some were mothers and fathers and grandmas," etc. Our son made us aware that as silent as is his nature on some things, this was a teachable moment.

Then the boys told us about the thousands of people who walked across their bridge—the one they cross every day to go to school—"because people wanted to show how they love instead of hate." Their father drove them (too small to walk) down that bridge and they commented on how long the line was, and then said, "We saw breaking news." It swelled our hearts. Values. Memories made that day. Mindful living.

Less than three years earlier, our son had had a professional collage drawn up in color that hangs in their home. It is of the kindergarteners at

Sandy Hook who lost their lives on the boys' third birthday. Very touching and shows the tenderness that surrounds his Marine heart.

Blessings on all families with parents who make such experiences happen!

ON THE 18ᵀᴴ ANNIVERSARY OF YOUR DEATH

> The mountain you went up decades ago
> rises pink before me in twilight. I can see
> a soft fog swirling. You climbed into night—
> a purple-black fantasia with living stars,
> gold eyes of seraphim set in cosmic skin.
> I hear the mountain calling, "Death will be
> what you saw from the foothills when he left.
> Your climb will be simple, and it will be soon."
>
> Icicles fall from my skin, and flowers bloom
> at the tips of each finger. I find a lamp
> beaming out of my third eye and my feet
> skimming rocks turned soft as pillows. On the other
> side of the sky are valleys filled with children
> we never had and words we never got to say.

WHEN STRIPPED BY FRAILTY

I always loved the Convent practice of once-a-month Silent Sundays and the hours of solitude, reading and reflection they offered. In the Motherhouse years I loved to sit on one of the green garden benches and luxuriate in the exquisite shrubbery and sculptured stone paths. The two fierce Sister-businesswomen who ran our bustling printing press and oversaw these Convent gardens as well were probably nature mystics at heart.

One year Silent Sundays became an agony instead. In the twenty years I spent as a member of the Community, I had, of course, many superiors—some fine educators, organizers, disciplinarians and some like quirky spinster aunts. At least two I consider mystics, highly enlightened beings.

In all that time I had only one superior who met my being like antimatter to matter. On multiple occasions early in our relationship, she accused me of pride when what I was actually experiencing in her presence was almost the opposite. Her disapproval of me seemed so strong at the time that I felt I had almost no right to exist. A near-absolute and irreversible rejection of my very being. Worse yet, she decided to have me come to her office each Silent Sunday to talk to her about my pride.

I was summoned to a cramped, dark, airless room dominated by an ancient wooden desk. A small, desperate discovery saved me. As soon as I sat across from her at that desk, I attached the softest parts of my fingertips beneath it. If I scraped them against the desk's rickety underside to the point of pain, an occasional splinter and blood, I could forget or outmaneuver the greater pain, the intimate cruelty of being there in the first place.

The only specific words I remember from any of these exchanges are hers. "You'll leave the Community too. Intellectuals always do." For her, very bright herself, my mind made me a leper.

After three or four such visits, determined that she would not break me, I left that room thinking, "If I have many more superiors like you, I probably will leave," and never returned to its confines. With no explanation or excuse to her, I simply stopped coming. To her credit—and my immense relief and surprise—she never sought my return. In fact, I think that unprecedented act of insubordination may paradoxically have won me some small respect in her regard.

There are those who thought then—and still think—that I should have felt and expressed rage. I didn't and I don't.

What I did was continue to take advantage of opportunities to mature, to individuate, to face more and more deeply my own shadow side, which certainly contained the pride she saw and the even more debilitating fear and desire to please that she seemed to miss.

The final time I saw her, I was at the Motherhouse for a resplendent celebratory Mass. Because of the crowds, I perched on the front right side of the choir loft where the panoramic view, as always, left me breathless.

After the service, I was swept along in the buzzing multitude to the Chapel stairway. As I reached the second floor, this very woman, shrunken but no less intense, sat in a wheelchair surrounded by many friends, waiting for the elevator ride to the first floor dining rooms.

Although I was by that time married, a mother, co-founder and managing partner of a small business, that familiar but almost forgotten terror welled up along with the desire to turn and run back up the stairs. Then, within myself I felt an instantaneous energy shift—I was no longer who I used to be. In her physical diminishment, if for no other reason, she was no longer who she used to be.

I stood tall and clear—and truly proud—in her presence. From somewhere deep within herself she welcomed what she saw.

A single look of recognition passed between us. I saw her stripped by frailty and she offered herself to be seen. Her bravely unashamed diminishment as well as my growth past an excessive need for approval blessed us, took both of us beyond forgiveness and the need for forgiveness.

Musings from an Eighteen-Wheeler

The life of a trucker is indeed "semi" cloistered, so it leads to miles and hours of reflection. My current pup Chase is almost twelve years old now and has been a true companion through three truck purchases.

Chase took over my newest cab once her name went on the door! I tell everyone she is the owner; I am the operator! What I call my Senior Studio, a place right in the cab where we can sleep, gets a lot of chuckles. The brethren out here on the road often need a smile and some conversation; I'm a sharing spirit. It works.

Pup and I are running the roads and enjoying spring across the US and Canada. Windows on this truck are my lifeline to world passage. In the rig at night, the moon is a welcome love-lamp for direction and reflection. The stars of the desert are endless, and I wonder if they were once the sands... yearning for home.

Rolling west in Nebraska today towards Oregon—Tuesday morning delivery in Portland. My search for Beauty is fulfilled passing miles of Mother Earth each day. Oregon is so rich with cascades of water and endless spruce; it lives in my heart forever. Spring carpeting rolls toward me from every direction; lively lambs and frolicking foals dot the farmscape creating what Angeles Arrien would call a "map of spirituality" totally unique. Beautiful sun and dry roads share today's Blessing.

My current home is near the entrance to Zion National Park. Its gentle Majesty reaches everyone's longing for the silent Presence within. Sharing that Spirit is my favorite pastime.

Our dying classmate Ann is in my thoughts and prayers. Out here on the Interstate I am quite connected to all our classmates and value so much our great contributions to each other's lives.

My years growing in heart and Spirit are the direct result of the Connection established in the Aspirancy! Pictures and thoughts of that precious time continue to drive my search and occasional discovery of the real world of the heart.

I thank all of you for the efforts borne in this book to close the circle from those earliest years to now. The soul of these messages surely speaks to mine, which makes us all true shareholders in the portfolio of love.

Truth be known, I don't get much time to read. That doesn't keep me from absorbing the human content of power born of the Spirit. In the world of transport, passing realities speak loudly from their core hunger for, you guessed it—Connection! It's taken me many years (and miles) to really feel the hunger of the human soul.

Because I don't have much reading time, I very much appreciate quotes sent by others. What a stunning thought of Martin Laird's, for example, that the mountains I look for every day when traveling west are really "looking" for me.

The union of global Spirit-driven love makes even the cobwebs, about which John Chrysostom speaks, a lace draping easy to penetrate. Out here on the road, the so-called space that separates us is a living landscape, however remote, that is wise in our attentive embrace.

As always, I serve you in prayer.

No Easy Exit

As a trucker, I have seen some sex trafficking over the years, more prevalent in the South. The poorest T Stops are usually where you see them. The big ones all have security guards.

In some border places, 11- and 12-year-old girls walk the trucks and try to offer services to those of us parked. About a dozen times I have been able to intervene, always a colorful experience.

American Truckers are required to stop the truck for 30 minutes within or immediately after the first 8 hours of driving, each day. We may choose a truck stop or rest area; occasionally we use a remote exit ramp with a parking area. On one occasion, I chose a numberless exit, somewhat remote with trees and a place to walk the pup. While lifting her back into the cab, I heard a woman's voice, "Go on! Go on!" Turning around I saw a young girl slowly come toward me (about 10 years old) big smile, beautiful face. Her mother (I guess) called out in broken English, "She good for you. She clean truck. She go with you, 100 dollar!"

I shook my head, gave the girl a $20 dollar bill and walked toward the 'mother.' I said, "Not good! Not safe! Take her home! God bless you."

They disappeared into the trees…. I geared up the truck and left, with tears in my eyes.

Parking Perils in the Darkness

At night, with trucks parked close together, there's room to get out with a flashlight, check tires, raise hoods, check oil, and perform the usual safety inspections.

But the darkness holds another dimension.

The long trailers hide women roaming from truck to truck, offering services. Truckers call them *Lot Lizards*. It's an old profession and, when I see them, I worry about the potential abuse and assorted other hardships they endure.

Nothing prepares me for the horror of watching them send a young girl up into a truck while they wait OUTSIDE. On one occasion, the little girl resisted getting into the truck. She was crying. God knows how many times she'd been sent on her 'mission'.

I'd seen enough. I came out of my tractor with phone in hand and walked up to the pair. "The next call I make is to the Police, Lady!"

The woman seemed stunned. I started to dial the phone; she said, "No! Wait! We're leaving!"

Then, to my surprise, two other MALE truckers were running toward us. They scolded the woman and urged her to take the child away from the area. Eventually, I walked back to my truck.

I sat in darkness for a long time. I missed the moon.

SOPHIA HOUSE

After working seven years at a retreat center in Notre Dame, the day came when I knew I could no longer work in a patriarchal institutional setting. I sat down at the typewriter and wrote my resignation. When I handed it to my boss, both he and the secretary were shocked. "Where are you going to go?" Without thought, my answer came, "I'll go back to Milwaukee and start my own center."

And so I did.

Some South Bend friends had a party and sent me off with $600. I tightened my belt and saved money that had been budgeted for daily needs. A friend invited me to stay with her until I found a small apartment, and I began going to homes and Convents to give spiritual direction to those who had kept contact with me through the years. Word spread; calls came in from individuals and sometimes churches. The spiritual directions increased.

After a few experiences speaking to church congregations, I knew I could not, even for one-time events, give presentations to those who were so very immersed in religion of any denomination. I was rapidly moving beyond a religion of dogma and doctrine into a spirituality that knew God as mystery and love.

After about a year and with much support and encouragement from friends, I knew that it was time to move on the earlier intuitive promise I made to myself as I was leaving Notre Dame. In April 1986, Sophia House became incorporated as a non-profit organization. In August of that same year Sophia House opened its first home in a rented neighborhood bungalow where we continued to gather until the landlord sold the house in 1994.

It was time to say who we would be. In a footnote of a book I was reading, I saw the name Sophia, Greek for Wisdom, the feminine presence of the living God. She is a beautiful and power-filled virtue we acquire with devotion and experience. There was no question—we were called to be *Sophia*.

When it was time for business cards, a friend asked, "What is Sophia House?" The same immediate knowing that is now a part of all important decisions of my life spoke: "A place of spiritual awakening and transformation."

Sophia House grew by word of mouth. We were able to pay the rent and utilities and to give me a sufficient stipend.

As we entered into the task of programming, I knew that what we were doing did not center around specific content. Content is only the vehicle.

The primary resource of every program needed to be the individual's own life experience. This truth was echoed during a scripture class when one of the women said, "Sophia House is not a what; it's a who and a where. Sophia House is there and there and there," she said as she pointed around to others in the room.

Some of our beginning and ongoing programs are meditation, scripture, book discussion, recovery and *shen* (a hands-on support for energy flow in the body). For awhile we had Thursday evening at the movies and various one-day workshops.

After the bungalow was sold, our next home was my tiny apartment where we sat on kitchen chairs, one easy chair and a small love seat, knee to knee in a space about twelve feet by twelve feet. We stayed there three years asking the question, "What kind of space do we need for spiritual awakening and transformation?" Together we responded from a place of collective meditation in order to tap the powerful energies of the deeper consciousness. Our programs at this time, some monthly and some weekly, added dream-work and a wellness group for women with cancer. Individual spiritual direction increased. Our mailing list was about fifty.

In 1997 we rented a spacious ranch house built by the School Sisters of St. Francis as a conference center and no longer needed for that purpose. The great room where we now hold our groups could have held my entire previous apartment.

Around 2001, a couple came asking for help in working through some difficulties in their relationship. After a few months, the husband asked me if Sophia House could have a men's group. "If you can get the men, yes." Within the month, the first three men, all of whom had wives affiliated with Sophia House for several years, came to the men's group. Now we have seven men in our group, which meets monthly and twice a year for a day-long retreat. There is also a couples' group that meets monthly.

Along with these programs, we sponsor an annual three-day retreat in Door County for women, several day-long retreats for women from Sophia House, and a journaling group that meets once a month. There are three book discussion groups and three process groups. This past year we introduced programming that allows for days of input to be incorporated into Sophia House teaching. Among these are the Enneagram, Eldering and Mystics.

As we continue to evolve as a community, we expand and deepen our sharing, contemplative practices and awareness of all the layers of the pain body within humanity and our Mother Earth. We become aware, too, of how often we create (or at least magnify) our own pain by dwelling on rather than releasing it and then we hurt others with it.

One powerful way we release our pain is by following our own bodies with as much ease as is true for each person's inner need (spiritual as well as emotional and physical) and learning to live in that Self Love that touches into the deep Self. We don't run away from the outside world but enter deeply into whoever or whatever we relate to in the depths of our own hearts (God, Divine Essence, The Holy One, Sacred Mystery) in which we all reside. We do this work in the company of Jesus and all the Holy Ones who have come before us, following their ancient spiritual steps opening us to transformation and inner peace.

Who we are becoming as we move further into the twenty-first century is reflected in our current mission statement:

> *In our fragmented and fear-filled world,*
> *we at Sophia House choose as our mission*
> *to grow in disciplined commitment to the awareness:*
>
> *That understanding and compassion*
> *are stronger than fear and hate*
>
> *That we allow the suffering of the world*
> *to touch and transform us*
>
> *That we seek to live our daily lives as co-creators*
> *manifesting the love that is God*
>
> *That to be fully human*
> *is to live within sacred mystery.*

IN THIS FEW GRAMS OF EMBRYO

Tonight, as on many recent nights before closing down my computer, I gaze into the mystery of our next grandchild shown on a nine-week ultrasound and feel I am peering into the vastness of the universe itself. My sense of time, space, life and all being shifts. In this few grams of embryo, about the weight of three paper clips, I feel my intimate yet infinitesimal connection with the entire sweep of creation, history and evolution in its billions-of-years of unfolding.

The experience of becoming a grandmother is having a profound and quite unexpected effect on me. Part of it involves a deepened sense of what I wish all birth could mean to the world.

Is not each birth divine in its miracle and its mystery?

Does not every child born on this planet deserve gifts from angels, common people and wise ones?

Recently, serendipitously, I stumbled upon a quote from David Whyte. "An ancient, much visited, but unverifiable human intuition says that we dwell not only in what seems like the immediate present but equally in a past peopled by those who have made us and a future for which our present seems to be but a slow preparation. In the very young child's face we have a sense, despite our daylight logic, of the unknown world from which they have come."

I believe the same can be said of the natural face after death. In the untouched-up face of one just dead we have a sense, despite our puny daylight logic, of the unknown world to which they have gone. That was certainly my experience of my mother's face in death. Craggy. Depleted. Exuding exquisite beauty and peace. These greatest of human events—birth and death—offer us portals into awe and mystery.

This year for some reason I was more struck than ever by the words of old Christmas carols, particularly this line: "While mortals sleep, the angels keep/ Their watch of wondering love…" In light of much of what is sadly dismissed as 'new age' writing, these words have unexpected implications and progressively deeper meaning. They seem to call us as a race to commit ourselves more powerfully to awakened consciousness. That is certainly the task to which I pledge myself, both in honor of and imitation of the great women, the grandmothers as well as all the sisters, in my life.

I welcome the expanse of such a view as many of us 57s, both current and former members, face the reality that the SSSF Community in the form we knew, entered and love may soon pass into history. After one recent phone conversation about its diminishment, in deep grief at such loss, I stared into space and heard/saw the words pass in front of me like a banner: *Cry, the Beloved Community.*

How much like death Bismarck's *Kulturkampf* must have felt to religious communities of that day. As a result, a small community of ten women was among those to whom the Archbishop of Freiburg in 1873 issued a directive containing three options: return to your families, continue teaching as laywomen or emigrate. Three of these ten, our own Mother Alexia, Mother Alfons, and Sister Clara, ultimately came to America to found a new community out of the ashes of the old. Out of such seeming death came almost a century and a half of life for thousands of women like ourselves.

Today many religious communities, in their declining numbers and rising median ages, face another form of death, one awaiting only the ability to see it as trans-*form*-ation. Recently I read an interview with a visionary Franciscan Sister possibly two decades younger than ourselves, Ilia Delio's "Seeing Christianity as a Religion of Evolution and the Implications for Religious Life." Here is hope. Here is challenge. Here is a future emerging from what looks and feels like death. She asks, "To what are we being attracted? What are the new unions forming in our lives? What are the greater wholes we are moving into?"

For years, some of us 57s have asked: "What, for young women today, could ever take the place of what we received as mere girls?" We would never wish to duplicate all aspects of our experience, of course. At the same time, we long for the emergence of new communities of seekers, places where young women can live and grow, have meaningful contact with strong women models on a regular basis—artists, mystics, activists, futurists, evolutionaries—as these younger visionaries ready themselves to take their places among committed women and men in a future we cannot yet even imagine.

May this tiny child—girl or boy—be blessed, as I was, to meet mentors, guides, inspirations along the path of life. May s/he carry forward the passionate dream of a grandmother's life.

PENTECOST GIFTING

This morning, Pentecost, my favorite feast of the year, I went to the Motherhouse for Mass. I had high expectations for the Spirit's working in me. My expectations were exceeded by the presence of my Sisters—so rich, so different from what I thought I wanted.

I sat in the chapel waiting for the Mass to begin, watching some Sisters with their walkers and rounded backs, others hanging onto the pews. These women who had taught me. Some I had idolized. Some I had judged in the past. Now, all that judgment gone, I watched as they took their places to pray.

Suddenly Pentecost in all of its promise was here. Each Sister present to pray in her own language, with her own fears, longings and personal relationship to The Presence. Each of us together became One. "This is my Body."

I've always loved this chapel; it was my safe place because God was here even in my times of No God. The space of the chapel oozes the lives of all the Sisters who ever sat here praying and yearning for their God.

This is a sacred space of the Eternal Luminous—made so by the intention of our Foundress, Mother Alfons, who oversaw the workmanship daily, creating the space worthy of the Holy. And made so by all those who've prayed here in their weeping and their profound joy—just as I. Though we have become many fewer over the years, my communion with my Sisters and our 140-plus year history continues to deepen—Pentecost gifting.

A Soft Day

It is a rainy summer afternoon. The Irish would call it a soft day. A gentle peacefulness hovers over the house. The aroma of the Sunday roast wafts from the kitchen into the den. The sounds of the Yankees-Red Sox game emanate from the TV in the corner. Our beautiful six-year-old granddaughter sings softly to her dolls and stuffed animals as she carefully places each one on the rug, forming a pretend circus parade. Her dad, our son, crouches his six-foot frame beside her, playfully assuming the voices of the various animals. In spite of the struggles and sadness of a difficult and painful divorce, the relationship of father and daughter remains strong and tender.

On the couch our daughter is nestled beside her husband. They are intently focused on the ball game, cheering and jeering in unison. Their love is evident, solid and strong. Both have met the challenges of mild developmental disabilities to find each other, marry, and build a beautiful and independent life together.

My husband is busy organizing materials gathered from his recent class trip to Italy. He will use them in his lesson plans for the coming year. A former Christian Brother, he has retired as an education and mental health administrator to find his bliss as a high school Latin teacher. For over forty-one years his love and encouragement have been my constant companions during my faith journey. He has always been at my side soothing my fears and encouraging me to open my heart to all of life's wondrous possibilities.

I sit here knitting the final skein of purple wool for a prayer shawl for a dear friend's grandchild who is very ill. I have found a ministry in the prayer shawl group of a small, caring, and Spirit-driven Episcopal community. This church has embraced me and my family and is our faith home. I find serenity in the sound of the clicking needles, a prayer of healing and a prayer of love woven into each stitch. So blessed has been my life.

I know the twelve years I spent as a School Sister of St. Francis have contributed mightily to the tranquility of this moment. Those great women—mentors, teachers, and friends—formed in me an openness to life, a joy in simplicity, a love and a belief in the basic goodness and worth of all people. This gift of the Franciscan spirit accompanied me in the South Bronx as I worked with families torn by the devastation of poverty and addiction. It was at the core of every lesson I taught to inmates learning the very basics of literacy and parenting in New York State correctional facilities. It prepared my heart to enjoy the blessing of so many women's friendships formed over the years.

So I sit here and smile, as I recall that evening last week, when our son, all dressed up to go out for the night, informed us that he had met a beautiful, caring and accomplished young lady. As he dashed out the front door, he turned and, with a devilish twinkle in his eye, smiled and said, "Oh, by the way, Mom, her mother used to be a Nun."

LOOKING FORWARD INTO DIMINISHMENT AND LEGACY

Recently I was talking with a dozen or so other SSSFs about Leadership because we would be electing our Community's Generalate leaders. Instead of talking about our way of life dying and our median age, someone said simply, "This is the time of diminishment."

As we writers are reaching the end of our stories, our book and the latter part of our lives—this *"last of life for which the first was made"*—we know we are not finished. We know, that though the religious life of women as it has been known is diminishing, we have the responsibility of leaving a legacy. A legacy that will provide rich soil for those who come after. A legacy that will meet the Evolutionary call of the day—that we, as a human species, one with "the One," co-create lives of consciousness and communion where all sentient being can thrive. We know we must continue deepening our faith in sacred mystery.

"Unless the grain of wheat fall into the ground and die, it will not live."

Today and into the future, there are and will always be young women seekers, creative and courageous innovators with vision for their future. Let us, in our seventh and eighth decades, dare to ask questions for a future that will involve them. How do we grow beyond what has been in order to leave the rich soil of transformation and evolving spirit presence for those who come after us in whatever communal or institutional forms their vision will take? How can the very way in which we live our diminishment inspire them to flourish?

I Buy Unopened Iris

I buy unopened iris
at the market.
Near my patio window
lizards bask—
those silent watchers.
I am waiting too.

I cut the stems
and set the flowers in a vase.
Water, warmed and sugared,
pulls the petals open.

Old now,
I do mostly quiet work
like this:
I'm called to witness
the opening of iris.

Companionship affirms:
without the need to forge ahead,
solve problems, worry about
the end of the world,
my steady gaze
will help the iris open—
and that's enough.

Chapter 10
Later Life Glimpses of the Sacred

Song for the Dying

A friend asked me to be part of her preparation for hospice work by simulating the breath of a dying person while she sang.

After receiving my instructions, I entered into the process. I found myself letting go of self-consciousness a breath at a time. My friend began to sing. Her task was to match the rhythm of her singing to my breathing.

She sang spirituals of various religions. My breath deepened beyond my will power. In and out, in and out. The vibration was filling my cells. Tears gathered in the corners of my eyes and soon overflowed. We continued. My life was in me without thought from very young until the present. My life with God filled me. Different belief systems flooded through me. But they were not many; they were one.

There was no thought—only awareness. The Oneness was the connection—a reaching, a searching for the Beyond. Form did not matter, the Beyond is always there and we are One. No separation, no contradiction. All is unified. All is One.

Dread Evaporates in Tenderness

All through my years since I was twelve, I've lived with an inside visitor, existential fear, that comes and goes. I didn't know its name, only its paralysis in my body and my mind. I named this the no-God-space. I lived the contradiction of fighting against and accepting this space in the name of being holy. Over fifty years have passed and paradigms have shifted rapidly. Being holy has become being whole. Surrender is not giving up but choosing life as it comes to me.

Over years of practice and search, this seeming enemy revealed itself as a friend. In the morning when I would wake and feel the dread of another day, I came to know I had a choice that was only a breath away. The breath, together with hands on my heart, evaporated dread into tenderness. When paralysis cut off feeling, I learned the vulnerability of relaxing into openness. I loosened my jaw, softened my forehead and allowed beauty to enter me. Even to this day, when feeling shame and no voice or what I previously judged as the wrong voice, I expand myself to feel and join all women who are suffering shame at this very moment. I am released and at one with them.

Now my no-God-space is simply and wonderfully the invitation to go beyond the limitation of present consciousness and enter into the vastness of mystery where there are no answers, only questions and possibility. I welcome this space because it truly belongs to me. It is the reason I came to Milwaukee—to learn to live a life of choice and creativity and move beyond the old limits and fear-based existence. This space has become the familiar friend and foundation of my journey. It has virtue now because it is my own.

APPROACHING PRAYER

> Cool morning air.
> Bars of salmon-violet cloud.
> It begins again:
>
> silence holding the fullness of the heart,
> melting and reforming like clouds.
>
> My hands move over my knees.
> Hands know something.
> They are writing something
> my soul has dictated to my skin:
>
> each of us is an earth
> with a single bird to fly around it,
> and the birdsong is a call,

"Where are you, dear heart,
dear heart,
dear heart?
My sorrow breaks the air.
Its shattered pieces pierce like glass,
pass through me as I fly.
Where are you, dear heart,
dear heart,
dear heart?"

In a place where sorrows
fall away like shining
nourishing rain.

Every morning
I am light enough to stand on lilies,
and by afternoon
I can move out into perfumed air

taught by the young hawk
who rises to her calling,
knowing air has subtle forces
real as rock,
and the nest will be there
when it's time for sleep,
and sleep itself
is another kind of soaring.

Entering a Space Very Different

As I reflect on these seventy-two years of my life, I have come to realize there is a hidden thread weaving a tapestry that one does not see as one awakens and moves through each day. Only in retrospect have I come to understand how a Loving Presence has pushed and hounded me into taking various steps throughout my life. Particular events are unimportant because those are unique for each of us. The experiences of pain, disillusionment, and joy provided the hues that made my life challenging and exciting.

I discovered that each major phase of life has been characterized by one or two major values that in some sense were my god(s) at that time in my life, i.e., those values were the principal driving force that governed that stage of my life. I am aware of a time during which I thought that I knew the questions and had the answers of an either/or nature. Then I realized that such a perspective is incomplete and biased.

Gradually, through living and ministering in various cultures, including war-ravaged countries, my heart was cracked open and I came to understand the Jesus of the Gospel in a deeper way. Everything is included in the two approaches of Jesus—an open inclusiveness towards others and the need for forgiveness, reconciliation within myself and with others. All of which is easier said than done. I learned that walking with the poor and needy helped me to begin to understand life from their perspective. And I came to believe that only by accompanying someone in real need does one develop a passion to do something about that need and to participate in movements to build a more just and caring society.

Today I am at another juncture in my life and perhaps beginning to pass through yet another doorway, entering a space very different from all that has gone before. Using an image shared with me recently, I feel as if someone grabbed me from inside my big toe, yanked on it, and turned me completely inside out, as one does with a stocking. Previous frames of reference, reasons for action, explanations of reality are incomplete for me. I know only that I am a vulnerable, fragile human being who is held in existence by a Loving Creative Presence, that I can only interact in the present moment to what is before me, and that I am called to be of loving service to victims of violence in one of the most violent cities of the world, Cd. Juárez, Mexico.

Deep within, it feels as if all of my previous life experiences have taught me something that assists me to live in this current reality. Here in Juarez I try to be simply present and extend my hand in compassion and support in whatever way is asked of me. Most often that means I offer psychological support to victims of violence and their families. I also provide relaxation treatments/stress reduction experiences to the staff and patients with whom I walk. Hopefully, a Loving God is experienced through my limited efforts, in spite of myself.

After the Opening
Fear of the Lord is the beginning of wisdom.
—Proverbs 9:10

I do not fear the moment when the door
clicks open. Years ago I heard that sound
and watched beloved souls fly through and hoped
their journey home came gently. What I fear
lies Clear beyond all clarity. Deep beyond
all depth: Pool of Bottomless Being.

Can my soul survive what it desires—
a Longing bigger than its own? I struggle
to keep my skin while mere anticipation
burns it off. Light bends me. Knees and forehead
arc to earth. A living silence covers me.
When it lifts, my fear has turned to Light
and Light to joy.

The Physicist in Me

The physicist in me knows and experiences God as energy. Even as a young child my interests have always been in science as experienced in nature. Is it any wonder that I know God as energy?

I hardly ever nap during the day, but I fell asleep on the couch one afternoon. I dreamt that I was on a couch in the middle of Highway 4 at the end of our driveway, and a bolt of lightning came from the electric wires right into me. I woke up with my hands and feet tingling and was about to explode with the energy that filled my body.

To my amazement, the next time I drove the one-third mile to the end of our driveway, I saw electric wires crossing the highway exactly where they had been in my dream. I had never consciously seen them before.

After that dream, I became much more aware of the energies that surround me—energy from people and nature or even energy entering me if I held my hands out, facing upward.

I've noticed that I can feel the energies coming from people in the same way babies seem to sense the goodness in people. If I am with a group of people I don't know, I'm drawn to a particular person and I find we have similar interests or goals.

My life experience is one of energy. God's energy in flowers, nature, or people. When I see a flower, it captures me in its colors. The colors draw me into the flower. We become one. I can no longer tell if I'm part of it or it is part of me.

That sense brings calmness and peace to me. I guess that is where I really feel a oneness with God. God is the energy in that flower and in me. I feel that God is pure energy, the source of all energy, and that everything is connected through energy. Everything is one. Everything is part of God.

I become one with what I am photographing. When I lose track of time it is because I have merged with the experience. Though I have been taking pictures for several hours, even a day, it seems like an hour.

The beautiful life energy I feel burning in my hands as I hold them open tells me that God's energy is present in my life.

I Came to Milwaukee

While driving from Iowa into Wisconsin, I stopped at a wayside overlooking the Mississippi River. This drive and the stop nudged me into questions about why I had entered the SSSF Community some thirty years before. In my journal I wrote:

I came to Milwaukee because I want to be united with God.

I realized these are the very words I had written to Mother Corona on my application to enter the convent. Then I continued to write about those important aspects of my life that would not be if I had not come to Milwaukee:

I came to Milwaukee to meet my lifelong friend, Diane.

I came to Milwaukee to pray in St. Joseph Chapel and Adoration Chapel.

I came to Milwaukee to hear beautiful music and to live with lovely artwork around me.

I came to Milwaukee to teach fourth, fifth and seventh graders about God and poetry.

I came to Milwaukee to meet two priests and a monk who is a mystic.

I came to Milwaukee to learn about opera and to love the soprano and the mezzo soprano whose voices rise above the orchestra.

I came to Milwaukee to learn to pray beyond the routines of time and books.

I came to Milwaukee to meet Raymond A. Parr, theologian, teacher and friend.

I came to Milwaukee to learn that there is no separation between God and humanity.

Now, nearly twenty-five years later, these truths are bearing fruit beyond the expectations of my youth.

I came to Milwaukee to learn that we, as a species, are becoming the Divine Presence we had projected onto the image of a superhuman man.

I came to Milwaukee to grow into the loving Presence of the Divine in all humanity.

I came to Milwaukee to learn that when I am not connected to myself and to life I cannot feel, see, touch or even believe in a living God.

I came to Milwaukee to experience the words of my teachers, "When you find yourself, you will find God."

I came to Milwaukee to found and foster Sophia House.

I came to Milwaukee to find my soul.

I came to Milwaukee to meet the challenge of interior demons and the acceptance of interior angels.

I came to Milwaukee to find my voice.

I came to Milwaukee to learn of evolution and the unified field that carries both science and spirituality.

I came to Milwaukee to learn that life is my teacher.

I came to Milwaukee to be at the deathbed of my lifelong friend, Diane, and pray her into the Heart of Love.

I came to Milwaukee and stay in Milwaukee to be united with God.

UNBROKEN SPIRAL OF GRACE

In addition to our shared outer experience, each of us Convent classmates has her own more intimate and hidden history. I can trace part of mine through books. Of the thousands of books I have loved between that first book of awakening—Caryll Houselander's *The Reed of God*, read at age fourteen—and now, these few here form an unbroken spiral of grace upon which I can trace the great loneliness of outgrowing one stage of awareness as well as the ongoing opening up and emptying out of my soul.

I returned to Houselander's lines each Advent for at least the next twenty years. I touch now a copy and finger remembered and cherished lines—"The pre-Advent emptiness of Our Lady's purposeful virginity," emptiness like the hollow in a reed, in a cup, in a nest.

Caryll describes as well an opposite emptiness in those who "have no sense of being related to any abiding beauty, to any indestructible life: they are afraid to be alone with their unrelated hearts." That rootless sense of emptiness bears little relation to the emptiness she describes as "that still, shadowless ring of light round which our being is circled."

Caryll would possibly not recognize the places her words have taken me, that weightless chain of grace begun by the power of her understanding of emptiness. Gradually, decade by decade, came further inner knowings, conversations, homilies, retreats, books, CDs and DVDs that expanded my experience of the fullness offered only by that virginal quality of openness to evolutionary emptiness:

> *The Cloud of Unknowing* by an anonymous fourteenth century English mystic,
> *Silent Music* by William Johnston,
> *Contemplation: Liberating the Ghost of the Church, Churching the Ghost of Liberation* by James Carroll,
> *At a Journal Workshop/The Practice of Process Meditation* by Ira Progoff,
> Eckhart Tolle's entire body of work—books, CDs and DVDs,
> *Journey of Souls* and *Destiny of Souls* by Michael Newton,
> Pema Chodron's entire body of work—books, CDs and DVDs,
> *Starseed Transmissions* and *The Third Millennium* by Ken Carey,
> Neil Douglas-Klotz's entire body of work—Books, CDs and DVDs,
> *The Wisdom Jesus* and *The Meaning of Mary Magdalene* by Cynthia Bourgeault,
> *Radical Amazement* and *Field of Compassion* by Judy Cannato,

Barbara Marx Hubbard's and Ilia Delio's entire bodies of work—books,
   CDs and DVDs,
My Bright Abyss by Christian Wiman,
The Grace in Dying and *The Grace in Aging* by Kathleen Dowling Singh,
Ancestral Grace: Meeting God in Our Human Story and the ongoing vision
   of Diarmuid O'Murchu.

I enter and re-enter the emptiness these pieces offer and, as I do so, their
advent-like emptiness, that greatest of all transformative gifts, enters me.

THE TONGLEN OF AWARENESS

Over the years, especially in the teachings of Pema Chodron on *Tonglen*,
I've come to recognize my soul's affinity to Buddhist practices. The word
itself is Tibetan for sending and receiving, a prayer form of breathing in,
receiving or accepting (Len) the sufferings of self and others and breathing
out (Tong) healing love and compassion. Pema describes it as "a gentle, step-
by-step process of opening the heart" that has deep, counterintuitive results.
"By embracing, rather than rejecting" what seems negative, "we overcome
fear and develop greater empathy." It is a simple practice that can be done
anywhere.

This past Sunday I had an experience that broadened my experience of
Tonglen even further. Late that afternoon I had to get some groceries. Here in
the sweltering South, many businesses hire people to stand on street corners
waving signs and wearing sandwich boards to attract customers from the
flow of traffic. Many in airless costumes and headpieces. From Jan. 1-April
15, for example, tax preparers advertise with people dressed as the Statue of
Liberty. Others year round are in rubber-headed animal costumes.

That afternoon, on her regular corner, I saw a middle-aged mulatto or
Hispanic woman walking back and forth waving her sign. Three worded-
feelings leapt out of me in quick succession: *I pray for you, I love you, I am
you.* Our identification was so total inside me that I wondered if there is such
a thing as the Tonglen of Awareness or Conscious Identification—Breathe in
the radical unity of all beings. Hold, experience and expand it within. Breathe
that enlarged sense of unity back out again to further energetic horizons and
deeper *real*-ization in our world.

ALL THESE YEARS I'VE PRAYED

All these years
I've slept,
waking sometimes
for a millisecond
to see
the blue heron
        stand on one leg
or the Harley
        on the kick stand.

All these years
I've prayed
for sight
for sleeplessness
so the bat
flying in the door
at dusk
is no stranger
but a welcome bedmate.

All these years
I've prayed,
and now the sleeplessness
and the blue heron
above the pond
        welcome the bat
who skims the skein of light
        dropping over the water.

And the water
        drops over me
as the air says,
        holy, holy, holy.

The red fox
      fights the wild turkey
while the cat
      mews from a window.
When the earth's shadow
      eclipses the moon,
the dark pond
      turns black,
the turkey feathers
      hold water and sink.

There the pond
      says glory,
the light
      sings hail,
while the bushes
      whisper hush.

FULL CIRCLE

In a strange way, my life has come full circle. Now, in a retirement community of about four hundred others, I am again in a vibrant, life-giving, supportive community. Here, on an almost daily basis, I can find the intellectual stimulation that I found in the Convent. There I lived with college professors, musicians, artists, innovative teachers, writers, mystics, composers, chefs, linguists, nurses, hospital administrators—those deeply perceptive, fascinating Nuns. How I missed their inspiration and support when I left!

Full circle. Now in our retirement community affiliated with a university, my husband and I live with retired university professors, attorneys, medical professionals, successful business people, musicians, artists, etc., who add to the good of the community. In a sense we are united in a common bond—to live the rest of our lives as best we can and to die with grace and peace. Here again can be found daily inspiration and support. The words of de Chardin in his *Christianity and Evolution* give me peace. I embrace his statement: "Now adoration means the giving of our body and soul to creative activity, joining that activity to God to bring the world to fulfillment by effort and intellectual exploration."

I find myself creating as a kind of meditation. I am happy, I am home as best it can be here. In a way, I have returned to the Convent, a truth hard for my friends to understand.

If you ask about my religion now, I will say only that beyond the strictures of organized religion lies the Source. My husband will tell you of my years of doubt, of emptiness. But as I reach into these elder years, older in body and still searching, I'm reaching beyond *nothing* to the powerful, creative energy of *All*. There, can be, finally, a relaxation, a letting go, a peace in *That Which Is* beyond all understanding.

MOMENT OF MY FREEDOM

While working on this book, I wrote to a classmate: "I am a living bundle of questions around a core of hope and a sense of the sacred everywhere." She responded with surprise that she had always considered me as someone living with serenity and certainty.

Almost immediately a realization flashed: My serenity comes precisely from having been relieved at a very young age of the burden of needing certainty. Serenity, yes. A gift from my father. Certainty, no. I felt no need of it and to this day am largely unable to take literal certainty seriously.

I was four or five when the burden of needing certainty was lifted. My childhood understanding of heaven involved being able to do what you wanted all day every day. At that time, such a heaven for me meant picking blackberries with my grandparents.

One fateful day it occurred to me that perhaps that was not what my grandparents would want. Anguish seized me—*How could we all be happy forever with possibly different wishes for our heavens?*

That was the moment of my freedom. It happened so young I hadn't yet built up much of a residue of needing to believe at face value all I was told. The experience taught me to hear almost everything as a story. Nuanced. Well-intentioned. Aiming at something far beyond itself. In reality, my introduction to metaphor. Levels and layers of truth and meaning.

The girl who entered the Convent a decade later was that girl—far removed from needing any doctrines and dogmas to be literally true. Content to be living in a parallel universe, as it were. Largely unaware that many others throughout history and right around me staked their lives on and promised their lives to literal truths I regarded as symbolic.

My years in Central America solidified that uncertainty aspect of my interior life. They called into question all manner of presuppositions resulting from the cultural and religious isolation and ignorance of living in the United States. Questions and healthy doubt became the lifetime allies and teachers I still cherish.

Today my questions are deeper than ever. Riskier. More poignant. Fed by ongoing scientific research and near-relentless human violence and greed. Through it all and beneath it all, I still sense that core of hope and of the sacred flaming out.

Silent Remembrance

Through the long, thick darkness
tongue reaches into the heart's hollow:
prayer-words usually lie there,
like sleeping fish in a pond.

Tongue comes up dry
as tearless eyes that turn
to the terrible place where God would be
if I could see God.

So I sink myself
down among lotus roots,
wordless as a sleeping fish,
eyes locked in prayer.

Suddenly There Was Hope!

It was a cold, gray winter Sunday afternoon in Albany, New York. I had just heard a two-hour talk given by former Maryknoll priest, Roy Bourgeois, who was expelled from his religious order and excommunicated from the Roman Catholic Church because of his support of the ordination of women priests. His talk was eloquent and deeply moving. The standing-room-only audience was filled with supporters, whose questions and comments appeared saturated in a cloud of hopelessness and despair. There was little doubt that the attendees shared a deep and tender love of their church, but we were saddened and confused by the failure of the church to allow even the discussion of women's ordination. We were angered by the disrespect and poor treatment experienced by our beloved American Nuns at the hands of the Catholic hierarchy. We felt that, for the most part, the American bishops had lost touch with the community of the faithful. Churches were closing at alarming rates, and so many young people felt that the church was no longer relevant in today's world. We felt a longing in our hearts for a spirit of renewal and love. We sang and prayed for it.

After the meeting, during my ride back home, I experienced a deep feeling of loss, almost a kind of mourning. As a young Franciscan Sister in the 60s, I had been driven by the challenges of renewal inspired by Vatican II. The church seemed alive and vital. We were encouraged to embrace all of God's creation with love and tenderness. Compassion and kindness became our standards. Even though I chose to leave the Franciscan Sisters, the gifts of love and compassion, a part of my life with those wonderful women, never left me. But where was the Church of Vatican II today? The American church seemed obsessed with abortion, homosexuality, suppression of nuns, and covering up their own responsibility for the sexual abuse of innocent children. There was no hope! The gray winter continued.

Several weeks later, I was stunned by the news of Pope Benedict's resignation. I must admit, I really didn't think that even with a new Pope much was going to change.

I watched the ritual of the election of a new Pope on television with casual interest. Then the commentator announced. "He has chosen the name Francis." At that very moment, seeing that simple, humble man emerge and stand there before the crowd, asking their blessing, I knew without any doubt that something really wonderful was happening.

"All will be well." My eyes welled up with tears of joy. Suddenly there was hope!

LETTING GO IS NO EASY JOURNEY

Ask Merton
Ask Siddhartha
Ask all of us comedians
Trying to live a life of
  Simplicity
  Solitude
  Silence

That is
Ask any God-seeking hermit
  Empty-headed
  Mindful
  Blind visionary
On a cruise through time on earth
  Exploding new disguises
  Birthing with Immense Creation
    Without knowing
What to learn
  While flowers bloom and go to seed
  Friends depart and go their way
    And change never stops
      Except to say

The journey is now
  This moment
    For Love.

LASER-LIKE BEAM OF IMMENSE POWER

Some years ago I read A. H. Almaas's description of a real relationship as "an evolution of two waves of consciousness … interweaving as one field of consciousness, shifting form through the exchange." It seems a wonderful description of the Unified Field, what Almaas describes as the "relational field as a living medium." More and more it seems to me that relational living of any kind can evolve into such a medium. This morning, for example, in a garden spot at Church I stroked a plant leaf and it felt for all the world like the *skin of God.*

Recently I experience more and more often spontaneous outpourings of uncontainable, uncontrollable, undifferentiated love. I drive in a car and find myself repeating, "I love you, I love you, I love you" out through the raindrops on the windshield. I stand at the kitchen sink emitting love to the late afternoon light as it suffuses the room. The *YOU* I love is totally mysterious and totally real, without form and all form. Enormous and infinitesimal. Intimate yet impersonal because so far beyond all we know or experience of personhood.

At times the force of this love energy coagulates or condenses into a laser-like beam of immense power that I sense can be directed toward a specific receiver. There is much more to learn about what this beam can do or wants to do. I am grateful to be alive to learn more.

HONEYPRAYER

> If air could be honey,
> but still breathe-able,
> I'd say
> I'm living in air.
> Divinity so thick around me
> and sweet.

I ALSO AM CLAY

The pain, the fear, all my fumbling and mistake-making come from participation in the work of God-the-Maker, *Al-Musawir.*

Ecstasy-without-Making is like the gift of sleep. Making—that is the goal of Life-in-the-World. All the effort and fumbling involved is the stuff of creation.

That's why Living-for-Ecstasy is a child's attitude. A mature artist lives for the work. Such an artist—say, a potter—in her struggle to make something of the clay, develops a clearer and clearer understanding of her materials—of the clay and the wheel and the relationship between them. And her relationship with both of them. She develops that understanding both in her mind and in the cells of her whole body, especially the fingers. And with that understanding comes greater and greater love—of the clay and the process and her artist self.

So that, as the years go by, she becomes a bigger and bigger person.

And of course, she keeps producing artifacts that increase the beauty of the world.

And one day she says to herself: *Ah, I also am clay in the Hands of Al-Musawir, the Great Fashioner.*

I said that today.

MY HOURGLASS OF LIFE:
THREE RUNNINGS

i

i was born
  & then
i was born…
  & then
i wandered from my birth
  & then
i reclaimed my life
i own myself
i am myself

ii

I was born & then
I cried & then
I learned that crying is not all & then
I learned that other people cry and that I could do
    nothing to relieve the pain & then
I bore someone else's pain and that was like
    bearing a baby and then

She died & then
I died with her and in longing for her & then
All is silence for a while, silent aching for longer than I
    expected & then
I am here with silent crying on the inside of my skin.

iii

i was born and then...
the stars sang and then...
it pierced, it punctured, it rent asunder and then...
i saw that its name was the overarching agony of love,
    the passion to union through wholeness and then...
it pleaded over and over again: "be me, in disguise" and
    then...
i did and then...
i longed to know "are we any closer on this darkling star?"
    and then...
i felt the warmth of a single star swirl within my heart chakra
    as a response:

"Continue on. You will know.
Remember the real message of those itchy ashes of your
    childhood:
'*Stardust* thou art and unto *stardust* thou shalt return.'
You come from the stars.
You are destined to return to the stars.
All being shares that same destiny."

Now/Thou

"Your now is just so much larger than mine."

These words resonated deep inside me during an otherwise unmemorable conversation shortly after my fiftieth birthday. I sensed their importance years before I understood them.

In the many years since then, influenced greatly by Eckhart Tolle's work, I have come to understand the pulsating power of now. I continue to meet more and more people with radiating now presence, whose now expands to include progressively and simultaneously all that is, was or will ever be—the deep time of dimensions, galaxies, quarks, black holes and antimatter, futures and pasts, parallel universes. Among the multiple enviable traits I've observed in such people is their ability to live freer of the constraints of the daily mini-dramas and story lines of life.

As my commitment to living in such a Now increases, it is becoming clear to me that, just as a person's Now can expand, so too can her sense of Thou. With awareness and disciplined practice, it seems increasingly possible to enter into dialogic relationship with all that exists. To cultivate with all being an intimacy of luminous joy.

A woman I knew for only two short months taught me an initial lesson in expanded Thou-ness. In my early thirties I participated in a disaster relief mission. This woman, survivor of a holocaust concentration camp, was part of the same field team. When it came time to apply bug spray to protect the sick and wounded children in our care, this woman had to leave the compound. She was incapable of killing even an insect.

Much as I admired her sensitivity, I did not share it viscerally at that time. Today, although I still swat mosquitoes and kill cockroaches, I feel the life force that I am altering in ways I never have before. I pause to ask forgiveness of the small being I harm.

Recently, more and more as I touch paper, I feel within it the life a tree surrendered. Napkins and loose-leaf pages become diaphanous Thous.

As a girl of ten or so I used to wonder intently what event would mark the end of the world. One day an answer arose within me: *When everything in the world has at one time lived as part of a human body.* Such a possibility, though immensely intriguing, left me with another overwhelming question: *How would it ever be possible for the matter in a mountain to pass some of its time as human?*

As is true of so many long-forgotten childhood intimations, this one contains a kernel of great wisdom. Those early whisperings become the life metaphors we are given to ponder and enlarge as we age. They are the great shape-shifting teachers within our lives.

How might I respond today to that youthful question about the mountains becoming human? With a prayer-longing for the rest of my life:

With St. Francis and his Sister Moon and Brother Sun,
with all my personal beloveds,
with all the great ones living, dead and to come,
I ask for the eyes to see all time as present,
as a Now,
to see all being as alive,
as a Thou,
as equally valuable to the universe
and whatever future lies before us on this planet we share.

I ask within the unseen mystery:

Is my Now large enough?

In the beginning
in which we are
and that which we are,
In deep time
in which we live and move and have our being,
In kairos time,
In liminal time
that we enter each Now,
Sacred Mystery,
the Holy One who was, who is and who is to come,
(and who—shatteringly—we are)
is creating the heavens and the earth,
is sustaining all life and all death,
all resurrection
and all blowing of multi-languaged wind.

Come, let us worship.
Bending toward our beginnings,
come all being as the One Being,
come, let us worship.

Is my Thou large enough?
Am I large enough to accept
the reality of my co-being within the One Now/Thou?
All is metaphor.
All is approximation.
Eye hath not seen...
nor can words express.
But within the marrow of our bones and the fiber of our lives,
may we continue to open
and let the cosmic shining-through do the rest.

RELATIONSHIP WITH JESUS

After retirement my life became quieter and for the first time in years I had minutes/hours to pray and contemplate. Through the years my relationship with Jesus has grown from doing things for Jesus, to allowing Jesus to work through me as He wills. In the beginning, I hoped Jesus was pleased with my life and efforts to work for His people.

Gradually, I began to have a running conversation with Jesus about everything happening in my life. Slowly I began to realize that I was praying, and the intimate relationship with Jesus I longed for was beginning. Hopefully by the time I die, my life with Jesus will transcend all other needs. For now, my arms reach around Jesus as I take refuge in His embrace.

> O Burning Love,
> O heart on fire,
> You call me Beloved,
> And I call you
> My God.

THE ATHEIST AND THE BELIEVER

Increasingly, especially with the death of Christopher Hitchens, I have been venturing into the inner world and writings of atheists and finding powerful and painful resonance. To such an extent that I now wonder if one can ever be a believer who could not be an atheist.

For me it is only in accepting at deep levels the atheist rationale that I am coming to know where my faith lies. The atheism in me is completely rational. The faith in me lives in my bones and cells. Intellectually I am more than comfortable with the possibility of no god and nothing after death.

Nothing within me, however, experiences such a nihilistic future as a reality. When I visualize my own death, I feel expanded rather than obliterated, inserted into a universe of unimaginable—even if not personal—grandeur. That universe answers to no creed or dogma or absence thereof. It is its own reason for existence.

OFFERING

My gaze rests on that great pine tree
That blew down in the storm
Last November
And is spawled out before me,
Face down
Limbs stretching forward
In a deep bow
Now fully laden with snow
Enlarging its form to greater proportions than ever,
Transforming into a whole, new
Offering of Love.

AFTER WIDOWHOOD

Widowhood—twenty years of it. Twenty years of grieving, searching, reinventing myself in solitude. Circling back into the silence I learned to appreciate because of my years at St. Joseph Convent.

Nothing much else is possible, after all. And it's satisfying enough—a life rich with friends, books, and a bit of the teaching I love to do.

But wait—what is this? Who is this! A new love taking deep root during my 70s. Another person who has spent a lifetime looking for God, who wants to continue that journey by my side. Another Sufi woman who is clearly God's gift.

What does it mean to be loving a woman? Am I gay? Bisexual? Real love is beyond labels, and I repudiate them all. I am simply a person who was lucky to have been loved unconditionally, so I know love when I meet it, and I know how to give it. To anyone God sends.

THE EDGES OF MY CERTITUDES

In the mid-60s, I had the life-altering privilege of teaching and doing community development in Central America. What I couldn't even have begun to imagine then was how wondrously those four years would alter and expand my worldview about almost everything—God, social justice, structures of violence, human dignity, not least of all about life's relation to possible previous lives, to the *bardo*, to the afterlife.

I met and lived among people—the majority, if not actually Catholic, certainly Christian—who took reincarnation as a given. The edges of my certitudes softened. Lived and pulsating reality began to replace inert dogma.

By my early forties and back in the States for almost a decade, I began to have spontaneous flashes of some past lives of my own. They had such power as teachers, I felt no need to verify whether they were actual lives or dreamlike states of active imagination, what the Mayan shaman Martin Prechtel calls "buds on the tree of life, small leaks from the other world's story."

During a recent conference on Thomas Merton, Dr. Christopher Pramuk gave a powerful talk on Merton's view of Hagia Sophia, Wisdom-Sophia, titled in Merton's own words, "'She Cannot Be a Prisoner': The Lure of Wisdom as Bearer of Hope." In it Pramuk mentioned with passionate intensity the beauty of Etty Hillesum's diaries as well as Melissa Raphael's book *The Female Face of God in Auschwitz*. As he spoke, a very cherished incarnation flashed through me as it has before.

In this seeing, I am a non-corporeal being during the pogroms. (I don't know the country or calendar date of the experience.) I am flying over a burning synagogue inside which the congregation has been herded and locked as it is set afire. Glass is shattering Kristallnacht-like. From one small side door come women in flames screaming as they run down a dirt footpath.

The task I have been given is to 'drink' the screams as they come from the women's mouths. The moment I do so, the screams are transformed into indescribable joy. As that happens, I understand with my whole body in this current incarnation that "You turned my wailing into dancing" (Psalm 30:11), a promise in which I have always believed, one I then felt and henceforth know at the cellular level. While the promise in the psalmist's words never precludes nor supplants our mandate to work against such atrocities, it does give us that welcome glimmer of hope to support us in the work itself.

Indeed Santa Sophia, Wisdom-Sophia, our beloved Sister Sophia cannot be a prisoner, not inside any inferno, not in any belief system, not even inside our own bodies. She embraces all, transforms all, unifies all.

MATRIMONY TWO:
THE INVISIBLE WOMAN

someone is giving me a cup to drink from but s/he is enveloped in a mist. i can't see who it is. i am aware of a bond or air of presence but of no individuals. i feel no great need to talk my way into inner wisdom, which seems to be pouring in through every pore.

she focuses. she becomes the invisible woman. you know her. i know her. she is everywhere. sunken treasure of ships, of the ship of life. her invisibility is a power in her and around her, an aura, a glow.

  i speak to her:

  o invisible woman, i believe you are the deepest love of my life. you are a ragpicker here, a shopping bag lady here. they have let you stay as harmless. doorways and curbings you inhabit. so you are among the oldest dwellers here. you've certainly stayed the longest, possibly know the most.

by way of response she opens a grey-lipped, toothless smile to me as if to say:

> *it is the emptying.*

i open my mouth to feel what emptiness there is, to match hers.

> *o mother before there was a baby. o baby before there was a mother, what have you to say to me?*

she thumbs her rounded, soft gums with her tongue, mouthing words that have no shape or sound. her tongue is like undulating earth. it ripples so that wheat fields could grow there and wave in the wind. the quality of her smile fills her whole face, especially her eyes. the tongue continues working like that of a stroke victim or an infant. her eyes are convinced that she's telling me as much as a baby thinks it's babbling. i learned long ago how to talk to babies. they write on the whole surface of your skin. you drink a baby's words.

now i see the significance of the cup at the beginning. the old woman re-offers me the cup. it is filled with words. i can't read them. i must drink them. then some day i will hear them from inside when i speak them. i will remember her as they are coming out.

> *in memory of me,* her face says.

i say:

> *how could i ever forget you? if i forget you, o zion, there would be no self to remember...*

she begins to withdraw, not in fear, but with the same benign majesty that is always hers with me. she knows if she is seen too long talking to a newcomer in this place of ancient wisdom, someone will begin to suspect she belongs here and that will make it very difficult for her vision to be what it is. others will want to stone her or crown her—both the same act.

> *i thank you, o beautiful woman. it is so hard to let you go, even for a time.*

she retreats slowly, facing me all the while. finally she vanishes back into the mist.

GETTING THE ANGELS TO TALK

When I was a child
I made snow angels with bright wings.

Today I try to find angels again.

I say to them,
What do I need when I lie down and make angels?

You want to find God.

Yes, I want to find God, in the ground I lie on,
on the bed I kick my feet into,
on the sidewalk where I stumble up the curb.
It hurts.

And I do not find.

They are quiet now, these angels of childhood.
I hear others, perhaps an angel of death fluttering in the dark.

Are these winged ones in my head?
To whom will I tell these stories?

I lie, make my own angels.

MILD HE LAYS HIS GLORY BY

Since Midnight Mass two Taize-like lines have echoed as inner heartsongs
playing incessantly. Working around the house, I sang or hummed them over
and over until I began to wonder if my husband would think I had gone
bonkers.

The song itself is familiar—"Hark! The Herald Angels Sing," its final verse
not so well known. It has caught my attention in previous years but nothing

like this year. Those ancient lines seem to carry a welcome and expanded understanding of both heaven and earth.

> Hail the heav'n-born Prince of Peace!
> Hail the Son of Righteousness!
> Light and life to all He brings
> *Ris'n with healing in His wings.*
> *Mild He lays His glory by*
> Born that we no more may die,
> Born to raise us from the earth,
> Born to give us second birth.

Even though the two lines follow each other, they echo in me separately, with a distinct impetus or 'packet' of realization. The one that started even during Midnight Mass was the Ris'n line, the image of "healing in his wings." In it, I experienced Jesus himself as a winged being, himself a herald angel, as we are all called to be—heralds, heralds. Hark! A new time is coming, one beyond dualisms, beyond exceptionalisms of all kinds, be they cultural, religious, or species-related. Behold! All things are made new. Behold! All are One.

Bringing about such unity, according to Raimon Panikkar, will be the task of third millennium Christians because, as he declares "Christ vastly transcends Christianity… because it is a name that can and must assume other names, like Rama or Krishan or Ishvara."

The "Mild He lays His glory by" line describes the *kenosis* of Jesus, his self-emptying. He lays his glory by, sets it aside. At midnight with a mellow trumpet piercing all boundaries and an exquisite descant swirling out beyond those boundaries to primeval silence, I looked around that ever-darkening-skinned church and realized: Every person in this building and outside it has set her or his glory by, has actively agreed to walk this land at this time in disguise.

From what I saw in the Life Between Lives regression I had some years ago, this planet is populated by beings who have lain their glory by, who walk the earth shedding feathers of healing as they go. The very people Thomas Merton saw and loved that now-iconic day in Louisville on the corner of Fourth and Walnut Streets, a day he describes as waking from a dream of separateness. The ones I've seen on occasion while walking through crowded airports.

In truth, my core belief is that every human has lain her/his glory by. While we are enfleshed, we may forget or forego that commitment, but that forgetting does not change the reality of our however-shadowy participation in luminous, numinous glory.

Between Tuesday and Sunday, including a wonderful Saturday retreat with a woman shaman, I lived inside those two realities of healing wings and glory in disguise. So Sunday I got to Church and the opening hymn was "Hark! The Heralds" once again.

At that point everything just seemed to explode and I was grasping for all alienated women to be in that Church with me. We, who were born and raised in the seriously and sadly co-opted Catholic/Christian tradition, were nurtured subconsciously on the glorious words of these hymns. Now we need to reclaim worship, first by sharing with each other the distorted ways in which 'God' has been languaged to women and then to share more widely their possible real meanings, their deeper truths, how they fit with Teilhard, Jean Houston and Barbara Marx Hubbard, with Neil Douglas-Klotz, Brain Swimme, Joanna Macy, Cynthia Bourgeault, Judy Cannato, Ilia Delio, Diarmuid O'Murchu, the inclusive artistic vision of Janet McKenzie and what science is telling us about the history and future of the universe within deep time.

Each reading, each refrain drew me into orbits before and beyond our small moment in time into a world of cosmic unfolding, emerging out of the past and piercing into fiercely hidden, yet imminent and immanent futures. Then I heard within myself the words *the translator* as my name, my task, my role. *The translator between traditions. The translator midwifing transitions.*

As so often in these elder years, I longed to write what I was experiencing, all the while realizing that the best of what comes out of me in writing is very seldom done in any space reserved or designated for writing but rather during simple household chores that I then interrupt to scribble on scraps of paper. It feels almost like taking dictation.

More always escapes than I can get down. I've learned to trust that what needs to be written for whatever reason will cycle back, perhaps in a different form, and that what doesn't get written goes into invisible airwaves somehow. Nowadays I send more into the invisible airwaves than I put on paper, trusting that those wordless or at least unwritten transmissions are the more powerful energies anyway. What silent, rich hearts have always done across the miles and across the millennia.

We may be thousands, even millions of years yet, from such fullness. I just so long to contribute the wholeness of my part. Then I am very content to dissolve and disappear, if that is what awaits us. Dissolve to evolve, so to speak.

So may it be for us and for our world.

SONG OF THE COLLECTIVE VOICES

During my morning meditation I found myself kind of reviewing my life again, as I've done a lot lately. And I found myself thinking, *It's all been so good.*

Not like the life of a friend of mine who has undergone staggering pain. Wait a minute, I told myself. I've suffered too. We all have.

Then I felt the beautiful song of growth under all that collective pain. Our collective voices have transcended the pain and transformed it.

GOOD FRIDAY

One thing I know: we live in what we make—
the children, poems, dinners. All demand
our skins and spirits. Into them descend
our futures, our fingerprints and soulmarks.
Gasping for breath in the terrible heart-dark
between the moment a thought takes form and then
leaves with its own life, we convulse, bend
over in what has been called suffering, death.

If this is so—and all of us know it is—
the Maker Whose thought sustains our straining breath
suffers the same black chasms. And in sad,
lost moments, we don't pray to thank or please,
to placate or cajole. We simply rest
a silent moment in the pain of God.

FORGIVENESS

In early 2011, I began a meditation practice that takes me to the place of no contradiction. Pain—yes. But blame, denial and hatred—no. Or rather, when they are there, they soften. (I learned about softening from *The Path With Heart* by Jack Kornfield.) Since I've been praying in this way I've been having a new experience because it allows for the Unified Field to be opened and touched.

There was a Sister against whom I held a grudge for almost ten years. I didn't see her often but, when I did, I avoided her. I felt that she had wronged me. For years I wished and prayed to accept and forgive; I knew I would feel better and get the beast off my back. About two weeks after I started the practice, I saw the name of that Sister in a bulletin from the Motherhouse. With no thought or will power, words came through me: "Please forgive me. I'm so sorry. Please forgive me."

The grace of this powerful practice continues to carry me beyond blame into the Unified Field where I am able to experience and forgive my part in the daily energetic exchanges of life. Experiences like this happened with more frequency through the following weeks and months.

Now, where there had been aversion and hatred, there is communion. I still grapple with jealousy, anger, and cowardice, but it has taken on a different name. The Name: "This is mine."

In that name I become one with what is my own darkness and very possibly my own potential. This movement within me has a name, too. The name is God, Sacred Unity.

QUIET DISCARDING

Wise men do not grieve
having discarded sorrow.
—*Dhammapada*

Sorrow is to be discarded,
not thrown out like garbage,
not fingered or sorted
or given to the less fortunate,
but discarded like old cells,

like flakes of skin in the shower,
discarded like long hair
wound through a pointed comb.

A part that is not a part
anymore is not grieved.
Wise ones neither mourn,
nor weep, nor squint in pain,
but sit in sacred stillness.
Peace is the quiet discarding.

A Hermit's Perspective

Today a hermit friend asked me: "How long have you been a hermit?"

"A long time," I replied. I am not counting the years anymore. Maybe I have always been meandering in the wilderness, always lost in the desert. Maybe I have always been alone with the Alone.

I am at a place where I realize what drew me to the Convent was not so much a What as a Who, a nameless One still summoning me today. Sometimes I wonder if all the delays, detours and doubts were really worth it—until I realize there was a great teacher of patience within it all, the teacher of Life Itself, guiding me and inspiring me to become who I am meant to be.

Patience has opened up the whole world of Silence to me—the Silence within me, the Silence as vast as the universe where God dwells in pure mercy and love. A yearning for that Silence that set me on my journey, which still hasn't begun because it is hidden deeply in the mystery of Christ, the Beginning.

Luminosity
Poetry from a Hermit

What must I leave behind?
Everything
to be free as God is free.

Now is the time of the year
when the world appears luminous.
The leaves, the ferns, the grasses
are radiating light even as
the clouds hide the sun.
Amazing light arising from inside
calling out openness.
All is translucent, freshly born.
"I am," says God. "I really am
vine, seed, hidden treasure,
silent presence, light of the world.

"Leave behind all notions, judgements,
fears and doubts.
Be luminous.
Shine!"

I Lift My Cup

I thank You. I thank You for all of it—my long life this far. For my safe and secure childhood and the unhappy early Convent years that followed. For the wonderful Sisters I lived with there and for my roommate during the painful years after I left. For my prince of a husband and then for widowhood. Finally, for being led to Sufism, my spiritual path.

Above all, I thank You for life itself. The unfolding of it. Each moment-by-moment opportunity. Now, during my early seventies I take the Long Look. I can see how the segments of my life reflect and build on each other, how each of them involved Calling-and-answer, Calling-and-answer. How even choices I am not proud of were simply the best I could do at the time, and God's Mercy is greater than all my shame and regret.

I remember so well my confused and desperate twenties, years when I felt hopelessly trapped in myself and a life that seemed nothing but struggle. I'd have been happy to leave it. "Wouldn't you feel cheated if you died so young?" a confidante asked. I was emphatic in shaking my head *No*. I really wanted *Out*.

Now I want *In*. Into life. Into You. Into myself—the deepest part.

My husband has died; the children have left. When I moved into a smaller house I forgot to buy a television. I've given away the sets of dishes I used to entertain with, retired the Big Thanksgiving Turkey Pan. I've exited the classroom doors I used to teach behind and waved good-bye to many friends whose lives have led them elsewhere.

I am ready for The Great Descent. Take me down into prayer, into holiness, into the Core Reality I've searched and hungered for all my life. To the inner cloisters of Teresa of Avila and Julian of Norwich. To the creative chaos at the center of *The Cloud of Unknowing*. My cup is emptier than it's ever been; I lift it in hope toward the spout of Rumi's mystical wine jug.

CARVING SPACE FOR LOVE TO FLOW

Life moving through
Magnet draw from outer Fields
Coming in and carving out
Clear the way, Clear the way
Let it be You, Let it be You
It is You I want

Let Your name be Love, Your name be Love
  It is Love I want
  It is You I want

Communion—Entering In and Being Entered

Where do I end and You begin
  Communion
  It is You I want

Love, Ever Ancient, Ever New
  It is You I want

As She Lay Dying

R spent some time in the hospital with Ann, a fellow Nun.
When R walked in, Ann started to cry.

R: Annie, how are you?

Ann: I'm not doing so well. My family was here yesterday, seven of them, and we knew it was the end. One brother wants me to keep fighting, but I'm just too weak. I don't have it any more. There are too many things wrong. I'm giving myself to God.

R: Yes, give yourself over. You've had a really wonderful life.

Ann: I've had a wonderful life. God is so good. God has given me a wonderful life and taken care of me. I love my life. My teaching, the children. I loved being a principal for over twenty years. This summer I was still helping teachers even though I'm retired. I loved my life... and now I'm giving my life back to God.

R: Yes, give yourself to God.

Ann: It's too painful to go on, and I'm too weak. I can't do it anymore. There are too many things wrong. More and more goes wrong. They would have to do something with my heart and with my bladder, and I would have to stay on oxygen.

R: Those are the vitals.

Ann: Yes. More things keep happening.

R: Then maybe it is time to go to God. That's where your mother and father are.

Ann: No, just my father. My mother is ninety-six, and she isn't with it anymore. But I talked to her heart and I asked her if I should let go. She said yes, I should, that I shouldn't keep hanging on or I would be trapped like she is. I don't want to be trapped, so I'm giving myself back to God. I'll give myself to God.

   God has given me such a good life. I loved my life. I'm giving myself back to God.

I Buried Sister Ann in My Garden

I buried Sister Ann last week in my garden. She was constantly in my thoughts as I planted spring bulbs—daffodils, snow drops, alliums and grape hyacinths. I knelt for hours repeating the ritual of digging the hole, setting the bulbs and covering them with soil.

I was Ann's guardian angel when she arrived at the Motherhouse in our sophomore year of high school. We were all so young, earnest and dedicated, and we have all made this world a little better for our being here.

When I Say Your Name

I say your name and feel your touch
on the back of my throat,
in the breath heaving up from my lungs.

Your name is swirling in my blood,
pounding its rhythm along my arms,
into the deep creases of my elbows.

I place your name behind my eyes
wrapped in that secret
where only I can find you.

I lay your name
between the bones of my spine
where you hold me up.

I write your name carefully
with water, in the spaces between my fingers,
in the spaces between my toes in sand.

I say your name and it nestles in my ear.

When I say your name,
I hold you.

October Grace

The autumn sun-dance of gold and crimson brocade
gives way to the black lace of branches
against the morning-glory sky.
My soul wonders
will this be dying,
leaping to the Spirit-wind,
before the brilliant eternal day?
You will know, O Soul,
when you lie beneath the leaves.

Growing Old Is All About?

I am wondering: Is this what growing old is all about—becoming more
enlightened to see the true value of each person and genuinely loving each
one with great depth? I seem to experience it more and more. I keep wanting
to tell each person whom I treasure "I love You!" each time I say good-bye.

At Four O'Clock This Morning

Angels, the Great Ones, hovered a scant earth moment
(I felt them) and prepared to calibrate
the turning earth with a tuning fork.
Our souls, our skins, and the cells they hold
around themselves, vibrated like the instruments
we are as the Great Ones bent their light
like midwives delicately turning babies in the womb.
I felt their touch—and you beyond their touch—
turning along with me, along with stars,
their meteors loosening and falling like dead cells.

I drank some water to steady myself,
pressed tender feet against the trembling earth.
God of our humbled hearts, help us to hear
new music we are part of—and adjust our steps.

NESTING DOLLS OF THE NEBULAE

Just now I am sweeping leaves and pollen from our front entryway. A drab-but-stunning winged insect rests on the concrete wall near me. Of a sudden I see the eternity within that liver-of-a-day and know its majesty somehow surpasses consciousness, even metaconsciousness.

The ancient Sanskrit '*Tat Tvam Asi/ Thou Art That*' floods me and I know myself as both insect and eternity with no need *to be me*, to claim any future at all except that which is always around us, always present.

Long after I recorded this experience of the dragonfly in my Meditation Journal, I continue to live within it as another reminder of how immensely expansive our NOW/THOU must become. We humans are exactly those drab-but-stunning winged beings, livers-of-a-day within deep cosmic time. The Great Ones beyond us see us on our concrete walls and are themselves seen by others greater still. Nesting dolls of the nebulae.

AFTER THE DEATH

Be content now.
You, too, will approach,
someday,
the great womb of Spirit
and be embraced
into total mindfulness.
The Eternal Now is now.
How else could we enter?

MEDITATION

My whole life, I searched your name, down many paths. What is your Name?

>Most High, Omnipotent, Good Lord.
>That which Is. All that Is.

In the beginning was the Word and the Word was with God and the Word was God.

>The Silent One
>Who Is.

I search for the name, the One to whom I call, the Before, and Now, and After.

>I am but a blink in this eternity of energy.

Do I need a name? In this great sea of energy, I am protected. Safe. Before and after are taken care of. The Silent One knows all. Is All. All Is.

>*Be comforted. Rest easy. You do not need to know. Cannot know. That is Good. You cannot name, you just know.*

Now I lay me down to sleep. I pray the Lord my soul to keep. Comforted as a little child. Still comforted.

>*Be comforted. Rest easy. You do not need to know. Cannot know. That is Good. Because you cannot name, you know.*

The Formless, Timeless, Nameless One. The All whom we are. Who is.

Beyond naming, beyond thought. Beyond form. Beyond time. Being. The One in whom we all are.

In silence. In solitude. Now.

CONTRIBUTORS

Pat Baron Monigold
Shirley Baumert Bigelow (formerly Ursula Ann, OSF)[1]
Mary H. Ber
Gwen Blavat Drapela
Margaret Sue Broker, OSF
Ann Busch, OSF
Jeanne Checkal Ellison
Patricia Coffey Giglio (formerly Thomas Aquin, OSF)
Mary Colgan McNamara (formerly Marie Bernarde, OSF)
Faith Devine
Kathleen Donohoe, OSF
Sister Bette Edl, Hermitess OSF
Christopher Lee Ehrgott
Marilyn Fiduccia (formerly James Mary, OSF)
Charlita Foxhoven, OSF
Carla Gebhardt Bodaghi
Joan Gehant Davies (formerly Ruth Mary, OSF)
Gloria Gragnani (formerly Raynier, OSF)
Valeria Hersant Foster (formerly Magdella, OSF)
Frances Ann Hicks, OSF
Theresa Marie Jarvis, OSF
Patricia Kenny (formerly Alverne, OSF)
Mary Sue Koeppel
Mary Anne LeClaire Jackson (formerly Angelene, OSF)
Mary C. May (formerly Geoffrey, OSF)
Maggie McManamon Dohr (formerly Rosaleen, OSF)
Regina Pacis Meservey, OSF
Jo Ann Nadeau
Patti O'Hearn Vespalec (formerly Timothy Marie, OSF)
Marina Padilla, OSF
Mary Ann Schmieding, OSF
Marilyn Sebastian Robbins (formerly Marilyn Clare, OSF)
Jayne Steffens

---

[1]Some former members chose to include their names in religion, others chose not to do so.

Julene Stromberg, OSF
Helen Strueder, OSF
Rose Ann Trzil, OSF
Roseann Wagner, OSF
Rose Marie Weller Knoth (formerly André Marie, OSF)
Arlene Woelfel, OSF

GLOSSARY

Adoration chapel—a smaller chapel in a room behind the main altar in St. Joseph Convent Chapel, Milwaukee, Wisconsin, where Sisters and Postulants prayed in adoration 24-7

Aspirancy—building where Aspirants lived. Also, the block of time during which high school age girls lived with the Sisters, attended the convent high school, and prepared to begin the formal steps toward becoming Sisters themselves

Aspirant—a high school age girl who "aspired" to become a Sister. She received both a secular education and spiritual training at the Motherhouse.

Breviary— book containing the Divine Office prayed (sometimes chanted) every day by the Sisters

Cantor—a leader of the Divine Office when it was chanted. At the Motherhouse the cantor sang out from the choir loft behind and high above the congregation.

Cell—a private space for sleeping, curtained off, in a dormitory

Chapter of Faults—an event on Silent Sunday during which each Novice or professed Sister related her small infringements of the rule or customs (such as being late for prayer) and received from her superior a small "penance" (such as a short prayer) in order to help her overcome this fault

Custody of the Eyes—the practice of keeping eyes downcast, especially after night prayer, in order to keep one's mind centered on the Divine

Divine Office—Matins, Lauds, Tierce, Sext, None, Vespers, Compline - Prayers and psalms prayed (sometimes chanted) every day

Final Vows—Vows of poverty, chastity, and obedience made for life

Foundresses—three women—Mother Alexia, Mother Alfons, Sister Clara—exiled from Germany during Bismarck's *Kulturkampf,* who came to the United States and founded the School Sisters of St. Francis

Great Silence—time from Compline in the evening until after breakfast the next morning when no unnecessary talking takes place; designed as a time of uninterrupted communing with God

Gregorian Chant—unaccompanied sacred music of pure melody sung in unison, often during Divine Office and parts of the Mass. Composed for many kinds of liturgical texts, mostly scriptural, this sacred song is also called plainchant and dates back at least to the Middle Ages.

Guardian Angels—term given to Aspirants and Postulants who guided new Aspirants and Postulants into the life and culture of the convent

Habit—outer clothing worn by all Novices and professed Sisters. Before Vatican II, in our community it consisted of a white (for Novices) or black (for professed Sisters) veil over white linens that wrapped around the head and neck; a floor-length, black, wool dress under a scapular (shoulder to floor-length strip of black wool) and white collar. A black and silver crucifix hung down in front. A white, wool, knotted rope circled the waist and hung down on the right side and, after first profession, a large rosary hung from the rope on the left side.

HAC—Health Agencies Council, a province created in 1966 and consisting of SSSF Sisters in the health care professions

House Sister—Sister who managed the convent kitchen and the basic needs of the household

Junior Sister—Sister who has temporary vows, but has not yet taken final vows

Juniorate—place at Alverno College where some Sisters in temporary vows lived while completing their degrees

Marian Hall—building near the Motherhouse in Milwaukee where Aspirants lived

Mission/ on mission—the place of work to which a Sister was sent after she had taken vows. These schools, hospitals, etc. to which obedience sent Sisters were mostly in the United States, though a smaller number of Sisters were sent as missionaries (in the conventional sense) to third world countries.

Mistress—the Superior of a group of young women being trained for the Sisterhood, e.g., Mistress of Aspirants, Mistress of Postulants, Novice Mistress

Mother General—Elected leader of the entire Community of Sisters, after Vatican II called the President

Motherhouse—large building in Milwaukee where the Postulants, Novices, and many vowed Sisters live. This is the hub of the governance, finances, etc, for all the provinces.

Novice—title given to women who are received into the order; that is they dress in the habit, are given a new name, and live according to the rule, fairly separated from the rest of the world for two years

Novitiate—a large room where Novices congregated for instruction, study, and other activities. Also, the two years after the postulancy and before first profession of vows during which young women prepared for a vowed life

Nun—Nun is used colloquially in the press and in many conversations to mean anyone who has taken the vows. In *No One's Easy Daughter* nun is used interchangeably with Sister because so many people use it so.

OSF—Order of St. Francis; title used by the Sisters in legal and official documents

Particular Examen—a fault that is selected for eradication and "examined" daily in the hope that there were fewer incidents of it in the day just passed

Particular Friendship—the kind of exclusive relationship that could signal lesbianism. Because the term was never clearly defined for young women during the early years, its use as a warning often led to confusion.

Pastoral Ministry—a position that opened up in many parishes after Vatican II. Sisters often coordinated religious education programs in the absence of traditional Catholic grade schools and facilitated other parish activities such as study groups. Often they trained for this work by acquiring graduate degrees in religious education or pastoral ministry.

Postulant—name given to the women spending about nine months preparing to become Novices

Postulancy—a large room where Postulants congregated for instruction, study, and other activities. Also, the block of time during which young women were prepared for novitiate

President—the elected leader of all the Sisters

Professed Sister—One who has taken vows

Province (Provincial)—Provinces are the sections into which the entire community is divided. Each Province is led by a Sister called the Provincial and her team. There are presently five Provinces: USA, Latin America, Germany, South India and North India.

Reception—name of the ceremony admitting a young woman into the novitiate

Refectory—dining room

Rule—a written canon that governed the life of the Sisters

SSSF—School Sister of Saint Francis; the title for our specific community of Franciscans; used in less formal and more personal settings

Sacristan—one who laid out vestments in the sacristy and prepared vessels used during Mass, often arranged flowers and linens on the altar, cleaned the church sanctuary, and did other things to facilitate the liturgy

Second Vatican Council/ Vatican II—Called by Pope John XXIII from 1962-1965, this group of Church leaders initiated reforms in liturgy and other practices in order to bring the Church into the modern world. It authorized liturgical prayer in the vernacular, the modification of Sisters' habits, etc.

Silent Sunday—one Sunday a month dedicated to prayer, spiritual reading and other spiritual practices. Its purpose was to anchor women who were in professional service (or preparing for it) in their most important purpose, a spiritual life.

Table Reading—reading from inspirational books done in refectories during all meals except on feast days and Sundays

Temporary Vows—Vows of Poverty, Chastity and Obedience made three times for one year (e.g., in 1959, 1960, 1961,) then for 3 years (in 1962). Final vows followed these six years of temporary vows.

Vatican II—See Second Vatican Council (above)

ACKNOWLEDGMENTS

In our almost-seven years of shared work on this book, we have had both visible and nonvisible help. The most powerful nonvisible guidance continues to come from those who created the legacy we received and who mentored us to become the women we are—the deceased members of our SSSF Community.

During these years the book has become a daughter to us. Like ourselves, she has not been an easy daughter but has firmly led us where she needed to go, down paths we initially feared, hesitated about, did not want to travel. Those paths would never have opened without our most courageous and generous visible help—the 39 contributors whose Journeys of Transformation are the heart of this book.

We offer our heartfelt gratitude also to the entire reception class of 1957, living and dead; our endorsers for seeing deeply into the heart of our book and offering words of validation; Francis Rothluebber whose visionary endorsement became the book's Foreword; our spouses and friends for support, proofreading and unfailing belief in the work; Jayne Steffens and Jerry Cross for the use of their home in Door County, Wisconsin where we editors worked for a glorious week in the country; Dan Quigley for his insightful help with contract questions; Jane Ray for permission to use her visionary artwork as our cover image; Pat Baron Monigold for her intricate and vibrant graphite drawings on pages 21, 111, 235 and 331; Dick Martin for generously donating many hours of video expertise and for his discerning understanding of our spiritual journeys, and Leila Joiner for midwifing our daughter to publication.

CREDITS

The Poems and work listed here first appeared in the following places, some in slightly different versions:

American Zen: a Gathering of Poets (Bottom Dog Press)*:* "While the Wolf Walks the Edge of the Woods"

Between the Bones (Canopic Publishing): "Porous Bones," "Bewilderment," "The Art Is Not in the Pickle," "Setting Dobyns Straight," " Near Palms and Sea," "Forty-four Dresses and One Smooth Stone," " Invisible. Like the Pattern," "Getting the Angels to Talk," "When I Say Your Name"

Connecticut Review: "All These Years I've Prayed"

In the Library of Silences, Poems of Loss (Rhiannon Press): "All These Years I've Prayed," "Praise"

Kalliope, a Journal of Women's Literature & Art: "Myself Comparing Religions"

"Letter from the House" Autumn 2006 (Many Rivers Press): www.davidwhyte.com

Small Press Review and *State Street Review:* "In the Aids Hospice"

The Art of Survival — An Anthology (Kings Estate Press): "Quiet Discarding"

The Elderbook (Finishing Line Press): "The Widow"

The Little Portion (St. Joseph High School Literary Magazine): "The Annunciation"

Unexpected Harvest (Kings Estate Press): "Andante"

*Vision (*Alverno College Literary Magazine): "One Grain," "Novena," "Prayer," "Maranatha," "Eschatology"

EXPANDED CHAPTER CONTENTS

PART 1 – EARLY LIFE

Chapter 1—Why We Came

Chapter 2—Aspirancy

Chapter 3—Postulancy

Chapter 4—Novitiate

Chapter 5—Early Life Glimpses Of The Sacred

PART 2 – MID LIFE

Chapter 6—Critical Decisions

Chapter 7—The Powerful And Passionate Mid Life Years

Chapter 8—Mid Life Glimpses Of The Sacred

PART 3 – LATER LIFE

Chapter 9—What Sustains Us Now

Chapter 10—Later Life Glimpses Of The Sacred

ABOUT THE EDITORS

Mary H. Ber – I learned to read at age six and started writing poetry at age seven. I have been writing ever since. In addition, I've created literary magazines for students in most of the schools in which I spent 50+ years as a classroom teacher. From 1995 through 2008 I served as co-founder and editor of *Moon Journal Press*, a feminist venue that turned out two magazines and two chapbooks yearly. I consider myself a bridge person, dedicated to a spirituality of unity—at home in churches, temples, mosques. Any place that holds the hearts of sincere worshippers.

To contact, email maryhber@gmail.com

Mary Sue Koeppel – I find life-giving energy in teaching, writing and making visual art. Through forty-four years of full time teaching, I experienced how education, especially in the humanities, changes and enriches lives. From 1988-2005 I was Editor of *Kalliope, a Journal of Women's Literature & Art*; then my husband and I created the literary website, www.writecorner.com. I co-founded Women of Vision, an arts program replicated nationally for the visually impaired. While my college texts and books of poetry invite reflection, my visual art offers serenity and joy. Creativity, I believe, bonds us to the Energy of the Universe.

Copies of *No One's Easy Daughter* are available for purchase
through Amazon.com and BarnesandNoble.com

Mary Colgan McNamara – I grew up loving silence and words almost equally—and longing for an older sister. Convent life offered all three. There silence deepened, words expanded and sisterhood became a way of life. After returning from Latin America, I continued working in education and gave seminars/retreats on spirituality, women's issues and liberation theology. Today my husband and I, in between grandparenting trips, are part of a retreat team on Contemplative Eldering at a Trappist Abbey. My segment involves writing as a contemplative practice. The words I write as I age carry me ever closer to the awe-filled Great Silence.

For news on upcoming YouTubes and website, marycmc@aol.com
For information on Contemplative Eldering Retreats:
https://bookwhen.com/mepkinabbey

Rose Ann Trzil, OSF – Since very young I wanted to be a Sister. And I am. As an elementary school teacher and principal, I remember wishing I could teach about God and read poetry to children all day. After receiving my Master's in Systematic Theology, I gave retreats around the country, worked for 6 years at Fatima Retreat Center in Notre Dame and then founded and have directed Sophia House, a center for spirituality, for the past 30 years. I am a lifetime student of spirituality and live and teach from the belief that, as a species, we are evolving into the One, the Presence that is God.

sophiamilwaukee.com
http://www.sssf.org/SSSF.htm

Copies of *No One's Easy Daughter*
are available for purchase online through
Amazon.com and BarnesandNoble.com

All proceeds will be donated to the
School Sisters of St. Francis
with gratitude.

CPSIA information can be obtained
at www.ICGtesting.com
Printed in the USA
FFOW03n1341040617
36256FF